D1520705

Channeling the Future

Essays on Science Fiction and Fantasy Television

Edited by
Lincoln Geraghty

THE SCARECROW PRESS, INC.
Lanham, Maryland • Toronto • Plymouth, UK
2009

SCARECROW PRESS, INC.

Published in the United States of America
by Scarecrow Press, Inc.
A wholly owned subsidiary of
The Rowman & Littlefield Publishing Group, Inc.
4501 Forbes Boulevard, Suite 200, Lanham, Maryland 20706
www.scarecrowpress.com

Estover Road
Plymouth PL6 7PY
United Kingdom

British Library Cataloguing in Publication Information Available

Library of Congress Cataloging-in-Publication Data

Channeling the future : essays on science fiction and fantasy television / edited by
Lincoln Geraghty.
    p. cm.
  Includes bibliographical references and index.
  ISBN 978-0-8108-6675-1 (hardback : alk. paper) — ISBN 978-0-8108-6922-6
(e-book)
  1. Science fiction television programs—History and criticism. 2. Fantasy television
programs—History and criticism. I. Geraghty, Lincoln, 1977–
  PN1992.8.S35C43 2009
  791.45'615—dc22

                                                   2008054534

∞ ™ The paper used in this publication meets the minimum requirements of
American National Standard for Information Sciences—Permanence of
Paper for Printed Library Materials, ANSI/NISO Z39.48-1992.
Manufactured in the United States of America.

Contents

Acknowledgments

This book has come a long way from the original proposal I sent to Scarecrow Press, and several people have helped in its development. I would like to thank my editor, Stephen Ryan, who saw potential in my idea and supported it at every stage. I had valuable assistance from the staff at The Kobal Collection at Picture Desk, Photofest, and Rex Features in locating and purchasing images for this book; to them I offer my gratitude. Thank you to my department for contributing toward the purchase of these images. I must also thank my colleagues in the School of Creative Arts, Film and Media at the University of Portsmouth, some of whom contributed to the collection, and in particular, Van, Dylan, and John, with whom I spent many hours in the corridor discussing the latest episode of *Battlestar Galactica*. Finally, my dearest thanks go to Rebecca Janicker; as ever, she was my rock.

-+-⇒

Introduction: Future Visions

Lincoln Geraghty

Channeling the Future focuses on the disparate visions of the past, present, and future that the science fiction and fantasy genres have offered television audiences. It not only shines new light on often overlooked and forgotten series but also examines the "look" of science fiction and fantasy television, determining how iconography (spaceships, machines, technology), location and landscape (space, Earth, the city, the countryside), mise-en-scène, CGI and special effects, art and set design, props, costumes, lighting, and manipulation of visual and virtual space contribute to the creation of real, fully imagined, and often all-too-familiar future and alternate worlds. Establishing how the medium of television can create a certain "look" for individual series leads contributors to discuss the cultural, historical, and political impact these series had on both the genre and wider society. However, the collection also locates their visual aesthetics within broader historical, industrial, and production contexts to fully understand their cultural value. Notions of history and historical periodization clearly influence how science fiction and fantasy television series were imagined by their writers and designers and received at the time of broadcast, but we must also consider how older series and their particular future visions are perceived and interpreted by contemporary audiences compared to the more modern series of today.

The book is made up of twelve chapters split evenly across four sections. Part I, "America's New Frontier," contains chapters on Rod Serling's *The Twilight Zone*, Irwin Allen's big-budget TV series such as *Voyage to the Bottom of the Sea* and *Land of the Giants*, and, in the third chapter, *The Man from U.N.C.L.E*. Part II, "British Dystopias and Utopias," contains chapters on the Supermarionation series of Gerry Anderson, dystopian visions of the British scientist on television in the 1970s, and screen adaptations of children's fantasy novels. Part III, "Fantasy, Fetish, and the Future," looks at the cofunded North American/European series *Highlander*, the style and dress of *Star Trek: Voyager*'s Seven of Nine, and the animated science fiction series *Futurama*. Part IV, "Visions and Revisions," brings the collection right up to date with chapters on late twentieth and early twenty-first century series *Angel*, *Firefly*, and the new *Battlestar Galactica*.

Part I: America's New Frontier

In "Retro Landscapes: Reorganizing the Frontier in Rod Serling's *The Twilight Zone*," Van Norris discusses the recurrent use of the desert landscape in the seminal science fiction anthology series, *The Twilight Zone*. He posits that the trope of the frontier, the wilderness, the desert, "is less about an outward exploration as much as an inner one" where Serling used the barren and desolate landscape as a backdrop on which he could cast his narratives about psychological turmoil. *The Twilight Zone*'s power to subvert notions of reality and human identity was mainly revealed through the use of mind games, the plot twist at the end of episodes which jilted the audience's perception about what is right and real. However, Norris argues further that the physical landscape was a symbol of this perceptive trauma and indeed linked to America's own love affair with the frontier as constructed through the myth of the West. This fascination for the mythic West and repeated use of imagery and tropes related to the American frontier is of course redolent of more obvious space operas such as *Star Trek*. Indeed, the two series are often discussed in relation to each other; however, Norris points out that Serling was using these generic tropes as signifiers of the human condition well before Gene Roddenberry's more futuristic take. He concludes that "the desert space now exists as a fixed convention of science fiction as much as any postindustrial cityscape, example of automated intelligence, or design of spaceship."

Oscar De Los Santos's chapter, "Irwin Allen's Recycled Monsters and Escapist Voyages," examines the four big-budget TV series *Voyage to the Bottom of the Sea*, *Lost in Space*, *Time Tunnel*, and *Land of the Giants*, showing how they can be understood as reflections of the popular culture and national interests of the period in which they were produced. He suggests that these series replicate 1960s attitudes toward gender and government authority, although each series is set in the far future. De Los Santos scrutinizes the changing look of each program, which grew slicker yet somehow more juvenile in scope to match degenerating storytelling as the series progressed. In the end, the chapter asserts that Allen must be credited for being discerning in producing shows he knew would interest 1960s TV viewers, but close analysis of his shows also reveals that Allen's creativity was largely stimulated by whatever was already "hot" at the time (or had been popular in the recent past). He took it, used it, produced his own version of it, and moved on.

People who knew and worked with producer-director Irwin Allen have talked about his childlike enthusiasm over launching a new television show. As time progressed, Allen would grow restless and move on to his next project, leaving his current hit drama in the hands of hired staff. These associate producers and writers were Allen company men. They knew what pleased their boss: action and more of the same, with the bare minimum of character development. As a result, they would come up with increasingly flimsy storylines. While the slick look of Irwin Allen shows remained a staple throughout their existence, the stories featured in these programs would grow increasingly threadbare and juvenile. The resulting four series were as unforgettable for their initial dynamism as for their significant deterioration, while at the same time they were handed to the public in a rich-looking package.

Moving on from the more fantastic TV of Allen, Cynthia W. Walker discusses in chapter 3 another popular (and now cult) series, *The Man from U.N.C.L.E.* Originally pitched as "James Bond for television," for the youthful audiences of the time, in the mid-1960s it was the hottest show on TV. At the height of its popularity, on Friday nights at 10 p.m., over half of all U.S. televisions were tuned to the show. Walker argues that a good portion of *U.N.C.L.E.*'s appeal can be attributed to its "style," which juxtaposed mundane reality with the futuristic, day-after-tomorrow fantasy, and light-hearted, fast-paced adventure with utopian politics. Each week, megalomaniac villains plotted world domination while average folks became involved in missions to defeat them. The main characters, Napoleon Solo and Illya Kuryakin, were agents working for a mythical top-secret, multinational security organization called The United Network Command for Law Enforcement. Their headquarters in New York City, located just blocks away from the United Nations, featured stainless-steel corridors connected by automatic sliding doors that led to rooms filled with banks of computers and communication systems. It was an environment that seemed even sleeker and more modern than the Starship *Enterprise* on *Star Trek* (1966–1969), yet it was tucked away behind a homely dry-cleaning shop. Pulling the coat hook in the middle dressing booth was akin to Alice falling down the rabbit hole, and many in the audience wondered whether the *U.N.C.L.E.* organization actually existed.

Although it was an espionage series, *The Man from U.N.C.L.E.* also included a number of science fiction elements. Episodes featured such concepts as intelligence-altering drugs, cyborgs, flying saucers, global warming, tidal wave activators, and long-range laser weapons. The agents themselves were equipped with a gull-winged car, a specially designed gun that could shoot both bullets and sleep darts, and a number of everyday objects like money clips and cuff links that could transform into technologically advanced communication and incendiary devices. Walker explores how the unique, groundbreaking aesthetic of *The Man from U.N.C.L.E.*, though based in the 1960s, looked ahead to a near-future world beyond the cold war, in which formerly antagonistic nations would unite to battle technological threats and global terrorism, and individuals would carry pen-shaped personal phones as a matter of course.

Part II: British Dystopias and Utopias

This section focuses on the British televisual form of the genre, looking at some of the more easily recognizable series created by the prodigious Gerry Anderson through to more obscure examples of children's fantasy television adaptations. In David Garland's "Pulling the Strings: Gerry Anderson's Walk from 'Supermarionation' to 'Hypermarionation,'" we are introduced to Anderson's animated science fiction television series, specifically exploring the look and sound of the work in relation to his ideology of realism and its operation in conjunction with a contradictory utopian vision of technological and sociopolitical progress. For Garland, a number of ironies inform the career of Anderson. He remains best known today for creating a succession of puppet shows ostensibly aimed at children (most notably *Stingray, Thunderbirds,* and *Captain Scarlet*) in a purple period of productivity during the 1960s. Anderson has, however, confessed in recent years to always hating the stringed process dubbed "Supermarionation" that originally brought him to fame. Indeed, his enduring ambition has been instead to produce live action work for adults, something only rarely gratified in series such as *UFO* (1970) and *Space: 1999* (1975–1977) and the film *Journey to the Far Side of the Sun* (1969). This period proved in retrospect to be a blip in a career trajectory taking Anderson back to children's animated television in the form of other techniques: from the Muppet-style hand puppets of *Terrahawks* (1983–1984) to a recent remake of *Captain Scarlet* (2005), which fused high-definition video and CGI in what he has described as a new "photoreal" method of making TV programs.

Garland feels this description evokes a second paradox in the puppet-master's work. Whereas Anderson over the years has obsessively followed a technological ambition of "incremental progress" in the context of a very cinematic realist aesthetic modeled on Hollywood, *Thunderbirds* remains his most famous and celebrated series, often praised by admirers for its opposing aspects, such as the out-of-proportion heads of the marionette characters and the extremely optimistic worldview (unlike, for example, the darker "adult" themes and plotlines of *Captain Scarlet*). Dismissal of his later, more realistic output has tended to bemuse and even infuriate the self-conscious auteur. For example, in a 1996 article for the Sound and Television Society, Anderson stridently defended his principles, arguing that "the fascination of our pictures is created by the realism and believability of the characters" and that every move made in the direction of realism has "produced a greater appreciation of our films," so "I will continue to move in this direction believing I am right."[1]

Perhaps a sense of contemporary realism is partly responsible for the spate of series produced in the 1970s centered on the notion of catastrophe and a dystopian future. For Laurel Forster, the 1970s was a decade of disruption and disquiet in Britain on both the personal and political fronts. A wide sense of unease emerged concerning the relationship between the governmental/industrial/scientific complex and the sense of being an autonomous individual, responsible for one's own fate and place in the world. There were many startling scientific developments in this decade regarding space travel, medicine, nuclear power, and visual entertainment: first landings on Venus and Mars intensified reflection on our place in the universe; heart transplants and "test tube" babies caused reconsideration of what it means to be human; nuclear energy and computer microprocessors gave pause for thought about the potentially self-destructive nature of mankind; and video games and realistic special effects made the futuristic seem a present reality.

In chapter 5, "Farmers, Feminists, and Dropouts: The Disguises of the Scientist in British Science Fiction Television in the 1970s," Forster argues that the television science fiction genre was best placed to respond rapidly to these cultural anxieties and that several important series addressed issues surrounding contemporary scientific developments, the "secret" work of laboratories, and indeed, the remote figure of the scientist himself/herself. She investigates the controversial and disputed role of the scientist and the responsibility for scientific experiments, as portrayed in much science fiction of the time. In *Doomwatch*, for example, the scientist as cold and amoral, pursuing his or her experiments without concern for fellow humans, is a regular theme. In *Survivors*, a catastrophic mistake made by scientists in a laboratory is the basic premise of the series. In addition, many other single dramas from strands such as *Play for Today* set modern technologies against ancient, more powerful systems. In many cases the antidote to out-of-control modern science was a retreat to the rural, embracing a state of antimodernity. This chapter raises interesting questions about the relation of science fiction not only to the scientific developments of the time, but also to the rise in popularity of the alternative "green" movement of the decade.

Continuing this environmental theme, in chapter 6 Dave Allen discusses the pastoral landscape in children's fantasy fiction as adapted for TV and film. For him there is much that is archetypally English about the various adventures of the now globally ubiquitous Harry Potter, not least that they take place largely in the equivalent of a co-educational "public" boarding school. But Harry Potter is not typical for the simple reason that he is a special boy who possesses magical powers, which he studies and develops at Hogwarts. Therefore, in "Secret Gardens and Magical Realities: Tales of Mystery, the English Landscape, and English Children" Allen examines the "magical" adventures that happen to children in narratives like *The Box of Delights*, *The Secret Garden*, and the various BBC and Disney adaptations of C. S. Lewis's *Chronicles of Narnia*. The central figures in these adventures are quintessentially middle-class English children from the first half of the twentieth century but, unlike Harry Potter, they possess no magic powers themselves beyond the capacity to believe and imagine. The magic happens around them and *to* them.

Allen's chapter considers how these tales draw upon and extend an older tradition of mysticism, magic, and fantasy in English creative practices and how these charmingly old-fashioned tales find an audience alongside the clearly more contemporary Potter stories. The chapter discusses both the original published versions alongside adaptations for the big and small screens. In the conclusion to his chapter, Allen states that "it is possible to see these fictions as part of a far greater continuum of English creativity around the English landscape—often with metaphysical connotations," yet he also questions to what extent these tales of magical escape for children are still relevant for a contemporary generation that would see such representations of a middle-class pastoral idyll as totally alien from their current and everyday experiences.

Part III: Fantasy, Fetish, and the Future

In his chapter "There Can Be Only One: *Highlander: The Series*' Portrayal of Historical and Contemporary Fantasy," Michael S. Duffy explores the notions of televisuality and the reimagining of a film franchise for the TV screen. For him, *Highlander: The Series* successfully expanded and reinterpreted the *Highlander* universe, introducing new characters and conflicts and increased characterization and atmosphere, proving itself to be one of the rare television spin-offs that creatively outshined its parallel feature film franchise. A Canada/France co-production, *Highlander: The Series* would film half the year in Vancouver and the other half in Paris, often on the river Seine, where the main character Duncan owned a barge. Duffy argues that its international filming locations allowed the producers to easily fabricate historical backdrops on low budgets, and the damp Paris streets perfectly complemented the characters' present-day melancholy.

While the series had its share of familiar genre elements—the introduction of a naïve teenager to be the audience's "eyes into the world," a villain-of-the-week formula that dominated the first few seasons—Duffy also points out that it introduced new approaches to television drama that were unconventional. *Highlander*'s frequent use of flashbacks to illustrate its immortal characters' pasts gave the actors and production crew new material to play with weekly. Its introduction of the "Watchers," mortal characters who have been keeping track of immortals for centuries, added another unique thread to the universe, and the franchise's association with contemporary rock musicians—Queen co-composed the original film's soundtrack—resulted in recurring acting appearances by Joan Jett, Roland Gift (of Fine Young Cannibals), and Roger Daltrey of The Who, among others. Additionally, *Highlander: The Series*' flashbacks often placed its characters in the middle of real historical events, giving audiences a personal insight into history (even though historical facts might sometimes have been "altered for dramatic purposes"), and its contemporary, realistic setting helped create a world that was believable in iconography, yet fantastical in purpose. Duffy concludes that in rooting its fantastical fictional characters in believable contemporary *and* historical "real world" settings, *Highlander: The Series* succeeded in giving more relevance and meaning not only to its audiences, but to fantasy television itself.

Notions of fantasy are taken a step further in Trudy Barber's chapter "Kinky Borgs and Sexy Robots: The Fetish, Fashion, and Discipline of Seven of Nine," where she argues that the Borg character Seven of Nine—from *Star Trek: Voyager*—acted as a metaphor fetishizing the Frankenstein body and is symbolic of contemporary culture's wider and long-lasting love affair with (and fear of) robots and cyborgs. She suggests that this fetishism is also evidence of our fear and suspicion of converging communication and entertainment technologies, loss of gender identity, and ubiquitous computing. The chapter explores the sexological attributes of the mechanistic and penetrating Borg and discusses the erotic allure represented in the mixture of machine and flesh. The character of Seven of Nine as fashioned and portrayed on screen is discussed with reference to specific sexual subcultures and their erotic fetish attire and demeanor. In contrast to already long-established discussion surrounding the iconic cyborg of Donna Haraway, the gendering and sexualizing of technology espoused by Mary Ann Doane and Anne Balsamo, and Jenny Woolmark's work on cyberfeminism, Barber readdresses notions of the sexy robot with women of discipline (in uniform) and the posthuman—which she argues are manifest in the Borg species—and brings into the discussion an "understanding and exploration of physical sensation, dominance and submission, sensuality, and arousal through the visual titillation of such on-screen science fiction spectacles."[2]

My own chapter, "'Welcome to the world of tomorrow!': Animating Science Fictions of the Past and Present in *Futurama*," analyzes the visual and cultural references at the heart of the *Futurama* series. Focusing on genre, animation, parody, and intertextuality, it highlights how familiar science fiction tropes such as the city, television, technology, and the alien were used and reused throughout the Fox series. I argue that such recycling points on the one hand to generic exhaustion, whereby original representations of the city or technology are no longer possible in a postmodern age, yet it also brings to light the notion of parodic reversion, where familiar elements are redrawn and reinvented for a contemporary audience predisposed to multichannel, multitext television. However, I also maintain that the use of parody, animation, and the depictions of aliens and new technologies in a thirty-first-century New York merely allow the series to revisit particular science fictions of the past.

As well as using generic themes and tropes, *Futurama* consistently drew attention to the medium of television itself, utilizing many fake futuristic advertisements, TV shows, and television personalities within the diegetic narrative of the series and outside it as exemplified by the referencing of old animation in every opening credit sequence. I contend that "*Futurama* was the product of a network and competitive industry struggling to keep up with advances in format and broadcasting technology." However, its primary concern was to use those new technologies and techniques in order to imagine the future by revisiting the past; that is why the iconography of the future city and ship designs hark back to a period more recognizable in the B-movie science fiction films and early television series of the 1950s. As the focus of this volume indicates, the look of science fiction and fantasy television, including visual tropes like spaceships and robots, locations and landscapes such as outer space and the city, special effects, art and set design, and costume, contributes to the creation of fully imagined worlds. However, audience expectations of science fiction television tend to center on a futur-istic aesthetic, one symbolic of the predictive nature of the genre. *Futurama*'s vision of a future New York based on a visual aesthetic more representative of science fiction media of the past is symptomatic of the dichotomy at the heart of the science fiction genre: it looks both forward and back, as Adam Roberts describes, a form of "prediction and nostalgia."[3]

Part IV: Visions and Revisions

As *Futurama* took science fiction television from the twentieth century to the beginning of the twenty-first century, the teen horror and fantasy se-ries *Angel* provided a bridge between both centuries. In "Plastic Fantastic? Genre and Science/Technology/Magic in *Angel*," Lorna Jowett explores how key examples of what she terms its "hybrid sci-tech-magic" draw on visual conventions from science fiction, horror, and fantasy, creating a distinc-tive look. She argues that representations of sci-tech-magic are vehicles for *Angel*'s thematic concerns, such as power, control, and the (hybrid) body. Continuing with some of the debates investigated by Trudy Barber in her chapter on Seven of Nine, Jowett discusses how the figure of the cyborg features in *Angel*, affording it an especially rich way of reading the melding of science, technology, and magic. This, she argues, is not unusual for a Joss Whedon television series since they often display overt genre references (as is discussed by Robert L. Lively about *Firefly* in chapter 11) but, like much contemporary television, they draw on a wide range of different genres. *Angel* has been examined as a superhero drama, a version of noir, a lawyer show, an example of TV horror, a vampire fiction, a critical dystopia, and even a musical. While Jowett acknowledges the notion of genre hybridity (as in-troduced by Geraghty in chapter 9 regarding *Futurama*), her chapter focuses on the ways in which different genres influence the show's representation of science/technology and magic.

Whedon's more recent but rather short-lived *Firefly*, a multilayered space western, is the subject of Robert L. Lively's "Remapping the Feminine in Joss Whedon's *Firefly*." While clearly using and subverting the typical tropes of the western—a gunslinger with a heart of gold, a hired gun, a preacher, a doc-tor, a married couple, an innocent young girl, and a prostitute—Lively argues that *Firefly* goes beyond typical western stereotypes to create complicated characters working on the margins of space and respectability. He analyzes the four main female characters, arguing that Joss Whedon has remapped the western feminine for an audience of twenty-first-century viewers. One might argue that the traditional western focuses on the comings and goings of the central male characters; however, for Lively, *Firefly* gives women as much of a role as the men. Zoe, Inara, Kaylee, and River all behave in very nontraditional ways, and *Firefly* draws upon western myth and archetypes using these cultural references to set predictable patterns that are then reimagined and subverted through the use of the female characters.

This sense of revision and reimagination seen in contemporary science fiction television is the focal point of the last chapter, "'Haven't you heard? They look like us now!': Realism and Metaphor in the New *Battlestar Galactica*." Authors Dylan Pank and John Caro argue that the series holds up a mirror to reflect the world as we see it today, a common science fiction trope, yet it does so through the playing down of a predictable futuristic aesthetic—most obviously seen in series such as *Star Trek*. They argue that the design and overall *mise-en-scène* of the series has an undeniable link to the now. Characters open hinged doors, listen to analog radios, record interviews on mini-DV camcorders, shave using Ikea mirrors, and escape from their Cylon pursuers driving Humvee vehicles. This all ties in rather effectively and conveniently with the series' imagined world, where one of the protagonists quotes freely from a Mario Savio speech and others paraphrase Shakespeare. Using the work of Isaac Asimov and Robert Silverberg, which posits that the transposition of seemingly familiar values to a distant context is a common science fiction technique, Pank and Caro speculate that in *Battlestar Galactica (BSG)* the audience may see rifles/pistols, audio cassettes, mini-DV cameras, telephones, door handles, books, etc., but it reads these items as representing "forms." Thus the design of the show creates a shorthand—a grammar—that develops an identity with which contemporary media-literate audiences can recognize and engage. Furthermore, they contend that this aesthetic—this representation of reality—is central to *Battlestar Galactica*'s engagement with contemporary social, political, and philosophical issues. This "fleshed out reality" manifests itself in the mise-en-scène, fitting with and fulfilling the metaphorical subtext of the series.[4] With the mirror of science fiction television, complex and painful topics—abortion, the war on terror, suicide bombings—are presented and represented with a slant, or from an alien angle. The audience (and the mise-en-scène is an important part of this) is encouraged to see the everyday in a new light. The familiar becomes unfamiliar. The future becomes a thing of the past and once-exhausted generic tropes and archetypes are revived and revised for contemporary television.

Battlestar Galactica is one of many extinct science fiction series to undergo a refit or reboot on twenty-first-century television. With a renewed focus on the fundamental nature of what it means to be human, *BSG* peeled back the superficial layers of special effects and technobabble associated with long-running franchises like *Star Trek* and instead focused on what science fiction does best—offer a window on the human condition. For C. W. Marshall and Tiffany Potter, *BSG* did not offer American audiences a salve for the psychological wounds inflicted after 9/11, rather, it commented on "contemporary culture by imagining dystopic alternatives, and by doing so it invites the viewer to interrogate notions of self, nation, and belief that are often taken to be nonnegotiable both on television and in our living rooms."[5] As part of the new generation of science fiction television, it not only visualized other worlds and alien species but it also managed

> to use those fantastic visions, in one of the abiding traditions of science fiction, to interrogate our own nature and our own condition, particularly as we confront an age in which history seems to have lost much of its relevance, the future is mysterious, and our humanity is often perceived as just a construct of various forces beyond our full understanding and control.[6]

Similar to *BSG*, the ever-popular *Doctor Who* underwent changes to its traditional narrative that both acknowledged its roots in the old series and reflected developments in British television drama inspired by U.S. series like *24* and *CSI: Crime Scene Investigation*, as well as *Buffy the Vampire Slayer* and *The X-Files*, that "were notable for their self-consciousness, visual stylishness and re-imagining of established genres for a postmodern popular culture."[7] Clearly Russell T. Davies, writer and producer, had to maintain the cult audience by following established norms and keeping favorites such as the TARDIS, but the new Doctor was reborn and his character fleshed out with a concentration on emotions and heroism that has never been seen before.[8] No matter the series, whether it be a revamped version of a seventies cult classic or a reimagining of a TV icon, current science fiction and fantasy television continues to offer a window on the "what if" possibilities of the future. However, it is important to remember that it is how that future gets envisioned and created on screen that continues to be the defining and appealing factor in the genre's continued popularity.

Notes

1. Gerry Anderson, "Supermarionation for 'Thunderbirds,'" *British Kinematography* (1966): 334.

2. See Donna Haraway, *Simians, Cyborgs and Women: The Reinvention of Nature* (London: Free Association Books, 1991); Mary Ann Doane, "Technophilia: Technology, Representation, and the Feminine," in *Body/Politics: Women and the Dis-*

courses of Science, ed. Mary Jacobus, Evelyn Fox Keller, and Sally Shuttleworth (New York: Routledge, 1990), 163–76; Anne Marie Balsamo, *Technologies of the Gendered Body: Reading Cyborg Women* (Durham, NC: Duke University Press, 1996).

3. Adam Roberts, *Science Fiction* (London: Routledge, 2000), 30.

4. A term used by series producer Ronald D. Moore, quoted in David Langford, "Infinitely Improbable—As Others See Us," *Ansible* 198 (2004), news.ansible.co.uk/a198.html (accessed May 31, 2007).

5. C. W. Marshall and Tiffany Potter, " 'I See the Patterns: *Battlestar Galactica* and the Things that Matter," in *Cylons in America: Critical Studies in Battlestar Galactica*, ed. Tiffany Potter and C. W. Marshall (New York: Continuum, 2008), 6.

6. J. P. Telotte, "Introduction: The Trajectory of Science Fiction Television," in *The Essential Science Fiction Television Reader*, ed. J. P. Telotte (Lexington: University Press of Kentucky, 2008), 26.

7. James Chapman, *Inside the TARDIS: The Worlds of Doctor Who* (London: I. B. Tauris, 2006), 185.

8. Kim Newman, *Doctor Who* (London: BFI Publishing, 2005), 115.

PART I

AMERICA'S NEW FRONTIER

Cast of *Land of the Giants* (1968–1970). *Courtesy of The Kobal Collection.*

CHAPTER ONE

⤙⇒⊙

Retro Landscapes: Reorganizing the Frontier in Rod Serling's *The Twilight Zone*

Van Norris

Unlimited Vision

Conventional wisdom states that on-screen visualizations of the rugged, nonurbanized American landscape are endemically tied to the western genre. Recent generations, however, have had their on-screen conceptions of this space forged *not* solely through the films of John Ford or Howard Hawks but primarily through U.S. science fiction television and cinema. And as time goes by it is undoubtedly within the original five-year run of Rod Serling's seminal CBS television anthology show, *The Twilight Zone* (1959–1964), that the first stage in this reordering of the symbology of the plains took place. Through a set of intense reinforcements the show provided a transformative bridge that traversed genre boundaries and shifted common understandings around the American desert away from classical definitions and into something more fittingly fragmentary and ambivalent.

The Twilight Zone was built on the auteurist reputation of chief writer and executive producer/overseer Serling in U.S. television's formative years. Since its initial broadcast it has become revered as something of a high-water mark and has continued to assert an almost primal fascination for historians and fans alike. Not only have many of its plots, characters, and conceits entered the American consciousness, but through worldwide syndication and constant quotation across numerous film, television, literary, and multimedia forms, the show continues to inform international culture to this day, supplying a rich bank of iconic images. This status was achieved through not only an acute awareness of its own form and of the medium of television itself but also, as Rodney Hill notes, through its "fine grasp of psychological, mythological, and cultural structures."[1] This saw the series function as an important barometer of change through its self-conscious reordering of fable and myth. Certainly this aids the significant fashion by which the show has marshaled a cultural memory of the wilderness, in that it offers a connection between the interpretations presented by John Ford et al. in the 1930s and the mine-stripping of a history of conventions collated by the likes of George Lucas and George Miller in the 1970s and 1980s. Serling's model of outward space simultaneously supersedes previous conceptions, creates a signature platform, and also predicts the next significant step in the reframing of scenery that is found within Franklin J. Schaffner's (and notably the Serling-scripted) *Planet of the Apes* (1968). It is his refashioning of this mythic space that finishes what *The Twilight Zone* starts in comprehensively dragging associations away from the western and over to science fiction. Certainly J. P. Telotte's call that science fiction television has consistently tapped into prevalent cultural anxieties is pertinent. Through television's penchant for "deformation and transformation," that reallocations of meaning occur in this setting appears entirely appropriate,[2] for not only has television maintained a complex two-way interrelationship with cinema, but the medium also has proffered a consistent cultural hum throughout our lives. Its sociocultural centrality, its immediacy, and its very pervasiveness make it the perfect conduit of metaphor and meaning.

The Cultural Desert

As a visual index, the rocky plains have functioned as generic off-world environments throughout a range of science fiction texts, usually tied to transfigurations of the pioneer narratives, with George Pal's studio-bound *Conquest of Space* (1955) through to the Death Valley exteriors of Byron Haskin's *Robinson Crusoe on Mars* (1964) springing to mind. But the road to a transmutation in perception is complex. It must be observed at this point that our expectations around the desert space received a key cinematic reordering through Fred M. Wilcox's 1956 *Forbidden Planet* as one of the few films of the 1950s that treated its pulp-inspired thrills with a modicum of gravity. The pastel plains of Altair V retrospectively operate as a premonition of Lucas's revisionist space operas and are a vital step in this recasting process. However, it is Schaffner's use of the locations of Glen Canyon, Utah, and Lake Powell and Page, Arizona, for the film version of Pierre Boulle's 1963

La Planètes des singes that now appear as the culmination of a broader cultural shift in understanding. The opening "Forbidden Zone" section of the film quickly became (bound to Jerry Goldsmith's groundbreaking atonal score) a definitive cinematic marker of the "familiar" substituted for the "alien" and cemented the desert as existing away from the western forever. Eric Greene, via Richard Slotkin, cannily ties deployment of landscape to the star of the film and the invulnerable icon of "Western imperial privilege," Charlton Heston.[3] Greene and Slotkin see that the desert and Heston's star persona were intertwined: "Heston appeared to be perpetually fighting a 'last stand' battle to defend a fort or outpost of Western 'civilisation' against the on-slaught of hordes of non-Western, dark-skinned 'barbarians.'"[4] Greene thus extrapolates that the film (and for us the representations of scenery therein) supplies an inversion of the Western myth by "denying the Western hero both victory and the mythological gesture of martyrdom."[5] This is rendered in explicit terms through Serling's typically sour ending when Heston's as-tronaut, George Taylor, discovers that the "madhouse" of the monkey planet he has been negotiating is in fact a postapocalyptic Earth of two thousand years into the future. Whereas the Western space in previous incarnations had implied spirituality and positivity, here it is transformed into a postcoun-tercultural wasteland of desolation and dislocation. By 1968 the frontier had shed any redemptive coding and was now a darker, more pessimistic environ-ment that suggested failure as much as survival.[6]

As a result of the film's success and reacting to the post-1960s mood, dys-topian visions soon became de rigueur within mainstream cinematic science fiction. The embrace of flats, mountains, and bleak exteriors soon became enmeshed within the slow ascendance to the quiet respectability enjoyed by the form. Treaties such as *No Blade of Grass* (1970), *THX 1138* (1971), and *A Boy and His Dog* (1975) and the cunning hybridity found within Michael Crichton's *Westworld* (1973) all contributed to this framing process. *Westworld* retained classical notions of the landscape as a site of contention but posited two versions of the frontier at the same time to indicate the breadth of man's folly. One version was a postmodern facsimile and reimagining of an antiseptic classical framework, the other a more deliberately post-Schaffner/Serling, Darwinian landscape that backdrops a struggle between man and machine. This impression flourishes in 1970s cinema right up to George Lucas's *Star Wars* (1977). The enormous impact of that film now ex-ists as a cultural, industrial, thematic, and formal "ground zero," as not only did it reconfigure the way filmmakers approach science fantasy/fiction, but also through the usage of desert space it offered another notable shift point. Though obvious nods toward the western were detectable in the Tatooine shantytown of Mos Eisley, these references were submerged into a plethora of highly self-conscious quotations accessing a patchwork of references from Herbert to Kurosawa and Tolkien. The Tunisian location supplied a New Hollywood verisimilitude and also marked an aesthetic release from the now over-familiar locations of California and Arizona. This newer "elsewhere" provided spectacle and demarcation and pointed toward our current cultural state of hyperfragmentation.

"Distance" Memories

Intersections with the generic expectations found in the western appear unavoidable here. If we work from the premise that iconography reinforced through repetition works to construct a consistent genre for the viewer/reader, then surely the appropriation of such familiar signs creates uncertainties. Before proceeding we have to indeed ask, is *The Twilight Zone* even *science fiction*? Historically it is certainly deemed to be. But confusions are apparent. In terms of generic continuity, arguably the presence of Serling himself (as John Tulloch and Manuel Alvarado express) promotes a kind of typology. Through the self-contained narratives this is managed not by sequential, diachronic continuity but via his weekly introductory narration.[7] The show's association with science fiction is also often reinforced through its alliance to recognizable visual iconography, much of which is bound up with convention. Common generic elements such as the varied elements of the fantastic that are present—rocket ships, time-travel devices, robots, and futuristic cities—and other aspects of the speculative are explicitly allied to an accepted canon of science fiction literature with the inclusion of writers like Ray Bradbury and Richard Matheson. Vivian Sobchack's observation of the visual style of science fiction cinema, that it is "a genre which is un-fixed in its dependence on actual time and place," further permits such an expansive show to perform generically as science fiction.[8] This is aided by Annette Kuhn's comments (fed through Sobchack's work) stressing that sci-fi is defined by "themes, iconography, its modes of address and its uses."[9] Such a fluid understanding is useful in that this genre is also primarily considered (by Robert Scholes, Bruce Kawin, and Barry Keith Grant) a "cognitive," cerebral set of conventions that prize an exploration of new ideas and a "sense of wonder"; all of this can be located within the series' less-than-rigorous scientific demands.[10] Yet *Twilight Zone* overlaps into magic realism, poetic realism, fantasy, and comedy as much as it does with science fiction. Thus bearing in mind Serling's penchant for jarring emotive reactions, perhaps we also need to be aware of the makeup of horror. Grant, via Linda Ruth

Williams, offers that through the genre's very name there are inherent implications of a predominantly "emotional" register at work and this tends to be based around "psychological" factors placed to elicit audience response.[11] Emotional effect prized over scientific exactitude is a characteristic feature of the show. The definition that seems to cover the most ground and hold the most purchase here is Lester Del Ray's 1979 summation of the fantasy genre, which he sees as preoccupied with "alternative impossibilities."[12] Serling's show consistently crosses many lines to facilitate an entrance to the realm of the allegorical, which adequately serves our case and plays into deeper concerns that will be addressed later.

Besides assessing generic boundaries, other factors in this reordering process need to be accounted for. Jason Mittell rightly asserts that "texts do not interact on their own; they come together only through cultural practices such as production and reception."[13] This makes it impossible to divorce history and lineage from the process of assessing genre within television studies. He goes on to say that "genres only emerge from the intertextual relations between multiple texts, resulting in a common category," and even though these may bear the imprint of understood conventions, they don't actually *define* the genre but in fact present artifacts that "exist only through the creation, circulation, and consumption of texts within cultural contexts."[14] Mittell's position that genre needs to be understood through cultural discourses alongside an acknowledgement of the inherent fluidity and hybridity of the medium itself is worth considering, especially when compiling a lineage around our cultural memories of the frontier. Lincoln Geraghty and Mark Jancovich follow this up by concurring that genre today is increasingly less defined by production, cycles, conventions, or sequence and that cultural memory now appears as a valid tool in judging boundaries: "Memory therefore plays a vital part in our understanding of genre. It can help us to remember that which has been excluded or repressed by historical processes, or to change the agendas of previous commentaries."[15]

It is of course apparent that a cultural studies–based model, based on socially defined individual memory, can be compromised. Cultural and individual memory can be subjective, random, biased, and transient. It is reliant on the processing of critically approved canons of thought in collusion with a heavily mediated experiential account. Inevitably, personalized frameworks of assessment are open to refutation when defined through a differing set of social precepts and expectations. My own thoughts here are filtered through keen attention to American popular culture and, as such, one must be aware that these reflections are informed by the consumption-informed histories so highlighted by the likes of Richard Terdiman.[16] Without wishing to be drawn at this juncture into the ongoing methodological debates over collective and individual memory, Jan Assmann's summation of this set of readings as allied to a "body of reusable texts, images and rituals that are specific to each society in each epoch whose 'cultivation' serves to stabilize and convey that society's self image" serves us here as a pertinent observational platform.[17]

Shifting Sands

My entire argument is based around the merging of boundaries, and this sits central to the show in terms of genre, theme, and representation. M. Keith Booker asserts that the series, "despite its lingering love of the Western literary tradition and its modernist aspiration to the condition of High Art, contains some of the clearest signs of postmodernism in the long 1950s, especially in its incessant interrogation of conventional boundaries, such as those between Self and Other and between Reality and Fiction."[18]

That *The Twilight Zone* plays a vital part in the beginnings of postmodern American television is a valid point that aids an understanding of how frontier symbology has been mutated. Its place at the final years of what Derek Kompare calls the "Golden Age of Television" (i.e., the first decade of production, between 1948 and 1958) is telling also, as the show entirely points toward broadcasting future rather than past.[19] The extension from modernist sensibilities dictates the deployment of landscape and reinforces that television has served culture profoundly as an incubator of imagery. All of this is paralleled by the downgrading of iconography incurred as a byproduct of the western's incorporation into 1950s mainstream television. Along with the boom in advertising, the success of shows such as *Have Gun Will Travel* (1957–1963), *Rawhide* (1959–1966), *Gunsmoke* (1955–1975), and *Bonanza* (1959–1973) enforced, through reiteration, a sense of exhaustion, as well as indicating the pace of an accelerating postmodern condition. This is detailed in John Cawelti's breakdown of the processes of generic transformation that inform 1970s cinematic revisionism and provides a useful conceptual model. In discussing exemplars of postclassical film, evidence suggests that these reconfigurations had actually already occurred within the arena of prime-time television. Cawelti argues that several stages of generic reordering, as enforced by New Hollywood, culminated around the time of the late 1960s into the 1970s. While Serling's 1950s deployments of landscape avoid the process of burlesquing that he highlights, the usage of Death Valley and the wide plains of Nevada therein do strike a necessary ambivalence with nostalgia. He isolates this state as the invocation of an original conception that has been consistently replayed to the point where the cultural understanding of an image is *so* embedded that it becomes "demythologized" as a result.[20] In turn this leads to a "generic exhaustion" that promotes a desire for a more complex, knowing take on overrecognized signifiers within a text.[21] Serling reorders the frontier for a new generation of TV watchers through such repetition across various key episodes of *The Twilight Zone* that feature inhospitable locales as central to their narratives. This, in Cawelti's words, serves better the "imaginative needs of our time," and off the back of an overfamiliarity these representations were revelatory of a geographical shift away from the sweeping grandeur of John Ford's beloved Monument Valley. The relocation of frontier imagery to the arid expanses of regular location shoot Death Valley, in effect, facilitated a fresh, more potent postmodern conception of the outlands.[22]

Now this procedure is both further aided *and* confused by the pervasiveness of the studio back-lot aesthetic. Here actual location becomes irrelevant and precipitation and perception are fundamental. For a generation weaned on a diet of television throughout the 1970s, this all-purpose "elsewhere" has profoundly contributed to this fragmentation of perception. This phenomenon is also bound up with the forces outlined by Kompare. He refers to "television heritage"[23] as linked to changing perceptions around the cultural and critical status of TV itself and suggests that our perceptions of imagery thus become embroiled with processing of twenty years of production, syndication, and repackaging: "Television, in its unparalleled accessibility, its endless flow of processed sounds and images, its connection to economic and state institutions, and its constant repetition, is thus the most prolific heritage generator in our culture."[24]

The studio back lot was an aesthetic built on expediency that became a convenient solution to presenting imaginative locations. It permitted a welcome visual contrast with claustrophobic, unconvincing studio interiors and in turn helped to offset budget and design limitations and restrictive deadlines. Within television production, this idea of desert as convenient "fantasy space" through its bland "openness" soon suggested a kind of oblique opulence. In reality, of course, it simply detailed a visual continuity borne of the same restrictive industrial constraints that defined the B movies of the era, located within any Allied Artists B-films, from *World Without End* (1956) to *Queen of Outer Space* (1956). While little was offered in the way of any true spectacle or any attempt to seriously detail a cohesive off-world ecosystem, the back lots did provide a platform for various alien minions/stuntmen to face off in unconfined, "realistic" surroundings.[25] Thus, real estate like the 40 Acres site (originally established by RKO and attached to the Desilu studios from 1957 to 1967) regularly passed for a range of continuums in which any number of protagonists could then face their ultimate tests of endurance.

Of course, this is merely a continuation of a tradition forged within the factory-line production ethos of classical production. The Universal International ranch in Culver City, California, stood in as an all-purpose battlefield for Buster Crabbe in *Flash Gordon Conquers the Universe* (1940), and lesser efforts like Republic's *The Adventures of Captain Marvel* (1941) and *King of the Rocket Men* (1949) were all filmed on the Iverson Ranch, also in California. But primarily studio-bound shows, from Stefano and Steven's *The Outer Limits* (1963–1965)[26] to Allen's *Lost in Space* (1965–1968) and *Time Tunnel* (1966) (see De Los Santos's chapter in this volume) to Roddenberry's *Star Trek* (1967–1969), all benefited from this option.[27]

Serling circumnavigated this trope by taking full advantage of the more expansive budgets allocated to the show, which allowed his production crew to present a visual extravagance that set it apart from other similar anthology series. As Serling himself stated in 1959, these would be "high quality, extremely polished films"[28] and this desire was maintained by director of photography and noted perfectionist George T. Clemens, who is often hailed as one of the primary contributors to *The Twilight Zone*'s consistently high-quality visual style. Arlen Schumer quotes Clemens from 1961 when he confirms there was a palpable sense of rigor around the visual presentation of the show with an uncompromising "Everything has got to be just right."[29] Interestingly, this flies in the face of tired critiques offered over the years around television's "artlessness" as the show regularly used gaps in budget or absences in detail to move into the realm of the poetic to remain consistently strong on visual signifiers and creative uses of space, exterior and interior.[30]

Dust to Dust

Dust features prominently in the show as interior and exterior incarnations of the wilderness, signifying varying degrees of resonance across all five seasons. The show broadly marshals desert in several interesting ways. (There is of course some potential slippage between each of the models I discuss here, and word constraints do not permit full analysis or indeed a comprehensive list for each category.) The first framework that reoccurs throughout the show can be defined as in service to *Historical/Contemporary*.

These depictions can be perceived as relatively straightforward indexes of place, such as in the case of "You Drive!" (1964). These can invoke either current temporal or historical backdrops. The historical indexes can often play into the more overtly sentimental detours and the longing for simpler times that permeates some of Serling's work. Such representations conform to the nostalgic "tranquil, Victorian times" that he uses to map out a sense of lost American societal innocence,[31] and this is explicitly acknowledged in episodes that stress a sense of reclamation, such as the Capraesque "Walking Distance" (1959). This model also features in the numerous stories that make explicit links to the western genre such as "Mr. Denton on Doomsday" (1959) or "Mr. Garrity and the Graves" (1964), among others. It also includes most of Earl Hamner Jr.'s writings for the series that exist almost as a subgenre, with its folksy "preference for earthiness and decency over the freeway glitz"[32] and thus covered in "Come Wander with Me" (1964), "Still Valley" (1961), "The Hunt" (1962), and "The Last Rites of Jeff Myrtlebank" (1962), to name but a few.[33]

The second typology found within the series is *Future/Off-Worlds*. This usage of scenery is often bound up with literalism and acts as rugged backdrops standing in for planet surfaces, asteroids, or futuristic landscapes. Episodes such as "Elegy" (1960), "People Are Alike All Over" (1959), "Probe 7—Over and Out" (1963), "Death Ship" (1963), "The Little People," (1962) and "Two" (1961) all conform to this and, like each framework here, can easily slip into allegorical registers. This configuration also includes examples like the celebrated "Time Enough at Last" (1959) and the equally gloomy "The Shelter" (1961), which construct studio-bound wastelands to simulate postnuclear devastation.

The third model is an unspecified *Anyspace*. This operates as a more neutral paradigm. Through its deliberate ambiguity, this depiction often forms the basis of the trick denouement and thus can be required to act immediately as an explicitly symbolic canvas. This is arguably the most potent category, which through its very blankness facilitates access to a deeper cultural resonance. Shows like "King Nine Will Not Return" (1960) and "It's a Good Life" (1961) conform to this model to lesser or greater degrees. The frontier paraphernalia suggested by Agnes Moorhead's cabin in "The Invaders" (1961) is deployed to wrong-foot us when it is revealed that we have been witnessing not Earth and a "home on the range" but in fact an alien world all along, thus sliding us to a location within the Twilight Zone itself. The curious blend of past, present, and future that serves the Hamner episode "Spur of the Moment" (1964) also comes to mind here. But it is in "The Rip Van Winkle Caper" (1961), "I Shot an Arrow into the Air" (1960), "A Hundred Yards over the Rim" (1961), and "The Lonely" (1959) where the strongest examples reside.

The Back of Beyond

One of the most potent examples of how *The Twilight Zone* contributes to the recasting of desert space undoubtedly came with the season one opener, "The

Lonely." As scripted by Serling and directed by Jack Smight, this emblematic story was shot over a grueling 130-degree, two-day location schedule in
Death Valley during June of 1959.[34] "The Lonely" commences a love affair
with frontier space that extends as an abstracted continuity across the entire
run. Indeed, this recurrent use of landscape actually conforms to the thematic
heart of the show itself. Peter Wolfe hits on a related point here as he allies
Serling's appropriation of "twilight" to Wordsworth and thus correlates this
to the show's fascination with spatial hinterlands. He sees that Wordsworth's
"soft gray twilight as a realm unto itself" mirrors Serling's conception of
locative space between "science and superstition." For us this is literalized in
these rugged plains and ravines far away from the urban, the contemporary,
and, more metaphorically, the constrictions of any ephemeral morality that
is regularly contested throughout the series.[35] The scenery in "The Lonely"
is a confirmation of this: not only is Death Valley a canvas that provides a
stark natural relief from the Desilu back lots, but through the parched, desolate rock faces and the absence of foliage we can see the grim heart of the
show projected on-screen. The lexicon of bleak, open panoramas, the distant
empty horizons, the searing sun, the attendant scenes of climbing, sweating,
and negotiation of hostile environments across several episodes all perform
as highly symbolic moments that embody an existential questioning that, in
retrospect, actually helps define memories of the show.

Within "The Lonely" there are thematic points that Serling and his staff
of writers would repeatedly return to. Lincoln Geraghty is not alone when
he notes the progressive intent behind the show.[36] Stewart Stanyard too
embraces a positivist reading of Serling in his collection of interviews on the
production of the series. He feels that among the prevailing themes addressed
across all the seasons is that of redemption, the offering by the fates of a second chance.[37] Wolfe concurs when he maintains that Serling optimistically
believed that even in the "most ugliest, squalid settings," a salvation can occur.[38] But while it is true that Serling's liberalist idealism is palpable across all
five seasons, what truly resides as a trace memory is a bitter pessimism. The
cruel, sour twists of "Time Enough at Last," "I Shot an Arrow into the Air,"
and "It's a Good Life," among many other episodes, reiterate this.[39]

It is no coincidence that the signature arid narrative contortion that
punctuates Serling's *Planet of the Apes* script had already been played out via
the "dry run" (as it were) of the first season episode "I Shot an Arrow into
the Air." Tellingly this story presents a lodestone of predictive images in the
Arizona exteriors that predate Schaffner's "Forbidden Zone." Serling revels
in the potency of the surroundings to convey murderous self-protection when
his astronauts, seemingly lost on a barren asteroid, enact the pioneer survival

impulse to its logical conclusions ("telephone poles . . . you were trying to draw telephone poles . . . we never left the Earth . . . !"). As in the similarly themed season two episode, "The Rip Van Winkle Caper," the desert is offered as somewhere where morality dissolves and abnegation of duty to fellow man is rewarded with ironic retribution. Serling has a taste for penalizing his characters in unforgiving outcomes that is matched by the nature of the locale. Thus the romantic notion of redemption is roundly undermined here also, in arguably one of Serling's bleakest tales.

Booker cites "The Lonely" not only as an appropriate introduction to Serling's continuum but also as an exemplar of the show's Menippean satirical register, which is a Bakhtinian emphasis based around fusing abstract and topical concerns within a fantastical setting.[40] Although much of *The Twilight Zone* can be seen to directly reference the contemporary, with episodes such as "The Mirror" (1961) nodding toward the events surrounding the Bay of Pigs and "The Monsters Are Due on Maple Street" (1960), "The Shelter," (1961) and "Four O'Clock" (1962) all explicitly aligning themselves to a McCarthyite critique, the show functions at its most effective in this context as a broader philosophical analogy. The identification of a satirical address at work (highlighted by Joshi, Wolfe, and Wolcott, among others) sees the choice of landscape here as evidently extending beyond simple convenience.[41]

Loneliness is, as Wolfe notes, a staple motif of the series—whether this is detailing people in transit from one world to another or in situations where they cannot transmit their experiences of the unknown, or people being cast out into unfamiliar landscapes.[42] Serling's title in itself indexes the inevitable loneliness that awaits us all and to emphasize this, the central character, James A. Corry, is described in the opening narration as a man "dying of loneliness." Corry is, as Booker correctly identifies, a typical *Zone* protagonist in that he is "alone in the face of strange circumstances that confront him or her."[43] This is heightened by the introductory motif of space travel that is another recurrent central concern of the series. Apart from existing as a metaphor that for Booker is all about being "ultimately alone in the world," it is also one that inevitably plays into grander cultural narratives of isolation, paranoia, and anxiety so emblematic of a cold war–obsessed America.[44]

"The Lonely" concerns convicted criminal Corry (Jack Warden), abandoned on an unnamed asteroid for fifty years for killing in self-defense. In an act of pity, his sympathetic jailer and regular supply man, Allenby (John Dehner), delivers him a female robot, Alicia (Jean Marsh), to alleviate the intense loneliness. Initially rejecting her, in time Corry slowly comes to accept and then fall in love with the automaton and soon believes that she is a real woman. When Allenby returns some eleven months later to inform Corry that he has been granted a pardon, he also tells him that he needs to abandon his accrued belongings for the journey back to Earth. Corry refuses to leave Alicia behind, resulting in Allenby having to shoot the robot in the face to shock him from his delusion. This leaves Corry in a typically Serlingian situation. He has been granted the thing he most desires but at an ongoing cost that he could not have possibly foreseen. He will be lonely now for eternity and the irony is that the Eden he found was merely (and will remain) in his head and the most inhospitable place conceivable.

Crossing Boundaries

As stated earlier, Booker's assessment of the show's intersections with post-modernity rests upon the way it interrogates boundaries. Arguably this fluidity also extends to the jumble of self-conscious stylistic flirtations which include a convergence of surrealist, expressionist, and classicist modes. Certainly the deployment of expressionist imagery throughout the series maintains the predisposition toward horror that lazily defines its application within American mainstream settings.[45] And away from theatrical appropriations of chiaroscuro on one surface level, it could be argued that the bleakness of Corry's landscape is a purely expressionist statement, a literal manifestation of the character's desolate inner self.

This also further plays into the fusion and confusion that commercial fantasy has often displayed when approaching surrealist modes. Arlen Schumer quotes Andre Breton himself in his 1990 introduction to *Visions from the Twilight Zone* when he allies the show to a definably surrealistic impulse.[46] As this is a form that has always embraced the uncanny, Schumer's reading is highly appropriate. Surrealism is detectable through the challenges to understood reality that provide the focus of so many of the show's narratives. Incongruous flourishes can also be detected in the manifold juxtapositions of the mundane with elements of the fantastic or the unexpected. Signature fixations on death, as one of the prime drives of our collective existence, are also dissected in many episodes such as "The Hitch-Hiker" (1960) and "Nothing in the Dark" (1962), adding more weight to this assessment. But we must acknowledge that this is a diluted, fragmented refraction and one that offers an often deliberately muddled political intent. Any shocking explorations of psychology and sexuality are of course neutered by prime-time imperatives and thus are revelatory of a distinctly American desire for rationalization. An understandable denial of a Bretonian automatistic practice is apparent in the necessary service to commercial pragmatism, yet the show manages to effectively synthesize formal narrative concerns with random, disturbing images. The blurring of styles works within the context of the show, as a pertinent aesthetic summation of twentieth-century art practice.

Within "The Lonely" it is notable that surrealistic dialogues work alongside elements of classicism to create a unique visual space. Several totems manifest themselves as entirely dreamlike in their construction and aid this postmodern confusion. The opening sequence in itself offers a Bretonian gesture with the placement of a vintage car parked on a roadless desert next to a cabin, smeared into a bleached rocky expanse. There is no fixed geographical point of reference visible as Serling's narration informs us that this is, ostensibly, a science fiction setting. This canny bricolage subverts the signifier of the automobile as marker of industrialization and as a signal of finality (essayed vigorously by the likes of Sergio Leone and Sam Peckinpah).[47] Corry's self-built "old touring car that squats in the sun and goes nowhere" is a jarring vision that suggests decay, defeat, and isolation and exists as a futile gesture toward an abandoned self-reliance. For a more shocking, disturbing register, the smashed face of Alicia, which is used to shake Corry from his self-delusion at the episode's finale, provides the series with one of its key surrealistic signature images. It is also this visage which drags him from one unreality to another and acts as a revelation of Booker's Bakhtinian "reversals" or "inversions."[48]

This alliance to carnivalesque subversions as "an image of capitalism" is perhaps a little convenient as an observation, but the show's postmodern credentials continue through its late-1950s subjectivity and its defiant free-play with extant signifiers.[49] The big-band jazz music Corry plays on his decrepit gramophone, the strangely appropriate but wholly illogical telegraph poles glimpsed in backgrounds, the 1950s speech idioms, Allenby's print book, and the outmoded paraphernalia that now charmingly infers high-end technology endemic to an unspecified techno-dominant Earth all go toward suggesting the contemporary. Yet the narrative implies we are in an unspecified future temporality, which creates a further disorder. This all contributes to an experiential schism for present-day viewers that colludes with the already inherent transgressions of narrative, generic, and temporal boundaries and actually complements the series' examinations over what constitutes authenticity.

Space Invasion

Slippage is permissible within such a symbolic setting. As located in the convergences here, there is an acknowledgement (as well as a breakdown) of what has gone before. "The Lonely," in typically muddled late-modern fashion, can be considered as much evolution as quotation, especially when one considers the term *new worlds*, as this is a projection that appears somehow embedded within associations around this kind of open space. J. Hoberman insists that the western form persevered throughout the 1950s as part of "the celebration of national expansion . . . implicitly supported by the dominant Cold War ethos of limitless growth and personal freedom."[50] Thus depictions of the desert space through this period would perhaps appear to suggest continuities based on a broader contemporary optimism. In cultural terms, however, much has been expressed over the duality of the American mood at that time, when an unresolved pessimism enforced by nuclear uncertainty and postwar doubt countered a consumer-based optimism. Serling's recasting of landscape taps into this and offers a less forgiving, more ambiguous sardonic extension. Corry's asteroid is no compromised 1950s space reconfigured by leisure and expansion. It is far removed from carving a simple home in the land. This is a frontier that tests and reveals spirit, soul, and mind, and is a defiantly paranoid space that actualizes the existential anxieties founded during the Great Depression and the fallout from a devastating world war.

In line with classicist definitions, Serling's conceptual bridge remains a site of Darwinian struggle, coterminous with an aesthetic and moral dimension.[51] Yet this is a complex gesture as it is at once entirely in service to the postmodern proliferation of signs as well as functioning simultaneously as both upgrade *and* continuity, as this lineage contains seemingly traditional mappings of pioneer narratives founded within visual representations of the West. Edward Buscombe's notes on Arizona within the films of John Ford (in his study focusing primarily on Monument Valley and the Grand Canyon) confirm this, and through such tales a rich set of significations have gradually become embedded within America's sense of self.[52] Jan Johnson-Smith takes this further when summating the convergence of these genre-bound frameworks into science fiction. Through the accumulation of nineteenth-century romantic fiction and art and early twentieth-century cinema, these potent myths have become (leaning on the definitions offered by John Conron) an amalgam of signifiers bound together within a familiar lexicon of images. The core understanding is still that of a romanticized conception that bears roots back to a specific historical moment yet retains links to the heart of American identity. Johnson-Smith states that

> the western landscape ceases to be one of reality: it is instead a composite of what the West as a symbol has come to represent . . . it is not a landscape painting of an actual place, but instead a collection of images and narratives,

gathered and relocated into a single picture, carefully balanced with a false but strong sense of human perspective. It is as if key components of Monument Valley, Yosemite and Yellowstone, the Catskills and the Rocky Mountains co-exist in one location: the sublime wonders of the Wild West are framed and tamed.[53]

The suitably ironic conceit at work here is acknowledged by both Buscombe and Johnson-Smith. Johnson-Smith states, "For a nostalgic genre it seldom spoke of its present but of the future—of what would happen when the wilderness became a garden."[54] What tempers this classical reading of mountains, skies, and plains is a set of narratives forged around the desert as site of "potential." This is seen as a predictive space where civilization itself is born; one which stresses wilderness as a testing ground, where the strength of the individual's will to survive is assessed, where there is a possibility for self-definition (and *re*definition), and where liberation itself can occur. Along with speaking of the past and the future simultaneously, there is also another palpable tension residing, an inherent religious coding that infers that the location or establishment of a Utopia, a Garden of Eden, is imperative. This founding myth, complete with the darker, parallel dialogues with undercurrents of dominance, colonization, and exploitation buried within, are at once recognized, incorporated, and subverted by Serling.

Buscombe asserts that through photography and paintings from the 1830s onward, the role of landscape was that of an aesthetic object to be gazed at "in an act of reverential contemplation."[55] Citing Roderick Nash, he describes this as an unspoiled summation of a romanticized obsession with panoramic vastness, a "primitivistic idealization" of a life close to an unspoiled nature. Notably, humans are deployed primarily as "markers of scale."[56] Through this compositional emphasis, implicit religious and spiritual dimensions are at work. Recognition of the sublime, access to awe, and insight are traditionally enforced within classical art by the inclusion of a contemplative figure. This provides a psychologized context and a contemplative gesture that sets up a profound connection to the higher power that created the land. The requisite idealistic "elevation" that Johnson-Smith observed in the art of Albert Bierstadt, Thomas Cole, and Frederick Church is now transferred to the mise-en-scène of American science fiction television but with these positivist qualities absent.[57] Serling offers us a nominal staffage index in the tortured form of Corry, but this is at once a nuanced reframing as it is a deliberate citation, not in fact to highlight the wonders of this new world but to provide a contrast that points out its overwhelming "lack." Johnson-Smith notes that frontier art of the late 1800s was translated into classical cinema forms appearing as a symbol for "divine destiny and potential glory."[58] The patriotic dialogues rooted within Bierstadt's celebrations of America's natural wonders are inverted toward an ambivalent reading that suits a more jaundiced, precountercultural mode of questioning. Corry's take on this space is resentment and is a premonition of the weary cynicism soon to be made explicit in *Planet of the Apes* as well as in films like Peckinpah's parallel disillusionment, *The Wild Bunch* (1969).[59]

Serlingian irony continues. Corry's criminal status is not posited, so the landscape can function not as a redemptive space but more as a dead end. He is not here to propagate but to exist in the barest terms and in fact to rot, to decompose physically and mentally. This further distorts continuations extended from cinematic pioneer tales where the protagonists within John Ford's films were, as Jim Kitses identifies, often "mavericks, underdogs, outsiders—driven heroes," which in turn leads to the conception that America's cornerstone society was forged by the criminal classes.[60] Here the central characters are no longer establishing a "socially regulated"[61] community, as the concept is roundly mocked with the appearance of Alicia as a sterile, male-constructed Eve to soothe Corry's abandoned, defeated Adam. Comparisons with Ford's 1939 *Stagecoach* are evident as shown by the high contrasts between the stasis and claustrophobia of Corry's studio-bound cabin set against the light-drenched locations. These echo the deliberately cramped interiors of the titular stagecoach to Lordsburg in Ford's film and the possibilities presented through the expanses of Monument Valley. Fordian expectations receive their most profound inversion with Corry's subjugation by the landscape itself. He is eventually, as revealed through the bleak denouement, psychologically branded by his surroundings. The rugged vista is not here to be admired, but feared and respected as the location emerges as the dominant character in this play and thus the ultimate victor.

Apart from Serling's opening statement, the visual assumes primacy in the episode. Dialogue is abandoned briefly as setting is revealed through a succession of long shots presenting an extreme vision of parched floors, distant mountain ranges, endless undisclosed space, and cloudless skies. It is entirely appropriate that color is missing as the neutral whites and greys propagate a blankness that complements Serling's existential play. That Corry's desert is scored by minor string tones and muted horns as a universe away from the declaratory fanfares and triumph that conventionally accompany the pioneer saga are appropriate and necessary reframing devices. As now stripped from its romanticized foundations, there is at work in these images a philosophical recasting of emphasis. Serling's analogy that this place is a "microscopic piece of sand that floats through space" is useful. This is no latent Eden but simply a confinement that stretches "as far as the eye can see," a stark, unforgiving space that refutes reclamation. It is devoid of clues that can provide the viewer easy purchase or any predictive or assumptive pleasures. Serling's frontier is an explicitly allegorical, unknowable, open-ended space and one that refutes any inevitability. This desert is about banishment, about facing absence, madness, and the barrenness of the infinite; this is a place to witness outer *and* inner space merge. Part of Corry's mission is to not only reconcile himself with this "dungeon nine million miles from the Earth" but to find a place within it. The parallels with traditional conceptions are intentional to deepen the despair. Punishment supersedes aspiration.

All in the Mind

This key shift in the perception of the landscape exists as much as prediction as it does continuation and quotation. As the classical reverential gaze toward the landscape was supplanted and refracted into a cultural space that now bears so much more meaning than just "the frontier," thus the statement, "the location of the story is perhaps less important than the perception of that location," holds true here.[62] Referring to elements of the "traditional" located within Gene Roddenberry's *Star Trek*, Johnson-Smith rightly sees the science fiction genre as the natural repository not only for the exploratory narrative but also for the attendant visual signifiers. However, in this televisual context it is of course Serling who first reasons that this final frontier is less about an outward exploration than about an inner one a good few years before Roddenberry. Arguably the desert space now exists as a fixed convention of science fiction as much as any postindustrial cityscape, example of automated intelligence, or design of spaceship. If, as Sobchack states, the fantasy or science fiction genre is defined by "a phenomenology of vision,"[63] then the barren vistas so unique to *The Twilight Zone* are surely a prime exemplar of this.

Notes

    1. Rodney Hill, "Mapping the Twilight Zone's Cultural and Mythical Terrain," in *The Essential Science Fiction Reader*, ed. J. P. Telotte (Lexington: University of Kentucky, 2008), 124.

    2. J. P. Telotte, "Introduction: The Trajectory of Science Fiction Television," in *The Essential Science Fiction Reader*, ed. J. P. Telotte (Lexington: University of Kentucky, 2008), 7.

    3. Eric Greene, *Planet of the Apes as American Myth: Race, Politics, and Popular Culture* (Hanover, NH: Wesleyan University Press, 1998), 48.

4. Ibid., 41.

5. Ibid., 45.

6. Ibid. This predicts the all-purpose apocalyptic space that reaches apotheosis with Miller's *Mad Max* films.

7. Jan Johnson-Smith, *American Science-Fiction TV: Star Trek, Stargate and Beyond* (London: I. B. Tauris, 2005), 52.

8. Vivian Sobchack, "Images of Wonder: The Look of Science Fiction," in *Liquid Metal: The Science Fiction Film Reader*, ed. Sean Redmond (London: Wallflower, 2004), 5.

9. Annette Kuhn, ed., "Introduction," in *Alien Zone II: The Spaces of Science Fiction Cinema* (London: Verso, 1999), 3.

10. Barry K. Grant, "'Sensuous Elaboration': Reason and the Visible in the Science Fiction Film," in *Alien Zone II: The Spaces of Science Fiction Cinema* (London: Verso, 1999), 17.

11. Ibid.

12. Ibid.

13. Jason Mittell, *Genre and Television: From Cop Shows to Cartoons in American Culture* (New York: Routledge, 2004), 8.

14. Ibid.

15. Lincoln Geraghty and Mark Jancovich, "Introduction: Generic Canons," in *The Shifting Definitions of Genre: Essays on Labeling Films, Television Shows and Media*, ed. Lincoln Geraghty and Mark Jancovich (Jefferson, NC: McFarland, 2008), 8.

16. See Richard Terdiman, *Present Past: Modernity and the Memory Crisis* (Ithaca, NY: Cornell University Press, 2003).

17. Assman in Wulf Kansteiner, "Finding Meaning in Memory: A Methodological Critique of Collective Memory Studies," *History Theory* 41, no. 2 (May 2002): 182.

18. M. Keith Booker, *Strange TV: Innovative Television Series from The Twilight Zone to The X-Files* (Westport, CT: Greenwood Press, 2002), 60.

19. Derek Kompare, *Rerun Nation: How Repeats Invented American Television* (New York: Routledge, 2005), 107. Kompare sees this as an era where "program forms and norms were not yet entrenched, and the level of ingenuity and sheer talent on display was unparalleled."

20. John G. Cawelti, "*Chinatown* and Generic Transformation in Recent American Films," in *The Film Genre Reader*, ed. Barry Keith Grant (Austin: University of Texas Press, 2003), 250.

21. Ibid., 260.

22. Ibid.

23. Kompare, *Rerun Nation*, 105.

24. Ibid., 106.

25. On a speculative level one has to wonder if this device has served cultural memory in a fashion unpredicted by filmmakers. Such representations surely became embedded as an attainable imaginative space for any impressionable youngster with access to a playground gravel pit or piece of neighborhood rough ground. Thus Altair

V or the Earth of 3056 could be handily reconstituted and re-staged, in the young mind, at any point in the pre-VCR culture.

26. *Outer Limits* episodes such as "The Zanti Misfits" (1963) and "Keeper of the Purple Twilight" (1964) through to "Cry of Silence" (1964) all undoubtedly play a part in this chain of influence.

27. One of the most memorable examples of this aesthetic would have to be James T. Kirk's *mano-a-mano* exchange with The Gorn, filmed at Vasquez Rocks in Los Angeles County for *Star Trek's* "Arena" (1967) and reused in the following episode, "The Alternative Factor." The back lot remained a fixture in the range of low-budget sci-fi "chase" shows fashioned after *The Fugitive* (1963–1967), such as *Planet of the Apes* (1974), *Logan's Run* (1977–1978), and *The Fantastic Journey* (1977), where the California hills continued as a marker for self-contained societies, alternative worlds, exiled spaces, and hinterlands well into the 1980s.

28. Serling cited in Gordon F. Sander, *Serling: The Rise and Twilight of Television's Last Angry Man* (New York: Dutton, 1992), 150.

29. Arlen Schumer, *Visions from the Twilight Zone* (Vancouver, BC, Canada: Chronicle, 1990), 21.

30. A high-end consistency is also played out in the interior set designs. "The Obsolete Man" (1961), "Number 12 Looks Just Like You" (1964), "The Long Morrow" (1964), and "The Trade-Ins" (1962) all infer futuristic spaces through simplicity of staging and effective, expert lighting and photography. These sets highlight limitation but still project alienation and unease.

31. Peter Wolfe, *In the Zone: The Twilight World of Rod Serling* (Bowling Green, OH: Bowling Green State University Popular Press, 1997), 43.

32. Ibid., 8.

33. Slippage occurs with "A Hundred Yards over the Rim," which begins in 1847 as Cliff Robertson's Christian Horne searches New Mexico for a mythical California. New is then juxtaposed against old as harmonica and soft strings recede to staccato, reverb piano, and punctuations of harp arpeggios and vibraphone to mark a subjective schism from the familiar to the alien. In this case, this is twentieth-century America. The shock of modernity sends Horne back to face a preferable certain death in the desert.

34. Death Valley wasn't the only desert shoot utilized. Associate producer Del Reisman recalls the "intense heat" of the exterior locations of the Mojave Desert for "King Nine Will Not Return" (1960) and the flats of Lone Pine, Nevada, are used in "A Hundred Yards over the Rim." Stewart T. Stanyard, *Dimensions behind The Twilight Zone: A Backstage Tribute to Television's Groundbreaking Series* (Toronto: ECW Press, 2007), 114.

35. Wolfe, *In the Zone*, 14.

36. Lincoln Geraghty, "Painted Men and Salt Monsters: The Alien Body in 50s and 60s American Science Fiction Television," *Intensities: The Journal of Cult Media* 4 (December 2007).

37. Stanyard, *Dimensions behind The Twilight Zone*, 46–47.

38. Wolfe, *In the Zone*, 10.

39. Booker states that "in keeping with the individualist ideology that permeates the series," Serling's characters tend to receive a sympathetic treatment. M. Keith Booker, *Science Fiction Television* (Westport, CT: Praeger, 2004), 11.

40. Booker, *Strange TV*, 53–57. Booker acknowledges the uncomfortable objectification dialogues in the text but also praises the story's prefiguring of the cyberpunk subgenre.

41. See S. T. Joshi, "The Life and Work of Rod Serling," *Studies in Weird Fiction* 7 (Spring 1990): 22–28; James Wolcott, "On Television: X-Factor," *New Yorker*, April 18, 1994, 98–99; Wolfe, *In the Zone*, 79–80.

42. Wolfe, *In the Zone*, 10.

43. Booker, *Science Fiction Television*, 13.

44. Ibid.

45. Expressionism palpably defines episodes like "The Four of Us Are Dying" (1960), "The Howling Man" (1960), "Eye of the Beholder" (1960), and "The Obsolete Man" (1961). These all foreground an emphasis on claustrophobic composition, studio-bound interiors, shadows, and distorted angles in service of narrative/thematic tension.

46. The show majored in a procession of eerie visuals, from Anne Francis cast as shop dummy in "The After Hours" (1960) to the nightmarish "Eye of the Beholder" and the glimpse into foreign dimensions within "Little Girl Lost" (1962), among others.

47. Both have cast motorized vehicles, in *Once Upon a Time in the West* (1968) and in *The Wild Bunch* (1969), as signaling the demise of the pioneer phase, the onset of industrialization, and a loss of innocence.

48. Booker, *Strange TV*, 60.

49. Ibid., 69.

50. J. Hoberman, "How the Western Was Lost," in *The Western Reader*, ed. Jim Kitses and Gregg Rickman (New York: Limelight Editions, 1998), 86.

51. Borne from the weight of cultural saturation, Sergio Leone would later recast the Fordian landscape in a more problematic (yet still celebratory) light in *Once Upon a Time in the West*.

52. See Edward Buscombe, "Inventing Monument Valley: Nineteenth Century Landscape Photography and the Western Film," in *The Western Reader*, ed. Jim Kitses and Gregg Rickman (New York: Limelight Editions, 1998), 115–30.

53. Johnson-Smith, *American Science-Fiction TV*, 52.

54. Ibid., 44.

55. Buscombe, "Inventing Monument Valley," 118. It is indeed an irony, postmodern or otherwise, that the American landscape has always been intertwined with commodification. Buscombe stresses the immense demand for pictures, stereographs, postcards, photographs, and paintings of mountains and canyons across the world in the later part of the nineteenth century.

56. Ibid. The indexical figures of Native Americans in the work of Edward S. Curtis had a profound effect on Ford's projection of the West too, as noted by Mick Gidley, *Edward S. Curtis and the North American Indian, Incorporated* (Cambridge: Cambridge University Press, 1998).

57. Johnson-Smith, *American Science-Fiction TV*, 39–61.

58. Ibid., 45. Buscombe too offers this, as mirrored throughout Ford's work, most notably in *Stagecoach* (1939).

59. When faced with a vista of Bierstadtian beauty early on in the film, the only commentary the soon-to-be-extinct cowboys can muster is a shrugged, "It just looks like more Texas to me."

60. Jim Kitses, *Horizons West: Directing the Western from John Ford to Clint Eastwood* (London: BFI, 2004), 32.

61. Ibid.

62. Johnson-Smith, *American Science-Fiction TV*, 48.

63. Cited in Kuhn, "Introduction," 5.

CHAPTER TWO

~≈≈≋

Irwin Allen's Recycled Monsters and Escapist Voyages

Oscar De Los Santos

Irwin Allen produced a string of popular television series in the 1960s: *Voyage to the Bottom of the Sea* (1964–1968), *Lost in Space* (1965–1968), *The Time Tunnel* (1966–1967), and *Land of the Giants* (1968–1970). He launched the "disaster film" decade in the 1970s with such features as *The Poseidon Adventure* (1972) and *The Towering Inferno* (1974). If nothing else, Allen's productions are marked by longevity. Reruns of his TV shows continue to be popular over four decades after their debuts. All have been released on DVD, allowing new viewers to discover them and old fans to revisit them. The same is true of Allen's most memorable theatrical films. More than thirty years after it was first screened, *The Poseidon Adventure* continues to run on television and it inspired two recent remakes. Other Irwin Allen critiques have trashed his TV shows as bad science fiction. My goal in this chapter is to weigh in on this argument and then argue that Allen managed to conquer 1960s American television not so much because he was indulging his own love of action and spectacle but because he satisfied his personal obsessions while producing programs that showcased viewers' pop culture interests and desire for escapist entertainment.

Irwin Allen TV Shows: Science Fiction or Sci-Fi?

In the twenty-some years that I've taught science fiction college courses, I've tried to help students distinguish between science fiction and that which might best be labeled "sci-fi," the term coined by *Famous Monsters of Film-land* magazine creator Forrest J. Ackerman. Print and visual science fiction, I explain, uses scientific principles and exponentiates them to concoct its "what if?" scenarios. Science fiction writers carefully extrapolate their premises. Whether writers tell stories involving time travel, genetic mutation, or artificial intelligence, they present their ideas in plausible fashion. Science fiction writers don't always get their suppositions right, but most use what we know now and might eventually know later as springboards into their stories. Sci-fi, on the other hand, is a threadbare science fiction sketch that doesn't work very hard—if at all—to explain its science and technology. Sci-fi is more concerned with dazzling the audience with spectacle than credible ideas. Sci-fi is closer kin to the fantasy genre than is science fiction. Indeed, sci-fi can be considered a subgenre of fantasy (see Jowett's and Pank and Caro's chapters in this volume for more on the relationship between science fiction and fantasy on contemporary TV).

That said, both science fiction and sci-fi can be immensely entertaining. Some science fiction fans who snobbishly privilege science fiction over sci-fi have forgotten (or are reluctant to admit) what led them to science fiction in the first place. In many cases, it was the sci-fi that many of us "consumed" in our youth that eventually led us to more rigorous science fiction stories and films.

Irwin Allen didn't create science fiction but he did produce a string of very good sci-fi TV shows throughout the 1960s. Scientific and technological premises introduced in the scripts were seldom correct. In the first episode of *Voyage to the Bottom of the Sea*, for instance, Admiral Nelson decides to counteract destructive tidal waves ravaging the earth's coastlines by traveling to the North Pole and setting off a nuclear bomb. Thomas Vinciguerra points out that "you don't need a seismologist to tell you this isn't a good idea."[1] More often than not, the longer an Irwin Allen show remained on the air, the further it moved into fantasy territory. No matter. As the *New York Times* remarked of *Voyage*, "From the beginning, plausibility was never the show's strong suit."[2] The same might be said of *Lost in Space*, *The Time Tunnel*, and *Land of the Giants*. And yet, these shows were immensely popular with many viewers because they were fun, escapist distractions produced by a man who tapped into a pop culture goldmine during a turbulent decade. Jon Abbott asserts correctly that "Irwin Allen may well have demonstrated how not to do serious, precognitive, or scientifically accurate SF for sniffy purists, but it was never his intention to do so. Irwin Allen's TV shows were made as commercial entertainments, not to comment on the human condition, deliver dire warnings, or speculate about the future (although on rare occasions they did all three)."[3]

Perhaps nowhere is the latter point most evident than in the array of aliens and monsters showcased in Allen's TV programming. Other science fiction shows of the era featured more thoughtful renditions of aliens. Quite often, when an entity with an outlandish exterior was showcased, such shows as *The Twilight Zone* (1959–1964) and *The Outer Limits* (1963–1965) added depth to these aliens; at times, they outright humanized them. As Lincoln Geraghty observes, "*The Outer Limits* revelled in creating outrageously ghastly mutants, aliens and monsters, although . . . these alien others were often presented sympathetically despite their visual differences, and were often presented as a friend or benevolent helper in relation to the human protagonist who was often presented as ignorant or violent."[4] Another classic science fiction TV series, *Star Trek* (1966–1969), showcased some of the best examples of sympathetic aliens with odd exteriors. In "The Devil in the Dark" (1967), for instance, an alien "Horta," which resembles a bulbous lava rock with shag carpeting around its circumference, turns out to be killing mining colony inhabitants because the miners are unwittingly destroying its eggs. Irwin Allen didn't bother evoking such sympathies. More often than not, aliens were created to torment the cast of *Voyage to the Bottom of the Sea*, *Lost in Space*, or some other Allen TV show. Monsters had no depth. They had to be eradicated, period.

IAB60TV (Irwin Allen before '60s TV): Intimations of Things to Come

Before Irwin Allen infused his distinct form of dynamism into 1960s television programming, he had already done the same thing on the big screen. His theatrical projects revealed that he had a pulse on moviegoers' hunger for adventure and the unknown. 1950s cinema showcased a substantial number of horror and science fiction adventures. Many—particularly the scores of giant creature and outer space invasion films produced during the period—were forged from meager budgets. A few were high-dollar projects. Somewhere in between were such documentaries as Louis Malle and Jacque Cousteau's *Le monde du silence* (*The Silent World*, 1956), in which the famous oceanographer gave audiences the most extensive look at undersea life yet provided. The film won a deserved Academy Award for best documentary feature (1957). It also serves as an example of Irwin Allen's ability to zero in on audience interests and provide them with similar variations of the product.

The Silent World's success showed Allen that there was more to be mined from a subject he had already tapped. Several years before the Cousteau film, Allen wrote, produced, and directed *The Sea around Us* (1953). Based on Rachel Carson's book, the film won Allen a Best Documentary Academy Award. Not only did Allen beat Cousteau to the big screen, but his undersea feature also hit theaters before Disney's ambitious *20,000 Leagues under the Sea* (1954). The three features served as audience gauges for Allen, who recognized that filmgoers wanted more cinema that featured nature and adventure. He provided it with *The Animal World* (1956), a chronicling of the evolution of all life species through the ages. The film featured stop-motion animation by special effects masters Willis O'Brien and Ray Harryhausen.

Allen's follow-up film was an audacious fantasy that showed his awareness of America's growing concern with nuclear weapons development. In *The Story of Mankind* (1957), Allen and co-writer Charles Bennett conjured a drama in which a "council of elders," comprised in part by angels, debates whether humanity's violent tendencies throughout history warrant its extinction. Many science fiction films of the period—particularly the giant creature films—reflect the worry that increased development of nuclear weaponry was destined to bring about the planet's demise. These features echoed the age-old conservative sentiment that human beings should best leave some avenues of scientific inquiry unexplored. *The Story of Mankind* looks more at the past than at the present and future. At times, it seems to call humanity to the carpet for its violent impulses. At others, the film defends the human race and its flaws. Allen doesn't so much choose a position as lay forth a debate that was surely troubling the public with each report of ongoing nuclear development and weapons stockpiling.

Allen's next three motion pictures bear further proof that he had a very good sense of what was dominating people's minds during this period. He crafted *The Lost World* (1960), which substituted live lizards and reptiles for dinosaurs and provided audiences with still more exotic adventure. After this film, Allen turned his lens below the depths again to create *Voyage to the Bottom of the Sea* (1961), a feature that dared to posit that nuclear weaponry might be used to positive ends. When meteorites turn the Van Allen belt into a ring of fire, Admiral Nelson (Walter Pigeon) proposes to use his nuclear-powered submarine *Seaview* to launch an atomic bomb and eradicate the threat of global extinction. Against everyone's wishes—including United Nations delegates—the admiral forges forward with his plan. His scheme works and he saves the earth. *Voyage* is a mélange of genres scoring hits with film audiences during the period of its release. It harbors a mixture of pro- and antimilitary sentiment. Nelson is a military man but also a first-rate scientist and engineer. A pacifist (Michael Ansara) is rescued from the sea during the crisis and challenges the military mindset aboard the sub. Pop singer Frankie Avalon was featured in the cast to attract a younger audience. Moreover, the film tapped into the era's escalating cold war tensions: a saboteur may or may not be aboard the *Seaview* and working to thwart its mission. The film even provides audiences with giant creatures, which would become staples of its television counterpart. Following up on the success of the giant squid battle in Disney's *20,000 Leagues*, Allen created his own giant squid skirmish in *Voyage*, with the *Seaview* crew tangling with a similar beast while outside the submarine. For good measure, there's also a giant octopus that must eventually be electrocuted off the *Seaview*'s outer hull. (It was likely no coincidence that *It Came from Beneath the Sea*'s [1955] giant octopus had dazzled audiences at theaters a few years before *Voyage*.)

Allen moved from the sea into the sky with his next film, *Five Weeks in a Balloon* (1962). Once more, this production fed filmgoers' penchant for adventure and exploration tales. Allen didn't stray too far from what had recently won good box office returns: an adaptation of Jules Verne's balloon tale, *Around the World in 80 Days* (1956), Allen's adaptation of Conan Doyle's *The Lost World* (1960), and his Verne-inspired *Voyage to the Bottom of the Sea* (1961).

Irwin Allen's 1960s TV Shows: Subs, Spaceships, Time Travelers, and Giants

Voyage to the Bottom of the Sea
In crafting *Voyage to the Bottom of the Sea*, the TV series, Allen returned to the film that featured Admiral Nelson, Captain Crane, and the crew of the submarine *Seaview*. (He recast the leads for television: Richard Basehart essayed the role of Nelson and David Hedison played Crane.) The program launched on September 14, 1964. Exploration of the ocean continued to garner popular interest. (Two years after *Voyage*'s TV debut, Cousteau would premiere his long-running *Undersea World of Jacque Cousteau* series.) Like so much of Allen's large- and small-screen catalog, the *Voyage* TV show allowed viewers to revel in their current fixations. Along with adventure and sea exploration, the cold war, paranoia, and the threat of nuclear war were prevalent American concerns throughout the 1960s. The specter of the recent Cuban Missile Crisis reminded everyone just how tenuous global peace was and how quickly it could sour. James Bond spy thrillers proved extremely popular, as did such films as *On the Beach* (1959), *The Manchurian Candidate* (1962), *Dr. Strangelove* (1964), *Seven Days in May* (1964), and *Fail-Safe* (1964).

American TV spy shows set in this cold war climate—*The Man from U.N.C.L.E.* (1964–1968), *I Spy* (1965–1968), and *Get Smart* (1965–1969), for example—were hardly as sober as their cinematic kin. In truth, Irwin Allen's *Voyage to the Bottom of the Sea*, for all its shaky scientific hokum, treated its espionage content more seriously than other programs of the day. William E. Anchors Jr. points out that "since Voyage premiered not long after the Cuban Missile Crisis, the series, particularly in the first and second season, spends a lot of time demonstrating that America is made up of everything good and noble and is the country designated by fate or design to stop the spread of evil across the globe."[5] Several *Voyage* episodes featured a foreign power meddling with American military and political interests. Captain Crane went undercover a number of times ("The City beneath the Sea" [1964] in season one, "Escape from Venice" [1965] in season two) and spies infiltrated the *Seaview* ("The Fear-Makers" [1964]). Although the *Seaview* was ostensibly a scientific exploration vessel, the first episode's narration informs audiences that the sleek, glass-nosed atomic submarine is also "the mightiest weapon afloat . . . secretly assigned to the most dangerous missions against the enemies of mankind." Vessel and crew were often dispatched on assignments of military and political intrigue.

David Hedison (Captain Crane) accurately describes the tone of the show as "grim." His appeals to Irwin Allen to lighten things up went nowhere: "I would say, 'Irwin . . . There should be some sort of humor in the characters. Not so grim.' But he would have none of it. He just knew that he always wanted the action to be very grim and very solid and very tense. And that's what he got."[6]

Although Allen capitalized on cold war paranoia and nuclear Armageddon fears, he used both the big and small screen to postulate that nuclear power could be used for good as well as bad. The *Seaview* is powered by a nuclear reactor and carries a nuclear arsenal. In the aforementioned "Eleven Days to Zero" (1964), a nuclear bomb is used to stave off deadly tidal waves. In season two's "The Sky's on Fire" (1966), essentially a remake of the *Voyage* feature film), nuclear missiles are used to save the world when the Van Allen belt catches fire. Ever conscious of the need to capture young and old audiences alike, Allen added Crewman Stuart Riley (Allan Hunt) to the *Voyage* cast in season two. Riley was a young surfer type and little more than window dressing (not unlike Frankie Avalon in the *Voyage* motion picture). He disappeared after the second season.

Many people remember *Voyage* for the parade of monsters that appeared with increasing regularity in its second season. The first season also featured a few creatures, but their appearance was more thoughtfully explained than those that followed. In "The Price of Doom" (1964), a scientific experiment creates a gigantic plankton creature. In "Turn Back the Clock" (1964), which allowed Allen to cull footage from his *Lost World* film, a stretch of warm Antarctic territory harbors dinosaurs. In "The Ghost of Moby Dick" (1964), yet another misguided scientist enlists the aid of Nelson, Crane, and the *Seaview* to tangle with—what else?—a giant whale. And in "The Secret of the Loch" (1965), enemy spies use the famed monster's reputation to conceal a submarine base.

Allen didn't pursue extensive character development in any of his shows. Such revelations as the one in the first-season *Voyage* episode "The Traitor" (1965), in which we learn that Admiral Nelson had a sister, were rare. (She never made another appearance on the show.) More often than not, characters were sketched early in a series' life and never developed beyond a few interesting traits. *Voyage*'s complement was no exception. Too often, Admiral Nelson, Captain Crane, and other regulars seemed to exist only to be thrust into far-fetched adventures or to hunt monsters in shadowy sub corridors. Yet even with such threadbare ingredients, Allen scored a hit with *Voyage*. He learned early that ratings increased each time an episode included a monster. The more outlandish the show's plots, the more audiences reveled in its offerings. This held true for several years but the formula was visibly tapped out by the time *Voyage* wrapped its fourth and final season. Until then, however, Allen provided viewers with a seemingly endless pageant of fish men, fossil men, lobstermen, mermaids, werewolves, aliens, ghosts, deranged puppeteers, mummies, and abominable snowmen.

Lost in Space

By the early 1960s, the space race was well on its way. Russia beat America into orbit when it launched Sputnik, prompting President Kennedy to pledge a commitment to get America to the moon before the Soviets. Having already conquered the ocean depths with *Voyage*, Irwin Allen zoned in on the race to the stars and pitched a space series to CBS. It would be action-packed, family-oriented fare—a space variation of Johann David Wyss's *Swiss Family Robinson* (1812). Each week, the Robinsons would face new adventure as they struggled against alien environments and unknown life. The first show chronicled the Robinson family's blastoff from earth. Their goal was to make it to Alpha Centauri, where they were determined to find hospitable planets capable of sustaining human life.

Initially, *Lost in Space* was structured to focus on all members of the space expedition: Commander John Robinson (Guy Williams); his wife and scientist Maureen (June Lockhart); their children, Judy (Marta Kristen), Penny

(Angela Cartwright), and Will (Bill Mumy); Major Don West (Mark God-dard); "reluctant stowaway" Dr. (and Colonel) Zachary Smith (Jonathan Harris); and a sophisticated unnamed talking robot (voiced by Dick Tufeld). As time passed, however, Harris stole the show with his Smith characteriza-tion. Will Robinson and the Robot rounded out a curious triangle in which Smith behaves more like a scheming child, Will a cerebral adult, and the Robot a resigned butler to his human charges.

Lost in Space premiered on September 15, 1965. The first season was spent exploring one planet, as the Robinsons affected repairs on their damaged craft. The second season opened with the *Jupiter 2*'s liftoff from the disin-tegrating planet, but the characters soon landed on another orb. The third season featured a more mobile cast and ship. William Anchors notes that during the espionage- and adventure-focused first season of *Voyage to the Bot-tom of the Sea*, "When the story *The Price of Doom* (1964), about a destructive plankton creature, was shown, ratings picked up, as did interest in the show by the public."[7] As the series progressed, Allen gave his audience what it favored: increasingly bizarre monstrosities. The pattern was little different on *Lost in Space*, as a procession of aliens gigantic and furry, slick and bulbous, tormented Will, Dr. Smith, the Robot, and the Robinson family.

Irwin Allen cast a futuristic sheen upon his space show but used the old movie serial cliffhanger trick to entice audiences to tune into the next Rob-inson family adventure. The series was supposedly about Americans' future in space but it was really no more than a surreal transplanted variation of the castaway story. (Some may flinch at the comparison, but aren't there striking similarities between the surreal adventures of the "seven stranded castaways" on *Gilligan's Island* and the seven oft-stranded space explorers on *Lost in Space?*) Dr. Smith was the resident bad guy people loved to hate—per-haps American, but working for a familiar shadowy "Them" that so many paranoid Americans feared. Nor did Allen challenge traditional gender roles with his show. The female characters were allegedly part of America's inno-vative future—Maureen Robinson was a scientist—yet they were frequently relegated to cooking and laundry duties. And who proved instrumental in finding solutions to many problems plaguing the Robinsons? None other than young Will, which guaranteed the show a solid kids' audience.

As with *Voyage to the Bottom of the Sea*, *Lost in Space* is a reflection of vari-ous popular trends at the time it first aired. Action and adventure dominated the show, but Allen wove the espionage theme into the series by adding the villain Smith to the ensemble cast. Joining the endless line of aliens were characters whose types America had embraced. *The Beverly Hillbillies* (1962–1971) garnered a loyal audience, so *Lost in Space* featured interstellar variations in "The Space Croppers" (1966). When the hippie movement was peaking, Allen provided audiences with "The Promised Planet" (1968), an embarrassing exhibition that features Jonathan Harris dancing and trying his best to be "hip." The Robinsons also encountered intergalactic pirates, space magicians, menacing robots, and rebelling plant creatures.

Throughout its three-season run, the show's focus became increasingly fantastical and absurd—and juvenile—but such was the climate of American television and what the public seemed to favor, whether Irwin Allen productions, variety shows (*Laugh-In* [1968–1973], *The Dean Martin Show* [1965–1974]), or supernatural fantasies (*Bewitched* [1964–1972], *I Dream of Jeannie* [1965–1970], *Dark Shadows* [1966–1971]). Even ostensibly realistic crime dramas and westerns (*Mannix* [1967–1975], *Gunsmoke* [1955–1975], *Bonanza* [1959–1973]) could be accused of being too fantastic. (How many criminals and gunfighters can one private dick and marshal shoot down, anyway?) Many fans still favor the first season and it is arguably much better than what was to come, but at no time did *Lost in Space* try to adhere to the laws of science, space, and time as they were understood during the show's production. Professor John Robinson's first-episode survival of a space flight through the planet's atmosphere while wearing little more than a thin space suit supports this point. Irwin Allen may be accused of pandering to audiences' undemanding tastes; of flagrantly violating scientific theories; of favoring action over character development—but *Lost in Space*, like all of Allen's shows, was seldom boring.

The Time Tunnel

When *The Time Tunnel* debuted on September 9, 1966, Irwin Allen found himself with three television series on the air at the same time. ABC asked Allen to come up with a time travel show for the network. Such an endeavor surely seemed a minor gamble, given the theme's longstanding popularity in science fiction storytelling (for example, H. G. Wells's *The Time Machine*, Ray Bradbury's "A Sound of Thunder," and Murray Leinster's *Time Tunnel* [1964], an unrelated novel published prior to Allen's series but which likely led Leinster to be picked to do a novelized version of the TV show). Various films (most notably 1960's *The Time Machine*) had proven that audiences enjoyed time travel stories on the large screen. While Allen's *Lost in Space* had touched on time travel, this new program would focus exclusively on the concept.

The Time Tunnel's premise was very basic: scientists Tony Newman and Doug Phillips (James Darren and Robert Colbert) are part of a clandestine government research project conducting time experiments. Newman and

Phillips go through the time tunnel and visit various moments in history, famous and otherwise, with occasional jaunts into the future. In the present, scientists, military personnel, and technicians (John Zaremba, Lee Meriwether, Whit Bissell, Wesley Lau, and Sam Groom) monitor the scientists' journeys and work to fix the broken time machine in order to bring Newman and Phillips home.

Since each episode visited a different moment and place in history, Allen was able to use Twentieth Century Fox's back lots and sets to produce his show. *The Time Tunnel* also capitalized on stock footage from countless other films. Always one to use—and at times overuse—such cinematic gimmickry, Allen transformed his new series into something that looked quite expansive and expensive. Of course, he didn't skimp on the master "time tunnel" set, which though used sparsely, reflected the producer's penchant for mammoth set pieces and stunning special effects. Once again, Allen used this show to give audiences the kind of visual excitement and lightweight television entertainment they were looking for during much of the 1960s. As "real life" grew ever more troublesome; as race riots increased and leaders were assassinated and America's young men continued to be shipped overseas to fight in the Vietnam conflict, Allen offered viewers hour-long escape options. *The Time Tunnel* plots didn't steer clear of historical crises—stories centered on the *Titanic* disaster and Pearl Harbor, for instance—but audiences were frequently attracted to historical tales as long as the depicted period was removed from the present.

Ultimately, *The Time Tunnel* was only fairly successful. It aired for one season and outlasted another time travel program on during the same season—the comedy *It's About Time*—by four episodes. ABC kept strict watch on Allen and the series budget. Frequent Allen writer Robert Duncan enjoyed working on the producer's other series but found that budget battles made working for *The Time Tunnel* very unpleasant. The budgetary issues gave Allen the perfect excuse to keep his show slight on character development and in-depth drama. When one writer and director tried to argue for a dramatic scene to be put back into one particular episode, Allen came down from his office, heard the deleted scene read, then declared, "Jesus! That's just quibbling. . . . This is a running and jumping show!"[8] William Anchors believes "it is obvious that Irwin had no need for good scripts, as long as everything was kept moving on the show. More action, more explosions, more special effects. Forget the dialogue, forget the story."[9] Perhaps Allen's passion for streamlined action tales and visual spectacle damaged *The Time Tunnel* more than his other small-screen entries; perhaps the show's format proved a little too formulaic even for the easygoing 1960s TV audience. Maybe its predominant focus on the past didn't allow Allen to tap into enough 1960s cultural trends to make it appealing enough to viewers (even with minor pop singer Darren as one of the series leads). Ultimately, it was likely a combination of these factors that doomed the show after one season. Nevertheless, decades after *The Time Tunnel* was discontinued, other TV producers found greater success by utilizing its basic formula (*Quantum Leap* [1989–1993], *Sliders* [1995–2000]).

Land of the Giants

Harry Harris directed episodes on various Irwin Allen TV shows. He recalls that Allen's "sets were big. He took up the whole stage with all this stuff because that's what he wanted. He wanted big, big, big scale."[10] Given his fervor for large-scale visuals and giant creatures, perhaps it was inevitable that Irwin Allen would eventually produce a series about a group of humans in a *Land of the Giants*. Allen's decision to go in this direction is understandable if we consider that he always seemed to know what trend was hot in pop culture at any given time. The concept of gigantism had been extremely popular in 1950s monster cinema. Scores of big-screen bugs, reptiles, and forgotten dinosaurs were spawned or reborn as a result of atomic testing. Bert I. Gordon owes a substantial portion of his low-budget filmmaking success to giant creature cinema. (Gordon even capitalized on his initials—B.I.G.—to sell his pictures.) Even when gigantism declined on the big screen, it didn't go away completely. A short-lived syndicated TV show, *World of Giants* (1959), featured a pre-*Daktari* Marshall Thompson as a secret agent reduced in size and transported in an attaché case to whatever mission needed his attention. Gordon produced a film about unruly teenagers turned gargantuan in *Village of the Giants* (1965). Richard Fleischer directed an impressive tale showcasing a miniature crew and submarine's journey into a seemingly giant human body in *Fantastic Voyage* (1966). Godzilla films were still minor hits in the United States, and Allen, via the oversized creatures that tormented characters in his other TV shows, knew that American television audiences still reveled in gigantism.

Over the years, people who worked with Irwin Allen have talked about his apolitical approach to filmmaking. Director Harry Harris, for example, insists that Allen "never thought in terms of trying to get a message across to anybody. Never."[11] That such shows as *Voyage to the Bottom of the Sea* incorporated cold war espionage and political intrigue into their storylines may seem to counter such beliefs, but close examination of these episodes reveals that Allen was merely using popular subject matter, not trying to make strong political statements. Ironically, *Land of the Giants*, a show that was blatantly obsessed with gimmickry, may be the Irwin Allen series that packed the strongest political punch.

Set in the near future, the show focuses on the crew and passengers of the "stratocruiser" Spindrift jetting to London. (The cast was comprised of Gary Conway, Don Marshall, Steve Burton, Dan Erickson, Deanna Lund, Valerie Scott, Kurt Kasznar, and Stefan Arngrim.) They never reach their destination. Instead, the Spindrift is pulled into a glowing orb and lands in a world that resembles early twentieth-century earth but is populated by gargantuan humans. The travelers soon learn about the dictatorial Supreme Council that rules over its citizenry and the Special Investigations Department (SID) that strictly enforces the law. Perhaps inadvertently, Allen created a wonderful metaphor of the little guy fighting Big Brother. Gary Conway, who played Steve Burton on the show, elaborates: "*Land of the Giants* became a phenomenal hit in many countries that had what we would call totalitarian societies. And they said, well, this is the little people against the government."[12] Although audiences were initially intrigued by *Land of the Giants*, the novelty of characters tangling with enormous humanoids and oversized props eventually waned after two seasons and fifty-one episodes.

IAA60TV (Irwin Allen after '60s TV): Disaster as Creature

Throughout the 1970s, Irwin Allen continued to pitch television projects: *City beneath the Sea* (pilot, 1971), *Swiss Family Robinson* (series, 1975), *Time Travelers* (pilot, 1976), and *The Return of Captain Nemo* (pilot, 1978). Only *Swiss Family Robinson* was moderately successful. Perhaps the success of George Seaton's *Airport* (1970, based on Arthur Hailey's novel) gave Allen a hint to reclaiming his fading popularity. In 1972, he channeled his penchant for high-energy storytelling back onto the big screen with *The Poseidon Adventure* (based on Paul Gallico's novel).

Allen scored a hit with *The Poseidon Adventure* and *The Towering Inferno*, which gave audiences more of the same overblown action and thrills. The producer became known as "the master of disaster." His successes heralded a string of copycat films (like *Earthquake* [1974] and *Airport 1975* [1974]) produced by others. Allen himself continued to capitalize on his distinctive formula on the large and small screen. In the course of a few years, he churned out *Flood!* (TV, 1976), *Fire!* (TV, 1977), *The Swarm* (theatrical, 1978), *Hanging by a Thread* (TV, 1979), and *Beyond the Poseidon Adventure* (theatrical, 1979). As in his 1960s TV shows, Allen stuck to a simple formula in his disaster films: various characters' lives eventually intersect and they must deal with whatever disaster is the focal point of the film. In spite of all-star casts, it's clear that Allen's disaster scenario was the main star of the film, whether it was the capsized ship *Poseidon*, the "towering inferno" skyscraper, a "swarm" of killer African bees threatening to overtake the United States, and so forth. In some respects, Allen simply transferred his TV formula onto the big screen, merely substituting a disaster for a monster of the week. Unfortunately, he also seemed to forget that the weekly creature gimmick initially entertained viewers but ultimately exhausted their patience. By the time Allen brought together another impressive cast to produce *When Time Ran Out* (1980) (in which island resort guests are threatened by an erupting volcano), his formula had grown far too obvious and the era of disaster films was dead. Even so, Allen wouldn't accept that his trick had been wrung for all its worth. On the strength of his notoriety for lensing exciting action, Allen was allowed to produce *The Night the Bridge Fell Down* (1983) and *Cave-In!* (1983) for television before finally abandoning disaster storylines altogether.

Conclusion: Allen 1960s TV in Hindsight

Irwin Allen possessed a keen barometer with which he monitored American pop culture. He knew what thrilled him on a personal level, but he also knew what intrigued audiences. His declaration, "If I can't blow up the world within the first ten minutes, then the show is a flop,"[13] is often quoted because it so aptly captures the spirit of his TV shows and films, but Marta Kristen (Judy on *Lost in Space*) also provides us with insight into Allen when she marvels that he was "like a little boy, in a way. He loved all of the special effects."[14] Apparently, so did many other adults. In a 1966 interview, *Voyage* actor Richard Basehart (Admiral Nelson) claimed that his fan mail was "pretty well split between the thirteen and fourteen year olds and older people in their forties and fifties." He also shared that "Irwin told me the other day that they made some kind of survey. Actually, even though this is reputedly a kiddie show, eighty percent of our audience are adults."[15] Allen knew that his brand of escapism would help others forget—if only for an hour—the era's political and social turmoil.

Unfortunately, Allen television productions were as consistently promising in their initial stages as they were flawed the longer they remained on the air. John Clute and Peter Nicholls correctly sum up the producer's "limited repertoire of basic formulae—the Verne/Doyle 'expedition' drama, the juvenile sf-series format, the disaster scenario,"[16] which could yield only so many stories. There's also evidence of a restlessness that surfaced in Allen. Once he launched a show successfully, he shifted his creative energies onto a new project and his previous successes suffered. Certainly a major flaw in most Irwin Allen TV productions was their privileging action and spectacle above everything else. The heightened theatrics grew tiresome, regardless of the programs' impressive appearances. L. B. Abbott won two Emmys for his visual effects work on *Voyage to the Bottom of the Sea*, and Gerani and Schulman are arguably correct when they claim that "the true star of this show was the research submarine *Seaview*,"[17] but a series must have good stories to back its good looks—to say nothing of some degree of character development and continuity. One need only study a few of the later episodes of *Voyage* to understand how damaging a lack of these staples can be to a series. Why, after fighting countless fantastic creatures in the course of previous episodes, does the crew scoff when Captain Crane claims to have seen a mermaid swimming outside the *Seaview*'s observation windows? Why, after being enchanted by a mermaid, does Captain Crane declare, "I see it but I don't believe it" when he encounters a werewolf aboard the vessel the following week? Why, after the crew engages in a fierce battle against rock monsters one week, does Admiral Nelson choke on incredulous laughter when one of his officers claims to have seen a mummy lurching down the *Seaview* corridor? And so forth.

Allen's desire to make his shows look and sound great at their onset also eventually hamstrung them. He spent considerable amounts of money on sets—so much so, in fact, that at least two of Allen's shows (*Voyage* and *Lost in Space*) grew increasingly set-bound. No matter how good a set looks, a show can grow stale if everything but the week's new monster starts looking the same—and even some of the monsters surely looked familiar to fans of various Allen programs, since they too jumped from one production to another. For instance, an undersea gillman in *Voyage*'s "The Mermaid" ends up a space alien in *Lost in Space*, and a white-furred space alien in *Lost in Space* becomes "The Abominable Snowman" in *Voyage*.

Moreover, Allen's penchant for using stock footage was both blessing and curse. On the one hand, it provided a show like *The Time Tunnel* with a big-budget look; on the other, Allen culled from his own programs' spectacular effects footage to the point that certain sequences grew recognizable and wearisome to loyal viewers. Even today, almost fifty years after they were filmed, shots of *Voyage*'s submarine *Seaview* moving across the small screen look impressive. The same is true of some *Lost in Space Jupiter 2* flyby sequences. However, Allen wore out the use of one particular shot of a damaged *Seaview* crashing to the ocean floor. Another sequence depicting the Flying Sub crashing into the ocean was also recycled countless times, as was a scene of the *Seaview* being torpedoed by an enemy sub. During *Voyage*'s second season, the *Seaview*'s impressive observation deck was redesigned. The craft's nose was refitted with four windows instead of its original eight—yet Allen insisted that some of the eight-window submarine footage be used in later shows.

Apparently, nothing was the sole property of one specific Irwin Allen series. The producer even used music and sound effects from one show to enhance another. Such audio and visual cross-pollinations provided familiar resonance between programs, but they may also have given audiences too much of the same thing—too much of what they had only recently encountered elsewhere. Yet for all their flaws, Irwin Allen's 1960s TV shows were more often than not entertaining vehicles, thanks in large part to their creator's consistent fixations and ability to dole out what viewers wanted from their small-screen entertainment. As Jon Abbott notes, "Allen was no storyteller, like the other aforementioned giants of fantasy TV [Rod Serling, Gene Roddenberry, Leslie Stevens, George Stefano]—he was into spectacle, and to that extent, he delivered the goods."[18]

Notes

1. Thomas Vinciguerra, "Never Silent, Not Very Deep," *New York Times*, August 20, 2006, www.nytimes.com/2006/08/20/arts/television/20vinc.html?pagewanted=print.

2. Ibid.

3. John Abbott, *Irwin Allen TV Productions, 1964-1970: A Critical History* (Jefferson, NC: McFarland, 2006), 1.

4. Lincoln Geraghty, "Painted Men and Salt Monsters: The Alien Body in 50s and 60s American Science Fiction Television," *Intensities: The Journal of Cult Media* 4 (December 2007): para. 3.

5. William E. Anchors Jr., ed., *The Irwin Allen Scrapbook: Volume One* (Dunlap, TN: Alpha Control Press, 1992), 9.

6. David Hedison interview, in *The Fantasy Worlds of Irwin Allen*, dir. Kevin Burns, 95 minutes, Foxstar Productions and Van Ness Films in association with Twentieth Television, Irwin Allen Productions, and the Sci-Fi Channel, 2000, DVD.

7. Anchors, *The Irwin Allen Scrapbook*, 9.

8. Ibid., 157.

9. Ibid., 163.

10. Harry Harris interview, in *The Fantasy Worlds of Irwin Allen*.

11. Ibid.

12. Gary Conway interview, in *The Fantasy Worlds of Irwin Allen*.

13. Gary Gerani and Paul H. Schulman, *Fantastic Television* (New York: Harmony, 1977), 69; Abbott, *Irwin Allen TV Productions*, 8, 13.

14. Marta Kristen interview, in *The Fantasy Worlds of Irwin Allen*.

15. Richard Basehart interview, in *Voyage to the Bottom of the Sea*, DVD, Season 3, Vol. 2, Disc 3, 2007.

16. John Clute and Peter Nicholls, *The Encyclopedia of Science Fiction* (New York: St. Martin's Griffin, 1995), 20.

17. Gerani and Schulman, *Fantastic Television*, 69.

18. Abbott, *Irwin Allen TV Productions*, 8.

-+⇒

The Future Just Beyond the Coat Hook: Technology, Politics, and the Postmodern Sensibility in *The Man from U.N.C.L.E.*

Cynthia W. Walker

In the fall of 2007, Internet blogs that cover the latest in technology were buzzing with news of a new cell phone shaped like a slim silver pen. Supposedly a prototype under development by an unnamed Asian manufacturer, the pen phone featured an earpiece at one end and a receiver at the other with a digital readout along the side. Most of the bloggers assumed the device would be used more easily when connected with a Bluetooth earpiece.[1]

Not surprisingly, a few of those posting comments immediately noted the phone's eerie resemblance to the personal communicator used by the lead characters on the cult television series *The Man from U.N.C.L.E.* The show ran in the United States on the NBC network from 1964 to 1968 and was telecast around the world in sixty countries. It was especially popular in Great Britain, where it debuted in June 1965 on BBC1 and broke box office records in London with several feature-length film versions of earlier episodes.[2] Paul Ruppert, who writes the *Mobile Point View* blog, dubbed it the "Waverly phone" after Alexander Waverly, the chief of the mythical U.N.C.L.E. organization.[3] A poster on another blog enthused how the device would make the user feel like an U.N.C.L.E. agent. At last, one could pretend to be Napoleon Solo or Illya Kuryakin and recite into the receiver the famous greeting, "Open Channel D." The future had finally caught up with a forty-three-year-old television series.

The Mystic Cult of Millions

In today's world, with hundreds of global cable channels, video streaming over the Internet, and multiple ways to broadcast and receive programming, it's difficult to describe and understand how exciting a television series like *The Man from U.N.C.L.E.* was for baby boomer youth in the 1960s. Most households had only one black-and-white TV set, usually located in the parlor or "family" room and usually controlled by the father.[4] There were no DVD players, VCRs, or other devices to record a program (although some industrious fans attempted to employ miniature reel-to-reel audio recorders) and, with the possible exception of one rerun, when an episode was over, it was gone forever. Or so it seemed at the time.

On American television, children's programming was mostly relegated to early mornings and Saturdays. Early evenings were crowded with innocuous situation comedies aimed at families. Then, on September 22, 1964, *The Man from U.N.C.L.E.* arrived. It was not children's programming—the leading roles were played by thirtysomething actors Robert Vaughn and David McCallum—but young people all over the United States and around the world embraced it enthusiastically. It was not originally meant for them, but it was *theirs* in a way a prime-time program had never been.

By the time of its phenomenally successful second season, during which it attracted nearly half of the U.S. sets tuned in on Fridays at 10 p.m., *TV Guide* was calling it "the mystic cult of millions."[5] It was celebrated and referenced everywhere. For example, in the U.K., the already established British spy series *The Avengers* (1961–1969) gently spoofed its American cousin with an episode entitled "The Girl from A.U.N.T.I.E.," while in the United States, *U.N.C.L.E.* prompted a flood of spy-themed series on all three major networks.[6] Vaughn, and especially McCallum (who was himself a British import), were mobbed like rock stars wherever they went. "Nothing quite like *The Man from U.N.C.L.E.* has ever happened to television," wrote *TV Guide* contributor Leslie Raddatz, "not only in program content, which has spawned a host of imitators, but in the fact that *U.N.C.L.E.* almost didn't make it at all."[7]

Actually, the series shared some aspects in common with other spy-themed films and programs that had come before, most notably Ian Fleming's James Bond. Indeed, Ian Fleming had been brought in briefly during the series' early development, although in the end his contribution consisted of a weekend of conversation with executive producer Norman Felton, some notes scribbled on a few blank telegram pages, and the suggestion that the main character should be named Napoleon Solo.[8] Like *Danger Man* (1960–1962) and its retitled successor, *Secret Agent* (1964–1968), which starred Patrick McGoohan as agent John Drake, *The Man from U.N.C.L.E.* would combine elements of, and provide a kind of bridge between, the quasi-realistic—even paranoid—espionage programs of the 1950s and the romantic globe-trotting, Bond-derived secret agent fantasies of the 1960s.[9] Nevertheless, despite Raddatz's hyperbole, he was correct about one point: after debuting with minimal fanfare, the series was nearly cancelled within a few short months. The earliest reviews were mixed at best. *Time* magazine called Solo Agent "006 7/8."[10]

Postmodern Fantasy

Despite *U.N.C.L.E.*'s obvious association with the Bond phenomenon, the critics were not quite sure what to make of the series. Cleveland Amory of *TV Guide* found the series irritating and lacking charm, although he revised his opinion when it began to catch on some months later.[11] *Variety*'s reviewer complained that "you couldn't tell if they were playing it for satire or for real."[12] Even Ayn Rand weighed in, utterly appalled by the show's "muddled" politics and "woozy" values. She was also not pleased to see that Solo's sidekick agent was Russian, nor that the main character was being played with more humor than Bond. There was nothing particularly comic about the current international situation, she pointed out, and she could not understand why Sam Rolfe, one of the show's creators who was quoted in *TV Guide*, wanted to avoid all that "anti-Communist stuff."[13]

Of course, Rand and the other critics had missed the point. *The Man from U.N.C.L.E.* was not a true espionage series, any more than *Star Wars* (1977), arriving some fifteen years later, could be considered traditional science fiction. Nor was it simply "Bond for television," though it was promoted that way. Certainly, the success of the first three Bond films made *The Man from U.N.C.L.E.* possible, but when Felton, who had great success producing socially conscious dramas like *Dr. Kildare* (1961–1966), first conceived the premise for *U.N.C.L.E.* in 1962, he was thinking more of the espionage thrillers of John Buchan and Graham Greene than of the Fleming books or the Bond films.[14] Felton's original pitch, which he improvised at a breakfast meeting with advertising executives and Hollywood agents, concerned a "mysterious man," an adventurer who undertook dangerous and particularly sensitive assignments for the Secretary-General of the United Nations. These assignments, accomplished in secret against unspecified evildoers, would involve solving problems of international importance and the general welfare of the planet.[15] From the very beginning then, *The Man from U.N.C.L.E.* would be a spy story that involved no national rivalries. It would be a glimpse of a post–cold war world—an original, even startling concept, especially considering that it was pitched at the same time that the Cuban Missile Crisis was occurring.

An experienced writer/producer known for co-creating the popular western *Have Gun—Will Travel* (1957–1963), Sam Rolfe liked Felton's idea and agreed to develop it further after Fleming was forced to bow out of the project citing ill health. Rolfe created an elaborate and detailed global organization for Solo to work for, and filled it with an international, interracial group of co-workers, one of whom would be, notably, a Russian. Rolfe also agreed with Felton that the tone be kept light and that the stories would mix intrigue with humor, maintaining a careful balance between fantasy and reality. That balance was often disrupted, sometimes subtly and sometimes dramatically, from season to season, and even from episode to episode. Eventually, the arrival of *Batman* (1966–1968) pushed *The Man from U.N.C.L.E.* further into camp, a fact that some blame for the series' short three-and-a-half-year run and somewhat premature demise.[16] Nevertheless, *U.N.C.L.E.*'s particular style, which had more in common with the Pop Art aesthetic than with other American television shows airing in early 1964, was reinforced at every opportunity. An informal writers' guide for the series urged the writers to enjoy their work and have fun,[17] and the writers certainly did.

The episodes featured characters based on not only real-life political figures like Eva Perón, Mahatma Gandhi, Nikita Khrushchev, and François "Papa Doc" Duvalier, but also mythical figures like Lady Godiva, Tarzan, and Dracula. There were intertextual references to popular films like *Lawrence of Arabia* (1962) and *The Bride of Frankenstein* (1935) as well as literary allusions and even snatches of classic poetry. Westerns, gangster films, horror films, and thrillers; Nazis, gypsies, UFOs, abominable snowmen, and even a dancing gorilla—all of it was fodder for *The Man from U.N.C.L.E.* In one first-season episode, "The Giuoco Piano Affair" (1964) (itself a reference to a chess move), Felton, Rolfe, associate producer Joseph Cavelli, and director Richard Donner even appeared in bit roles in a party scene.[18]

This everything-but-the-kitchen-sink approach introduced a new sensibility, making *The Man from U.N.C.L.E.* arguably the first postmodern dramatic television series in U.S. prime time. One might consider it the American counterpart to the British series *The Avengers*, which followed a similar trajectory from black-and-white to color film, and from relatively serious plotting to a combination of techno-fantasy, parody, and pastiche, shifting emphasis over time from content to style.[19] Younger audiences "got" it even if the early critics didn't. The Nielsen ratings climbed and the series was saved midway through its first season when college students returned home for their winter break. Of course, parody, self-reference, and an emphasis on style can have a distancing effect for an audience, and actually undermine the "aesthetic illusion"—that is, the appropriating of the artistic daydream by the beholders who then make it their own.[20]

To ensure viewers invested in the series, the creators of *U.N.C.L.E.* introduced several realistic elements into their postmodern spy fantasy. The earliest episodes open with a pseudo-documentary prologue in which viewers follow the agents into U.N.C.L.E. Headquarters while an unseen narrator gravely intones, "In New York City, on a street in the East Forties, there's an ordinary tailor shop . . . or is it?" The U.N.C.L.E. organization is described and its headquarters briefly explored; Solo, Kuryakin, and Waverly break the fourth wall to introduce themselves before the credits roll and the episode proper begins. Because they were filmed in black and white, often using a handheld Arriflex camera, these first-season episodes have a sort of film noir quality, almost like a well-shot newsreel.

U.N.C.L.E.'s veracity was further enhanced, rather accidentally, when MGM's legal department worried that the "U.N." in the acronym might be construed as having some relationship to the United Nations. New York State law prohibits using the initials "U.N." for commercial purposes. Although Felton and Rolfe had intended to deliberately leave the meaning behind the initials vague, there is no doubt that some association with the United Nations, whether deliberate or implied, was on their minds from the very beginning. First-season episodes began with a shot of the U.N., and even episodes in later seasons featured the iconic building as part of the view from Waverly's office window. At the urging of the studio's lawyers, the producers reluctantly designated U.N.C.L.E. as an acronym for the "United Network Command for Law and Enforcement." Taking a cue from his own *Dr. Kildare* series, which carried an on-screen endorsement from the American Medical Association, Felton also proposed that at the end of each *U.N.C.L.E.* episode the producers would "thank" the fictitious United Network Command for Law and Enforcement for its assistance in making the series.[21] The acknowledgment had the unintended effect of hinting that, perhaps, an U.N.C.L.E. organization or some real-life counterpart actually existed. Amusingly (even to U.N. officials), visitors to the U.N. began asking to see U.N.C.L.E. Headquarters.[22] As a publicity gimmick, the show also distributed U.N.C.L.E. identification cards of various colors (gold was the most coveted). During the summer of 1965, requests for the cards exceeded 200,000.[23]

However, the most successful strategy for reinforcing *U.N.C.L.E.*'s aesthetic illusion was the inclusion of an "Innocent"—that is, an ordinary person—in the course of every mission or so-called "affair." The Innocent character had been an important concept from the very beginning, one that Felton considered integral to the format. "If we were going to have a [hero] who was a superman," he recalled in later years, "it was good to have someone the average person could identify with."[24] Innocents (usually, but not exclusively, female) ran the gamut from housewives and farm girls, to schoolteachers and secretaries, to college students and even children—characters who were similar to those found on the family sitcoms and, not so incidentally, very much like the people sitting at home watching the show. The result was a paradox: an elaborate, obviously outlandish fantasy that could, at times, feel that it might, just possibly, be real.

Turning the Coat Hook

If U.N.C.L.E. as an organization might exist, then the headquarters where its agents worked and the technically advanced equipment they used might exist as well. And why not? The invisible, undetected world inhabited by U.N.C.L.E. and its nemesis, Thrush, bumped right up against the mundane world, making it a kind of wainscot fantasy.[25] U.N.C.L.E.'s New York headquarters was tucked behind a mundane city block consisting of nondescript brownstones, an after-hours nightclub, and a parking garage. Like Harry Potter's wizard folk who tap a brick behind the Leaky Cauldron to enter Diagon Alley, U.N.C.L.E. agents passed through a seedy, below-street tailor shop called Del Floria's and signaled to the proprietor, who tripped the bar on his steam presser. They would then slip into a dressing booth and yank an antique coat hook, thus releasing a secret door that swung inward to reveal a futuristic steel-paneled fortress.

Once inside the reception area, agents and visitors were required to wear triangular color-coded badges that were activated by a special chemical on the receptionist's fingers. Afterward, the agents would proceed down smooth silvery corridors guarded by pulsing overhead security monitors and accessed through sliding pocket doors that opened automatically. In 1997, the science fiction fantasy film *Men in Black*, which began as a comic book inspired by *The Man from U.N.C.L.E.*,[26] borrowed the wainscot HQ idea and expanded upon it for laughs, as had the spy spoof series *Get Smart* (1965–1970) thirty years before. Not surprisingly, *Men in Black*'s climax was set at the site of the 1964–1965 World's Fair. The fair's shiny, optimistic vision of technology and peaceful globalism was echoed by *U.N.C.L.E.*, which even incorporated a kind of skeletal hemisphere into the fictional organization's logo. Inside, U.N.C.L.E. HQ was a gunmetal hive teeming with workers and crammed with blinking computer terminals, communication consoles, and flat-screen monitors. In addition to the badge system, various security systems included retina and biometric scans and an impregnable vault called File 40. Except for the armed secretaries, it was an environment in which any employee working in a corporate complex today would probably feel right at home.

Del Floria's was not the only access to the secret world of U.N.C.L.E. There were other U.N.C.L.E. offices tucked away behind other little tailor shops the world over—only the language of the ironic motto hung over the door ("Honesty is the Best Policy") changed. Moreover, just as U.N.C.L.E. was hiding in plain sight, the bad guys were, too. Although they occasionally occupied castles, uncharted islands, or remote caverns (and in one instance, a secret base built in Antarctica), unlike the megalomaniacs encountered by Bond, who enjoyed the benefit of larger budgets and designer Ken Adams's spectacular sets, *U.N.C.L.E.*'s villains had to make do with more modest surroundings. Lairs (or, in the case of Thrush, "satrapies") were located behind all sorts of everyday places like haberdasheries and beauty salons, dance schools and discos, schools, hospitals, factories, a vacuum cleaner repair shop, a mortuary, an art gallery, a car wash, a suburban drugstore, a college town bookshop, and the thirteenth floor of a Manhattan high-rise. The possibility that a high-tech headquarters or a mad scientist's laboratory could be revealed by the turn of a coat hook or the press of a button was often played for humor in the series. In "The Mad, Mad Tea Party Affair" (1965), which aired during the first season, the series purposefully addressed the wainscot fantasy aspect by organizing an episode around allusions to Lewis Carroll and *Alice in Wonderland*. As Kay Lorrison, a soon-to-be-wed secretary (played by Zohra Lampert) observes after accidentally stumbling into U.N.C.L.E. HQ, "I was just leaning against the wall one minute and wham! I was right down the rabbit hole or the looking glass."

The agents of U.N.C.L.E. not only lived and worked in these special places, they traveled all over the world as well—or, at least, as far as the MGM back lot permitted. David Victor, one of the three producers who worked on the series during its second season, argued to Jon Heitland that the artificial sets, which were used over and over again, actually diverted attention away from the background to the action and enhanced the fantasy aspect of the series.[27] Without VCRs to review the episodes, the audience hardly noticed. To the twelve-year-old fans, Solo and Kuryakin, traveling in smart business suits on missions to exotic locations, seemed the epitome of worldly, sophisticated style—prototypes for the globe-trotting executives that some of those twelve-year-olds would grow up to become.

Open Channel D

"Don't worry about gimmickry and gadgetry," *U.N.C.L.E.*'s informal guide assured its writers. "If the story and people don't grab—and excite and amuse—our viewers, all the visual effects in the world won't save the show."[28] More than forty years later, writer Dean Hargrove, director Joseph Sargent, and associate producer George Lehr express similar sentiments on the recently released DVD set.[29] Nevertheless, *The Man from U.N.C.L.E.* became known for its gadgets and day-after-tomorrow technology. Early on, test audiences remarked that they loved the gadgets and were looking for more.[30] These gadgets also attracted publicity,[31] and could be reinterpreted as toys and tie-in merchandise that funneled revenue back into production of the show.[32] At the same time, because Bond and other film spies featured similar spy technology, audiences came to expect it. If Bond carried a briefcase crammed with equipment, so did the U.N.C.L.E. agents. Indeed, briefcases filled with communication devices, weapons, and GPS-type units became so ubiquitous in spy series and films, that Paul Atkinson argues that the concealed technology aspect created a "macho mystique" for the briefcase that has transferred to today's laptop computers.[33]

Because James Bond had a signature gun, the Walther PPK, then the U.N.C.L.E. agents needed one, too. Actually, the U.N.C.L.E. Special ended up receiving as much—if not more—attention than Bond's PPK. Designed by prop masters Bob Murdock and Arnold Goode, the U.N.C.L.E. Special was an impressive-looking spidery gun based on the Walther P-38 automatic. It had a number of attachments, including a scope, a screw-on stock, a double magazine, and a barrel extension that could transform the handgun into a full auto machine gun. Eventually, the crew created six U.N.C.L.E. Specials at a cost of approximately $1,500 per gun, but only two had a full array of attachments. A few months into the series, investigators from the U.S. Treasury Department visited the set and subsequently fined MGM $2,000 for manufacturing automatic weapons without a license. The trouble and the expense were worth it, however. The U.N.C.L.E. Special became a kind of fourth star of the series, receiving some five hundred fan letters a week addressed specifically to the gun. The Ideal Toy company eventually manufactured a Napoleon Solo Gun Set, which sold for $4.99.[34] One interesting aspect of the U.N.C.L.E. Special was that it shot sleep-inducing darts as well as bullets, a concept promoted by Felton himself. "We don't kill anyone any more with the U.N.C.L.E. gun," Felton joked to *TV Guide.* "We just put them to sleep. And afterwards they're better off. They're nicer to their wives and kids after being hit with one of Mr. Solo's darts."[35] For creating the gun and other unusual props, Murdock, Goode, and their assistant, Bill Graham, were awarded a special Emmy in 1966.

In addition to a signature gun, James Bond also had a signature car, an Aston Martin DB5 introduced in *Goldfinger* (1964). It was specially equipped with machine guns, a smoke screen, an oil jet, a radar screen, a bulletproof shield, and, most famously, an ejector seat. In creating a car for *U.N.C.L.E.* designer Gene Whitfield, who also worked for the Speed and Custom Shop of the AMT model car company in Phoenix, Arizona, went one better. Because the *U.N.C.L.E.* producers were reluctant to award free publicity to a major car manufacturer, Whitfield chose the lesser-known two-seater Piranha as the foundation for his design. Low and sleek, sporting gull-wing doors ten years before the first DeLorean prototype, the U.N.C.L.E. car was equipped with even more futuristic features than the Aston Martin. Along with the required flamethrowers, machine guns, radar, and sonar screens, the car also had a laser beam, rocket launchers, a parachute, and propellers in the rear because it was also amphibious. Obviously, the mock spy features were nonoperative. Unfortunately, often so was the car. Stories have been told over the years of how the Corvair engine leaked motor oil by the quart and died every few feet, and how difficult it was to enter and exit gracefully by the gull-wing doors. The actors also suffered from an interior that featured wide, curved glass windows but no air conditioning. As a result, the car appeared in only a handful of third- and fourth-season episodes, and in a few episodes of *The Man from U.N.C.L.E.*'s sister series, *The Girl from U.N.C.L.E.* (1966–1967). Still, the low-slung, metallic-blue car looked fabulous on camera, the sort of futuristic-looking vehicle more likely to be found in a science fiction metropolis than on the streets of mid-twentieth-century New York City.[36]

Besides the iconic headquarters, the famous gun, and the cutting-edge car, *U.N.C.L.E.* was best known for the personal equipment carried by the agents. These weapons, communicators, GPS, and listening devices were inevitably disguised as everyday objects such as umbrellas, cameras, books, rings, wristwatches, buttons, tie tacks, money clips, and cuff links, making the agents veritable walking arsenals. This was partly due to the ingenuity of the show's prop masters and partly due to the limited budget. In "The Summit-Five Affair" (1967), we see that Kuryakin carries a picklock in one of his molars. In "The Five Daughters Affair" (1967), Solo combines one of his explosive shoelaces with vinegar to fashion a makeshift bomb. The writers of *Get Smart* spoofed this aspect of *U.N.C.L.E.* wickedly when they placed Agent Maxwell Smart's phone in his shoe, forcing him into awkward positions in order to answer calls from his superior. The pen communicator described at the beginning of this chapter was actually the third in a series. The first *U.N.C.L.E.*

Piranha from *The Man from U.N.C.L.E.* (1964–1968). *Courtesy of Cynthia W. Walker.*

communicator was a radio embedded in a fake pack of cigarettes that needed to be plugged into a power source like a lamp or an electric outlet. Eventually, the plug was eliminated, and in a season one episode, "The Gazebo in the Maze Affair" (1965), Solo informs his captor that his communication signal requires a moment to bounce off the Telstar satellite.

The rather homely radio pack was soon replaced by a sleeker cigarette case that opened like a small book and featured a row of real cigarettes that flipped over to reveal a microphone and receiver. However, Rolfe thought the case looked too bulky on camera and, reportedly, Felton was afraid that these communicators featuring cigarettes would make smoking appear too glamorous to the younger viewers.[37] Early in the second season, they were replaced once and for all by the iconic silver pen. The agents used their pens continually, much as we do our cell phones today, to keep in touch with HQ and each other. Interestingly, the only feature the communicators notably lacked was a vibrate function, which might have been useful when the agents were attempting to remain inconspicuous. Today, many of these props, along with Maxwell Smart's shoe phone and dozens of other television- and spy film–related artifacts, are owned by collector Danny Biederman and can be found on display at the CIA museum at CIA headquarters in Langley, Virginia, or as part of a traveling "Spy-Fi" exhibit.[38] Of course, when their equipment was broken, destroyed, or confiscated, the agents were forced to improvise, much as *MacGyver* (1985–1992) would twenty years later. For example, in the season one episode "The Iowa-Scuba Affair" (1964), when Solo finds himself locked in a hotel bathroom with poisonous gas spewing out of the showerhead, he blasts down the door by igniting a towel wrapped around a can of shaving cream.

Technology in *U.N.C.L.E.* was ubiquitous, even mundane, and prefigured many devices we take for granted today. In fact, some of the gadgets came very close to what the CIA and other espionage agencies were using in real life.[39] Associate producer George Lehr remembers being instructed by both Felton and Rolfe to make the technology appear both accurate and plausible.[40] In a memo to second-season producer David Victor, Rolfe explained, "I had always imagined that *U.N.C.L.E.* was taking place in the year 1969, and that science fiction devices that entered through our story were the sort that might be feasible by about 1979. Beyond that, I hesitate to go."[41] The writers' guide instructed that stories for *U.N.C.L.E.* should "take place in the present or in the very near future. If science fiction devices are used, they (1) cannot be of the type that are unlikely for generations, and (2) should be employed only as a point of departure for the story. The story itself must be contemporary."[42]

These warnings notwithstanding, *The Man from U.N.C.L.E.* was filled with science fiction elements. Episodes featured dozens of fantastic, futuristic devices and apocalyptic weapons, such as mind-reading machines; cyborgs; earthquake, volcano, and tidal wave activators; long-range laser weapons; a suspended animation device (SAD); a thermal prism; and formulas to promote intelligence, reverse aging, and inhibit human reproduction. Villains plotted to divert the Gulf Stream (shades of global warming!), extract gold from seawater, and turn African villagers into superwarriors and children into programmed assassins. In the season one episode "The Double Affair" (1964), we discover that U.N.C.L.E. is also the guardian of "Project Earth Save," a superweapon stored in a secret cavern, to be used only in the case of alien invasion. Not surprisingly, the series attracted science fiction writers like Harlan Ellison to contribute scripts. When Ace Books was contracted to publish a series of tie-in novels, assistant editor Terry Carr (who would go on to become a respected science fiction editor) recruited young science fiction writers David McDaniel, Robert "Buck" Coulson, and Gene DeWeese.

Although *U.N.C.L.E.*'s approach to good vs. evil was fairly clear-cut, its approach to technology was more ambiguous. If our heroes could employ advanced technology to save the world, the bad guys used equally advanced technology in their attempts to destroy or subdue it. Both sides had their scientists, their experts, and their banks of computers. The difference was, while U.N.C.L.E. used its computer for intelligence gathering and field support, Thrush, its primary nemesis, used its supercomputer—an infallible "Ultimate Computer"—to make policy decisions. "Computers are a valuable tool, but they can be dangerous," Felton told columnist Donald Freeman in 1967. "[They] should be put in their place." As for *U.N.C.L.E.*'s overall approach to science, Felton noted, "We kid the daylights out of the Brave New World."[43]

Things to Come

Over the years, everyone who had ever worked on *The Man from U.N.C.L.E.* has staunchly maintained that the show was meant to be nothing more than entertaining, escapist fare—a modern fairy tale—with no deliberate agenda, political or otherwise. But even fairy tales have morals, and with a show so groundbreaking, so successful, and so popular even to this day (a healthy fandom for the show and its stars still exists)[44] it is inevitable that cultural theorists would attempt to tease out deeper meanings from it. Some see the activities of U.N.C.L.E., particularly in its Manichean battle against Thrush, as a simple metaphor for the cold war.[45] This, despite the presence of the

Illya Kuryakin character and the decidedly left-of-center real-life politics of the producers and its star, Robert Vaughn.[46] "U.N.C.L.E. does not serve the interests that are peculiarly American," the writers' guide instructed. "The Cold War or any of its ramifications do not exist for us."[47]

A number of commentators have granted the series' vision a bit more complexity. Rick Worland, for example, argues that the use of satire and parody by U.N.C.L.E. and other 1960s spy series actually undermined the rigid cold war mentality of the previous decade.[48] Ignoring any political subtext, others point out how these series aided and abetted a rising culture of conspicuous consumption.[49] Although product placement within the series was limited to a few vehicles supplied by Ford and Chrysler, *The Man from U.N.C.L.E.* did feature an array of consumer goods and everyday objects. However, this may have been more in the service of reinforcing the show's aesthetic illusion than promoting any particular lifestyle. Indeed, as Kackman observes, many of these objects were actually lethal.[50]

Still, the question remains: from whom or what were the agents weekly "saving the world?" For an answer, it is instructive to follow the evolution of Thrush, U.N.C.L.E.'s primary adversary. Originally described in NBC's promotional booklet as a supranation without geographical boundaries,[51] Thrush morphed from a terrorist-like organization bent on taking over small countries and disrupting relations between the major powers, to a multinational, bureaucratic entity run by a board of directors advised by an infallible computer. Thrush employees vied for promotions and worried about project funding. For their efforts, upon retirement, they were awarded a gold watch that blew up. Although there were plenty of peons—guards, henchmen, and a private army (Thrush soldiers even had uniforms)—right from the very beginning, those in charge of Thrush were not mere thugs or grotesques as in Bond. Wealthy, educated, articulate, and sophisticated, they were the well-positioned and powerful of the world: industrialists, scientists, millionaires, intellectuals, owners of art galleries and vineyards, and leaders in the fashion industry. "Thrush is an organization that believes the world should have a two-party system," Solo says in "The Green Opal Affair" (1964), "the masters and the slaves." Thrush was composed of people who had the political, economic, and technological resources to exploit and prey upon those who did not. When Ace novelist David McDaniel added to the mythology by inventing an acronym for Thrush, "the Technological Hierarchy for the Removal of Undesirables and the Subjugation of Humanity," it seemed entirely appropriate.

So, perhaps, *The Man from U.N.C.L.E.* was a metaphor, but one more suited to a world that, in 1964, did not yet exist. Speaking to a younger generation, *U.N.C.L.E.* warned against decentralized but well-organized terrorist organizations disrupting sovereign nations; greedy, self-interested global corporate interests operating without civic responsibility; and well-funded scientific researchers working on commercial or military projects without accountability—the very issues that our post–cold war, postmodern world is grappling with today. "We're showing people things to come," Felton told *TV Guide* in 1964, "and we're doing it with a sense of humor. So, rather than make a comment on life as it is today, we are commenting on life as it will be in the future."[52] Applied to technology, aesthetics, and perhaps even politics, Felton's observation appears to have been entirely prescient.

Notes

1. Charlie White, "Cell Phone Design is Smallest Yet," November 8, 2007, gizmodo.com/gadgets/cellphones/pen-phone-design-is-smallest-yet-320328.php (accessed November 30, 2007). "Cell Phone Pen Coming Soon," November 30, 2007, www.geekologie.com/2007/11/cell_phone_pen_coming_soon_get.php (accessed November 30, 2007).

2. Craig Henderson, "The Films from U.N.C.L.E. Part Three: One Spy Too Many," *Cinema Retro* 4, no. 11 (Spring 2008): 42–47. Henderson notes that the opening day of the third *U.N.C.L.E.* feature film set a house record at London's Empire Theater, and during its first week of release in London the film outgrossed James Bond in *Thunderball* (1965).

3. Paul Ruppert, "Open Channel D, Please," November 24, 2007, www.mobile-pointview.com/2007/11/open-channel-d.html (accessed November 30, 2007).

4. David Morely, *Family Television* (New York: Routledge, 1988), reports what baby boomers knew growing up.

5. Leslie Raddatz, "The Mystic Cult of Millions: The People from U.N.C.L.E.," *TV Guide*, March 19, 1966, 15–18.

6. "Great TV Spy Scramble," *Life*, October 1, 1965, 118–20.

7. Raddatz, "The Mystic Cult of Millions," 16.

8. Jon Heitland, *The Man from U.N.C.L.E. Book: The Behind the Scenes Story of a Television Classic* (New York: St. Martin's Press, 1987).

9. For *The Man from U.N.C.L.E.*'s relationship to other spy-themed films and television series, see Cynthia W. Walker, "Spy Programs," in *The Encyclopedia of Television*, 2nd ed., ed. Horace Newcomb (Chicago: Fitzroy Dearborn, 2004), 2181–85. Also available online at www.museum.tv/archives/etv/S/htmlS /spyprograms/spyprograms.htm.

10. "Second week premieres," *Time* (October 2, 1964), 106–7.

11. Cleveland Amory, "Review: The Man from U.N.C.L.E.," *TV Guide*, January 16, 1965, 21. See also Amory's follow-up review, "Second Thoughts," *TV Guide*, June 7, 1965, A-1.

12. Review of *The Man from U.N.C.L.E.*, *Variety*, September 30, 1964.

13. Ayn Rand, "Check Your Premises: Bootleg Romanticism," *The Objectivist Newsletter* 4, no. 1 (January 1965): 1–4.

14. Norman Felton, *Quarterly Retrospective, Arena Productions.* Unpublished manuscript. Norman Felton Collection, University of Iowa Library, Iowa City.

15. The story of how *The Man from U.N.C.L.E.* was originally conceived has been reported numerous times over the years. In addition to Heitland, see also Cynthia W. Walker, "*The Man from U.N.C.L.E.*," in *The Encyclopedia of Television*, 2nd ed., ed. Horace Newcomb (Chicago: Fitzroy Dearborn, 2004), 1404–06. Also available online at www.museum.tv/archives/etv/M/htmlM/manfromun/manfromun.htm. The most recent version can be found in "The Cloak and Swagger Affair: The Untold History of *The Man from U.N.C.L.E*" on *The Man from U.N.C.L.E., The Complete Season One*, DVD, Disc 11 (Time Life, 2007).

16. See Heitland, *The Man from U.N.C.L.E. Book*, 188, also 175–92. *The Man from U.N.C.L.E. 1967–1968 Season Information for Writers*, available from the Norman Felton Collection, observes that the show had moved from straight adventure to high adventure with humor to broad comedy and satire, and was, circa 1967, trying to restore the balance between adventure and humor. It was probably too late, although scheduling a more serious *U.N.C.L.E.* just after the comedy series *The Monkees* (1966–1968) on Monday nights did not help. A public postmortem was written by Lloyd Schearer: "Life and Death of the Man from U.N.C.L.E," *Parade*, March 17, 1968, 16–19.

17. *The Man from U.N.C.L.E. Information for Writers* (circa 1966). Norman Felton Collection.

18. "Everybody Wants to Get into the Act," *TV Guide*, October 17–23, 1964, 10–11.

19. David Buxton, *From the Avengers to Miami Vice: Form and Ideology in Television Series* (Manchester: Manchester University Press, 1990) categorizes both *The Man from U.N.C.L.E.* and *The Avengers*, along with *Danger Man* and *The Prisoner* (1967–1968), as "pop" series that privilege style over content and emphasize modernity, technology, and conspicuous consumption. For discussions of *The Man from U.N.C.L.E.* as a postmodern text and its relationship to Pop, see also Toby Miller, *Spyscreen: Espionage on Film and TV from the 1930s to the 1960s* (Oxford: Oxford University Press, 2003); Michael Kackman, *Citizen Spy: Television, Espionage, and Cold War Culture* (Minneapolis: University of Minnesota Press, 2005); and James Chapman, *Saints & Avengers: British Adventure Series of the 1960s* (London: I. B. Tauris, 2002).

20. See the discussions of the "aesthetic illusion" in Leon Balter, "On the Aesthetic Illusion," *Journal of the American Psychoanalytic Association* 47, no. 4 (1999): 1293–1333, and how to undermine it in Werner Wolf, "Aesthetic Illusion as an Effect of Fiction," *Style* 38, no. 3 (Fall 2004): 325–51.

21. Norman Felton, personal memo sent May 21, 1964. Available from the Norman Felton Collection.

22. Reported in N. Robinson, "Our Man with UNcle," *Secretariat* 11, no. 3 (February 16, 1966): 13 (available from United Nation Headquarters, New York) and "The U.N. in U.N.C.L.E. is Evoking Letters," *New York Times*, December 26, 1965, section 6, p. 1.

23. For more on the creation and distribution of the U.N.C.L.E. identification cards, see Peter Bogdanovich, "With Gun in Hand and Tongue in Cheek," *TV Guide*, October 26, 1964, 10–13, and Heitland, *The Man from U.N.C.L.E. Book*, 157.

24. Norman Felton, personal communication to the author, October 2, 1995.

25. A "Wainscot" fantasy involves "invisible or undetected societies living in the interstices of the dominant world." Definition from *The Encyclopedia of Fantasy*, ed. John Clute and John Grant (New York: St. Martin's, 1997), 991–92.

26. Barry Sonnenfeld, Ed Solomon, Walter F. Parkes, and Laurie MacDonald, *MIB, Men in Black: The Script and the Story behind the Film* (New York: Newmarket Press, 1997), 19.

27. Heitland, *The Man from U.N.C.L.E. Book*, 104.

28. *The Man from U.N.C.L.E. Information for Writers*, 5.

29. Hargrove, Sargent, Lehr, and others are interviewed in "Guns, Gizmos, Gadgets and Garb." *The Man from U.N.C.L.E.: The Complete Collection*, DVD, Bonus Disc 1 (Time Life, 2007).

30. Memo from Sam Rolfe to Norman Felton, August 10, 1964, Norman Felton Collection.

31. For example: W. Stevenson Bacon, "Crazy Gadgets of 'The Man from U.N.C.L.E.,'" *Popular Science*, December 1965, 46–47, 186.

32. *The Man from U.N.C.L.E.* was one of the first television shows to be heavily merchandised. For a full listing, see Brian Paquette and Paul Howley, *The Toys from U.N.C.L.E.: Memorabilia and Collectors Guide* (Worchester, MA: Entertainment Publishing, 1990).

33. Paul Atkinson, "Man in a Briefcase: The Social Construction of the Laptop Computer and the Emergence of a Type Form," *Journal of Design History* 18, no. 2 (2005): 191–205.

34. See "What a Weapon for a One-Man Army!" *TV Guide*, February 6, 1965, 12–14, and Joel Cymrot, "The Cat with the Gat from U.N.C.L.E.," *Gun World*, May 1965, 24, 26–27. For an extended discussion of the history, development, and implications of the U.N.C.L.E. Special, see Cynthia W. Walker, "The Gun as Star and the U.N.C.L.E. Special," in *Bang Bang, Shoot Shoot! Essays on Guns and Popular Culture*, 2nd ed., ed. Murray Pomerance and John Sakeris (Needham Heights, MA: Pearson Education, 2000), 203–13. Images and modern replicas of the U.N.C.L.E. Special are available online at the Samaritan Arts website at www.theunclegun.com/.

35. "What a Weapon for a One-Man Army!" 14.

36. Today, the car has been refurbished and is owned by Robert Short, a professional special effects designer who lives in Southern California. For the complete story of the U.N.C.L.E. car, see Nick Whitlow, "Meet *The Man from U.N.C.L.E.*

Car," in *The AMT Piranha & The Man from U.N.C.L.E. Car from the shops of Gene Winfield*, 2006, www.c-we.com/piranha/UNCLEcar.htm, and "Behind the Wheel: U.N.C.L.E.'s Piranha" with Bob Short and Gene Winfield, in *The Man from U.N.C.L.E.: The Complete Collection*, DVD, Bonus Disc 1 (Time Life, 2007).

37. Mentioned by Danny Biederman in "The Spy-Fi Tour: Archives, Art and Artifacts," *The Man from U.N.C.L.E.: The Complete Season Two*, DVD, Disc 11 (Time Life, 2007).

38. Danny Biederman, *The Incredible World of Spy-Fi* (San Francisco: Chronicle Books, 2004). The archives can be viewed online at "The Spy-Fi Archives," CIA Museum, www.cia.gov/about-cia/cia-museum/spy-fi-archives/index.html.

39. The publicity department at MGM once received an inquiry from a CIA agent informing them that a microdot used in an episode was similar to the agency's own technology. Reported in "Crazy Gadgets of 'The Man from U.N.C.L.E.,'" 186. Also, according to Jennifer Hillner in "What the CIA Learned from *Get Smart*," *Wired Magazine*, www.wired.com/culture/culturereviews/multimedia/2008/05/pl_print (accessed May 19, 2008), such similarities were apparently more common than anyone realized.

40. Lehr, "Guns, Gizmos, Gadgets and Garb."

41. Memo from Sam Rolfe to David Victor, March 18, 1965, 4–5. Norman Felton Collection.

42. *The Man from U.N.C.L.E. Information for Writers*, 5.

43. Donald Freeman, "TV's Future Looks Good," *Dallas Morning News*, 1967, L-32.

44. See *The Fans from U.N.C.L.E.*, www.manfromuncle.org/ (accessed May 31, 2008), among others. There are also several discussion groups available on Yahoo Groups devoted to the series.

45. See, for example, Erik Barnouw, *Tube of Plenty* (New York: Oxford University Press, 1990), 366–77.

46. Rolfe's liberal politics at the time are reported by Todd Gitlin, *Inside Television* (Los Angeles: University of California Press, 2000), 222. Norman Felton is well known for his active role and financial support of liberal causes, in particular, nuclear nonproliferation, elimination of the U.S. death penalty, and media literacy. See Pam McAllister, *Death Defying: Dismantling the Execution Machinery in 21st Century U.S.A.* (New York: Continuum, 2003), 47–48, and "Norman Felton," The Center For Media Literacy, 2002–2008, www.medialit.org/felton_bio.html (accessed May 31, 2008). Robert Vaughn, who starred as Napoleon Solo, was an outspoken, high-profile critic of the Vietnam War. His political activity was well publicized at the time, most notably in Dwight Whitney, "The Other Bobby in American Politics," *TV Guide*, February 24, 1968, 14–17.

47. *The Man from U.N.C.L.E. Information for Writers*, 1.

48. Rick Worland, "The Cold War Mannerists: *The Man from U.N.C.L.E.* and TV Espionage in the 1960s," *Journal of Popular Film and Television* 21, no. 4 (1994): 150–61.

49. Leon Hunt in "Drop Everything . . . Including Your Pants! The Professionals and 'Hard' Action TV" puts it bluntly: "The men from U.N.C.L.E. were agents for conspicuous consumption first and the 'Free World' second." In *Action TV: Tough Guys, Smooth Operators and Foxy Chicks*, ed. Bill Osgerby and Anna Gough-Yates (New York: Routledge, 2001), 130.

50. See Kackman, *Citizen Spy*, 79–98.

51. National Broadcasting Company, "The Man from U.N.C.L.E.: Coming on NBC-TV, fall 1964, 8:30–9:30 pm NYT, Tuesday." Promotional booklet, Norman Felton Collection.

52. Bogdanovich, "With Gun in Hand and Tongue in Cheek," 13.

PART II

BRITISH DYSTOPIAS AND UTOPIAS

Captain Scarlet from *Captain Scarlet and the Mysterons*
(1967–1968). *Courtesy of ITV/Rex Features.*

CHAPTER FOUR

Pulling the Strings: Gerry Anderson's Walk from "Supermarionation" to "Hypermarionation"

David Garland

One morning his class was told to write a play to be performed the following day. When it came to Gerry's turn, he began enacting a love story before a giggling audience and a slightly nervous English teacher. "I shall be a wonderful husband for the rest of my days and, to prove it, I shall give you my heart," he declared, fumbling inside his cardigan and pulling out a home-made cardboard heart—not the traditional pink love heart, but, to his teacher's astonishment, an almost perfect replica of a human heart, complete with exposed ventricles.[1]

Gerry Anderson made his name during the 1960s with a string of science fiction children's television programs, most notably *Fireball XL5* (1962–1963), *Stingray* (1964–1965), *Thunderbirds* (1965–1966), and *Captain Scarlet and the Mysterons* (1967–1968). Yet, although these shows all famously featured marionettes and enjoyed considerable success around the world, there is little if any reference to them in scholarly works about puppets, which in their discussion of television have tended to focus instead on Jim Henson's Muppets. One clue to the reason for such neglect comes from Anderson's retrospective derogatory comments about working with puppets, expressed most succinctly perhaps in a 2004 interview: "Frankly I hate them."[2] Indeed, his prevailing attitude has seemed to be that the marionettes were the double-edged necessary evil that jump-started his career but ultimately frustrated his ambitions.

Hence, for example, Anderson's dismissal of the original *Captain Scarlet* while promoting the new, "improved" CGI version:

> *Captain Scarlet's* characters all looked so real that I remember looking at the show with some pride and thinking to myself, "It's wonderful, they look wonderful." The only thing is, they can't walk, they can't pick up anything and have no expression because the heads were made from fibre. I thought that if only I had a magic wand, where I could touch the screen and all these characters, who by then were world famous, would then spring to life and become flesh and blood like you and me. Well a while ago, I did get hold of a magic wand and I tapped the screen and now we're going to show the result.[3]

These words encapsulate the central theme that has run throughout Anderson's work: a self-reflexive obsession with an aesthetic of realism (or more accurately a surface realism often associated with naturalism), borne of an unfulfilled desire to make live-action films for adults. Ironically, however, notwithstanding Anderson's own disdain for the form, such a preoccupation actually locates his work very resonantly within both the long history of puppetry and the current theoretical debate about its future. In this context, Anderson's wand may have succeeded in removing the strings from *Captain Scarlet* only to reposition it at the vanguard of the contemporary craft.

As Pam Morris suggests, "realism" is a slippery word, inhabiting the realms of everyday and aesthetic usage, and entangled with other equally elusive concepts.[4] Raymond Williams notes that despite referring to much older methods, realism only emerged in critical vocabulary during the mid-1800s and became further complicated toward the turn of the century by attempts to distinguish it from naturalism. The terms for a time became so interchangeable that Strindberg's famous definition actually reversed the ultimate conventional distinction, which was that naturalism "merely reproduced the flat external appearance of reality with a certain static quality, whereas realism . . . was that method and that intention which went below this surface to the essential historical movements, to the dynamic reality."[5]

The word "realism" (and variations such as "realistic," "real," and "believable") dominates the retrospective commentary of Anderson and his colleagues regarding all of his work, but particularly the marionette television shows. Although also reflecting a general interest in the dynamic reality of an imagined future (most obviously in the utopian vision of a world government and cooperative global institutions), these individual instances typically show a naturalistic concern for the *look* of things, one that radiates outward from the marionette figures themselves to the entire world they inhabit, from explosions, vehicles, and other props to buildings and landscapes. Anderson's reaction to being typecast as a producer of children's puppet television led him on a lifelong quest to perfect a simulation of reality. As colleague Reg Hill acknowledges, when desperation for work led Anderson to accept a commission for his company, AP Films (APF), to make his first marionette production, *The Adventures of Twizzle* (1957–1959), the only way to make it bearable was to add something: "Everything we did, whether it was the detail of the sets or the advances in puppetry, was designed to seem as real as possible and was injected into the work to make it palatable for ourselves. Instead of following on the traditions that go back thousands of years with Chinese puppetry, we really branched out in another direction."[6]

Being Big(headed)

An actor who enjoys being a ham is no match for the puppeteer who wants to be the whole hog.[7]

Reinvention may have separated the APF productions from then-contemporary trends in puppetry, but it was a response to a dilemma shared by puppetry in general. During the 1950s and 1960s, puppet theater in the West had become increasingly marginalized to a niche, to an association with children's entertainment, so much so that a 1959 *People and Puppets* show in New York felt the need to proclaim itself "a production for adults at a strictly adult level." Poor critical reviews then led Vivian Michael in *The Puppetry Journal* to wonder if it were even possible to present puppet theater for adults anymore, clinging to the hope that maybe "if we all strive for just a little more perfection in our work . . . 'adult recognition' will come along some day.'"[8]

This comment would appear in one sense to encapsulate Anderson's attitude in the 1960s to his own career in puppetry, with the notable exception of course that for Anderson "adult recognition" ultimately meant the opportunity to make live-action feature films for grown-ups. Nevertheless, along the way he also targeted adults as collateral viewers of the marionette shows ("I deliberately made pictures which were for children but which adults could also watch"[9]), via among other things the use of humor and themes (notably the cold war[10]) not usually associated with children's television. Indeed, both Andersons of the husband-and-wife team have made great play over the years of the term "kidult,"[11] to suggest the wide, inclusive appeal of these programs, an appeal that endured despite ITV's original haphazard scheduling (in stark contrast to the relatively stable teatime time slot of the BBC's similarly targeted *Doctor Who*[12]). Above all, however, it was arguably the aesthetic of incremental realism that seemed designed most to appeal to adults, both regular viewers and industry professionals alike.

Perhaps the most articulate denunciation of Anderson's use of puppets (and by extension his aesthetic of incremental realism) has come from one of his former puppeteers, John Blundall, who worked on the APF science fiction shows from *Supercar* (1961–1962) to *Thunderbirds*. Although Blundall made and operated mainly peripheral puppets, the chauffeur Parker in *Thunderbirds* (based loosely on British comedian Ben Warris) is one of his creations and not coincidentally proved to be one of the most caricatured characters in this or any Anderson series. Parker, however, served mainly as comic relief and played most of his scenes with British agent Lady Penelope, well away from the main plotlines dealing with the Tracey family. (As such, he harks back in many ways to Victorian marionette culture's "pantaloon," a low comic figure that functioned as the butt of jokes and did not mix with regular dramatic characters.[13]) Puppets at this time also had heads out of proportion to the rest of their bodies, for aesthetic considerations rather than Anderson's logistical reason (of having to house the lip-sync mechanism there), the theory being that the head carried the puppet's personality, with the larger size further providing a sense of distance and perspective. Interestingly, the comic characters often tended to have the largest heads of all.[14]

In a 1985 interview with fan magazine *S.I.G.*, Blundall claims that Anderson's earlier puppet shows were best because they featured more peculiar creatures and unusual characters, whereas the later ones lacked imaginative qualities and focused on "little humans," trying to disguise the fact that they were puppets.[15] In Blundall's view, puppets need exaggerated, stylized features in order to develop their own personality and function properly. He particularly disliked Sylvia Anderson's practice of modeling puppets from photos (often of famous actors) and the increasingly realistic smaller heads that undermined weight distribution and made the puppets harder to operate. Ultimately, Blundall argues, the ongoing efforts at increased realism in puppet design squeezed the creativity out of the puppeteer's role.[16]

In his commentary on the DVD release of *Supercar* in 2005, Gerry Anderson somewhat disingenuously caricatures Blundall's position by claiming there to be two schools of thought regarding puppet strings (one arguing that everything should be done to get rid of the strings and the other that if you couldn't see the strings then they weren't really puppets), only to conclude: "If you couldn't spot a puppet was a puppet without the strings there was something wrong with your eyesight." A more textured and (for our purposes here) interesting defense of Anderson's vision of incremental realism comes in a 1996 article for the Sound and Television Society, in which he addresses the viewpoint that puppetry should not be realistic and its corresponding question: why not use real people if the real thing is wanted? Preferring not to acknowledge that "real people" had been his ambition all along, Anderson instead espouses the spectacular attractions of simulation and miniaturization:

> A beautifully made scale model of an ocean-going liner will always attract a crowd at an exhibition and, in the same way, the more accurately we copy life on a miniature scale the greater will be our success. Our history has shown that every move made in this direction has produced a greater appreciation of our films and so, despite this view point, I will continue to move in the same direction believing that I am right—only time will tell![17]

Actually, the degree to which Anderson in this regard was swimming against the tide of puppet history is implied by Steve Tillis in his discussion of puppets as a subset of the wider category of "media figures," defined as performance made possible via technological mediation:

> It might seem that the various figures I have mentioned do anything but "hold a mirror up to nature"—being, in the main, figures of fantasy; but this is as much a function of economics as artistry: Why bother with the expense of a "naturalistic" media image when an actor can perform such roles easily enough? Media figures are, thus, left most often to enact non-naturalistic roles, at which they happen to excel. In this regard, the figures are rather similar to puppets as we have known them, which have frequently held up the mirror less to nature than to the untrammelled imagination of the puppet-artist.[18]

These "puppets as we have known them" equate of course to the stage approach that lead puppeteer Christine Glanville originally brought with her to Anderson's shows, but which he dismissed as "pure" puppetry in favor of his own "more and more life-like" techniques,[19] encapsulated by the term *Supermarionation*. Sylvia Anderson openly admits that she and her husband created this term for status reasons because television was widely regarded as the poor relation of film, and puppetry as even lower than that. Consequently, "the name Supermarionation was to distinguish the pure puppetry of the stage from our more sophisticated filmed-television version."[20] Nevertheless, she does implicitly question the entire basis of Gerry Anderson's realist aesthetic in claiming that with *Thunderbirds* they "perfected the art of Supermarionation"[21] and that "we found by critical reaction that the audience was just not interested in the exact science of the perfect, humanized puppet. They preferred our *Thunderbirds* version."[22] *Thunderbirds* proved to be the last Anderson series to employ disproportionately large heads, of the puppet kind anyway.[23] By the time of *Captain Scarlet* technological advances meant that the lip-sync mechanism no longer needed to be housed in the head.

Ironically, the Andersons' move to distance themselves from the poor relation of stage puppetry (and later on from puppets and then television altogether) has a clear antecedent in the nineteenth-century marionette theater's own attempts to distinguish itself from other forms of puppetry (especially glove puppets), which also involved a tethering to the newly emergent realist aesthetic across the arts. The attraction of this aesthetic proved particularly strong given that, as McCormick notes, marionette shows were much closer in form and presentation than other puppetry to the actor's theater of the time:

> The nineteenth-century theatre was heavily caught up in notions of realism and in the idea of trying to deceive the audience into a belief in the reality of what was being presented. The patent unreality of the glove puppet allowed it largely to escape this concern, but in the case of the marionette there was an extraordinary degree of ambivalence.[24]

Consequently, marionette show people avoided the word "puppet" due to the association with street glove puppets, the Italian term *fantoccini* often prevailing instead until the mid-nineteenth century.[25]

Marionette theater further mimicked many aspects of its human role model, including retaining an equivalent of a stock repertory company of actors.[26] A century later, AP Films also had its stock company of puppets with interchangeable heads. Thus, for example, the puppet playing the title role in *Captain Scarlet* would later appear in a bit part in *Joe 90*, and the puppet character "stars" in general would invariably be introduced at the beginning of episodes in shows like *Thunderbirds* in the manner of actors playing roles on live-action television programs and films.

Trimming the Real

When asked if anyone on the expanded roster had particularly impressed him during the making of *Thunderbirds*, puppeteer John Blundall picked out two people: Derek Meddings and Mike Trim. This choice seems appropriate, because both became enormously influential on the later Anderson puppet shows, as concern with production design and special effects began to rival and even surpass that of the puppets themselves in terms of the concept of incremental realism. In some ways the challenge posed here proved even more daunting than that facing the puppet makers and operators, for clothing aside, the people populating Anderson's vision of one hundred years into the future seemed little different in appearance to those in the present day. However, the designers of sets and vehicles had to balance the conventional science fiction imperative of the "futuristic" with seeping hyperrealist concerns mandated by Anderson's approach to the puppets, a task perhaps somewhat oversimplified and underestimated by Sylvia Anderson when she recounts that for the *Thunderbirds* craft, Meddings "employed current technology and then took a giant step into the future. This explains why so many of our action sequences are credible years later: we were ahead of our time, not in a pure fantasy, but rooted in a future reality."[27]

The actual extent of the challenge can be suggested by two quite different descriptions of the specific roles of and relationship between Meddings and Trim. In his book describing his time at Century 21 as a member of the special effects team, Alan Shubrook notes that as Meddings spent increasing time "pursuing the art of realistic effects," he recruited Trim to assist in the design of the "futuristic vehicles and locations."[28] On the other hand, in his foreword to a book about Trim's art, Richard Taylor claims that Trim "added the stamp of realism and authenticity" to Meddings's work that "transported the viewer to another time and world."[29]

Clearly, this realism/futurism tension lies at the heart of a great deal of British science fiction television, which has frequently focused, in Mark Bould's words, on "the dialectical struggle . . . between tradition and innovation."[30] However, it is important to emphasize that for Anderson the genre functioned as almost as much of an unwanted diversion as puppetry did. After making two marionette shows for children's writer Roberta Leigh, *The Adventures of Twizzle* and *Torchy the Battery Boy* (1960–1961), Anderson chose the western as the genre for his first independent production, *Four Feather Falls* (1960). Despite being typecast as a producer of children's puppet programs, Anderson nevertheless saw the relatively greater freedom offered here as an opportunity to get closer to the film industry (an ambition signaled right from the start in the name of his production company, AP Films, and then maintained in Anderson's ongoing references to his television shows as "films"). As he remarked of the series, "It was really me trying to make the sort of films I used to see in the cinema."[31] The first of AP Films' productions for Granada's Lew Grade followed, and the success of this show, *Supercar*, further typecast Anderson even more narrowly into the niche of science fiction, yet the choice of genre this time proved purely instrumental.

Anderson's incremental realist aesthetic had run into particular difficulty in earlier shows with the technical challenge of getting the puppets to walk in a relatively believable way. A science fiction context, centering on the title vehicle, seemed to provide an ideal way out of this problem.[32]

This accident of genre, although never reaching the millstone proportions of puppetry for Anderson, certainly had important implications for the ongoing realism/futurism relationship in his shows. The overall balance between the two became even more of a high-wire act, as it were, given Anderson's continued central preoccupation with perfecting puppets as "little humans" running (or failing that, driving) around a believable environment. In short, this simulated world gave new meaning to the suspension of disbelief.

One consequence of this situation seemed to be a relative reining in of fanciful futuristic production design, despite the temptations of the significantly larger budgets afforded to Grade's ITC producers over their BBC counterparts on shows such as *Doctor Who* (the result in part of early successes and ongoing ties with American television).[33] Instead, the fantastic tended to be temperately grafted onto familiar foundations, as Trim describes it: "We took the world around us and nudged it towards the future, rather than trying to create something so outlandishly futuristic it was hard to accept."[34] Thus, the puppets of shows like *Thunderbirds* and *Captain Scarlet* may have been inhabiting a world set about a hundred years into the future, but the realism imperative ensured that the environment ultimately looked very much like that of the 1960s. This stylistic approach was retained even when Anderson finally left puppets behind at the end of the decade for the live-action science fiction series *UFO* (1970–1971) and *Space: 1999* (1975–1977).

In the same way that the Andersons often found the basic premises of their shows from science stories in the news (as in the invention of magnetic tape recording for *Joe 90* [1968–1969][35] and Christian Barnard's heart transplant procedure for *UFO*[36]), both Trim and Meddings in their vehicle designs looked to current technological development, most notably the U.S./USSR space race of the 1960s. This cold war inspiration built on the practice Samantha Holloway identifies in early American science fiction television of the 1950s, in which spacecraft typically echoed the German V-2 rockets of the Second World War:

The ships of these early shows were direct ideological descendents of the rockets that had starred in the previous decade's war: V-2s, tall, sleek, phallic, the cutting edge of rocket science, and, of all the vehicles known at the time, perhaps the most likely to get a man away from here, into space. In the early years of television, spaceships were almost always like them—sleek, silver, involving

vertical liftoffs and fire shooting out of the engines far below the cockpit. Although they were often modified from the rockets everyone knew from World
War II—by an added tail fin, perhaps, or a pair of short wings—they were still
essentially rockets.[37]

Thus, for example, Meddings took his Thunderbird 3 craft from a Soyuz
original, with the addition of extra fins and rockets to enhance its appearance on screen.[38] Trim also turned to Soviet technology for inspiration. His
Space Intruder Detector (S.I.D.) design for *UFO* featured an insectlike front
drawn from a Vostok spacecraft,[39] and a mobile drilling rig was influenced by
the chunky look of many Soviet military vehicles.[40]

Inevitably, given the specific nature of this realistic/futuristic dialectic,
the two designers found themselves in conflict on a number of occasions.
For example, Meddings rejected Trim's original Interceptor design for *UFO*
as too conventional and old-fashioned. Trim's focus here in the craft's details
on a "sense of realism" and "what viewers would expect" was discarded in
favor of a more streamlined version.[41] On the other hand, Meddings vetoed
Trim's original concept for the S.H.A.D.O. jet from "small and sleek" to a
more realistic "inverted version of the American XB-70 Valkyrie bomber"
(with a Concorde-style drop nose[42]). With Meddings otherwise occupied on
the second *Thunderbirds* feature film, *Thunderbird 6* (1968), Trim assumed
more responsibility and power on Anderson's final two marionette productions, *Captain Scarlet* and *The Secret Service* (1969). Ironically, however, he
often found his hands even more tied given the two shows' increased realist
slants, which intensified the conflict between the streamlined/futuristic and
mundane/contemporary. A case in point (although he eventually won the
day) would be Trim's fight against Anderson's original vision of the real
Eiffel Tower as the blueprint for the London Car-Vu building featured in the
climax to the first episode of *Captain Scarlet*.[43]

However, despite the undoubted significance of such conceptual macro-
dichotomies, perhaps even more important to the final look of Anderson's
shows, and particularly the miniaturized marionette ones, would prove to be
the techniques relating to microrealistic details, neatly encapsulated by "Realism Simulation," the title invented by Trim and colleague David Palmer
to market themselves to the film industry after the demise of Anderson's
Century 21 production company.[44] A focal point for such techniques, known
as the "dirtying down" department, featured the art of detailing models with
found objects ("gubbins") and then dressing them with signs of "real world"
wear and tear. Shubrook, for example, recounts a trip with Derek Meddings
to a number of local Slough department stores to retrieve colanders, mixing

bowls, etc., for the Mysteron complex in episode one of *Captain Scarlet*.[45] Similarly, attempts were made to conceal puppet strings using a film industry combination of antiflare (a grease mist spray) and puffers (bottles of dry powder paints), so as to match the background and reduce reflective surfaces.[46] Third, a process now often known as "artworking," involving the application of small bits of detail (such as grills and vents, hinges and handles), collectively "provided another level of realism and helped further the illusion the team was trying to create on screen."[47]

Stand By for Action

> The marionette is a puppet on strings, suspended from a control held by the puppeteer. It is versatile and can be simple or complex in both construction and control. Performances can be graceful and charming, and fast and forceful action is generally avoided.[48]

One of the most striking paradoxes about Anderson's science fiction shows in the 1960s is that they employed the type of puppet perhaps most unsuited to the action-oriented subject matter. Shadow puppets, for example, are, as David Currell suggests, far more able to handle "vigorous knockabout action."[49] Instead, the clarion call "Stand by for action!" uttered by Commander Shore at the beginning of each episode of *Stingray* (along with the accompanying claim that "anything can happen in the next half hour") seems more than a little ironic. As we have seen, walking always posed one of the greatest technical challenges for Supermarionation, so much so that vehicle-heavy science fiction became Anderson's preferred genre. *Stingray* thus focused enormously on the eponymous underwater vessel, and Shore himself was confined in the Marineville control tower to a futuristic hoverchair, the result of a war injury. The other main solution to this problem dovetailed with Anderson's long-standing ambitions. Consequently, even before the move to *UFO* and *Space: 1999*, his final marionette series *The Secret Service* blended puppetry with live action (and was uniquely set in the present day). Thereafter, when Anderson finally returned to puppetry in the 1980s after a long break, the unwieldy marionettes had given way to other types, such as sophisticated latex hand puppets (via a process dubbed "Supermacromation") in *Terrahawks* (1983–1986), animatronic heads (on live-action bodies) in *Space Precinct* (1994–1995), and stop-motion animation (wedded with computer graphics) in *Lavender Castle* (1999–2000).

The latter show set the stage in many ways for arguably Anderson's most groundbreaking production since the 1960s Supermarionation era. As the title suggests, *Gerry Anderson's New Captain Scarlet* (2005) retains the producer's self-consciously grandiose auteurist aspirations, something also apparent in Anderson's stated rationale for deliberately avoiding a commissioning broadcaster: "A broadcaster would impose itself on the script, appoint a producer to oversee it. I can't work like that. The whole thing about this production is that I have total creative control. That's not big headedness, it's about maintaining a vision."[50] However, as with *Lavender Castle*, this remake discards film entirely in favor of digital video. The ongoing aesthetic of incremental realism is once again foregrounded, most obviously in Anderson's assertion that the digital process employed should not be described as animation, but rather a new "photoreal method" of making television programs—a combination of high definition, Dolby 5.1 surround sound, and computer-generated imagery labeled "Hypermarionation."[51]

Like the original, *New Captain Scarlet* wedded a technologically aided leap in surface realism to a utopian but dark-edged vision of the future extrapolated from current events and issues. Set once again in 2068, the show features the exploits of the military organization Spectrum (headquartered on a mobile base in the sky), whose agents use a plethora of futuristic vehicles and weapons to protect Earth on the behalf of a world government from an extraterrestrial threat. This time, however, the Martian Mysterons' modus operandi of terrorizing rather than invading Earth holds particular contemporary resonance and the backstory has been updated to cement this link. Instead of the 1960s-inspired atomic war of the marionette version, the 2005 production notes reference the death of Captain Scarlet's parents during an outbreak of "world terrorist wars."[52]

Throughout the promotion of the show in interviews and via collateral texts such as DVD audio commentaries, Anderson took particular pains to point out how much more realistic the new technology had proven to be, most notably in the realm of his long-standing bête noire: character movement, and specifically walking. Indeed, these comments even spilled onto the DVD commentaries for *The Secret Service* box set, released in the UK in 2005 around the same time as the initial ITV broadcasts of *New Captain Scarlet*: "And now with the advent of computer animation we were able to bring them to life and they look very very real and it's a wonderful thing to watch. . . . The faces are flesh and blood, or they look like it, and of course the characters can hop, step, and jump at will. So it's a tremendous move onward." This preoccupation extends to director David Lane's discussion on the *New Captain Scarlet* DVD concerning the two main animation methods of key frame and motion capture employed on the new show: namely, how the latter eventually rose over the course of production from 10 to 95 percent because of its greater effectiveness in portraying human action scenes such as running, jumping, and fighting. The fighting scenes in particular evidence a continuation of the Anderson trademark desires to be both "up to date" (as in the use of kickboxing) and paradoxically, despite the move from film to video, "cinematic": "We didn't want it to be a close-up, close-up, close-up series. We wanted it to have a lot of weight, a lot of spectacular sets, and the general feel to be totally cinematic." Perhaps even as important to Anderson, the use of motion capture technology has also enabled the simulated feel of a live-action film, as suggested by Wayne Forrester's voice-over commentary to the DVD's "Production Tour": "All the scenes are acted out live on stage in time with the voice track, enabling the director to direct exactly as he would a live-action shoot."

Ultimately however, notwithstanding Anderson's attempts to put puppets behind him on *New Captain Scarlet*, to reach instead for a hyperreal simulation of his live-action film utopia, the term "Hypermarionation" maintains (at the very least etymologically) the link with his marionette past. Such a connection may be more "live" than Anderson appreciates, if we accept, for instance, the ideas of Steve Tillis regarding puppetry's future in his 1999 essay "The Art of Puppetry in the Age of Media Production." Although admitting that such figures offer the greatest challenge to puppet theory,[53] Tillis persuasively proposes integrating computer graphics into a contemporary (or near-future) definition of puppet performance. Following Kaplin's inclusive model of media figures as puppets, he extrapolates a revolutionary definition of puppetry: "If the signification of life can be created by people, then the site of that signification is to be considered a puppet."[54] In other words, this paradigm transcends the sense of a puppet's materiality to include not only stop-action and animatronic animation but CGI as well. By this reckoning, Gerry Anderson has become more of a puppet-master than he ever was before.

Notes

1. Simon Archer and Marcus Hearn, *What Made Thunderbirds Go!* (London: BBC Worldwide, 2002), 14.
2. Adrian Pennington, "Look No Strings," *Televisual*, June 2004, 26.
3. Stephen Payne, "Simply Red," *Starburst* 29, no. 11 (March 2005): 37.
4. Pam Morris, *Realism* (London: Routledge, 2003), 203.
5. Raymond Williams, "A Lecture on Realism," *Screen* 18, no. 1 (1974): 65.
6. Archer and Hearn, *What Made Thunderbirds Go*, 62.
7. George Latshaw, *The Complete Book of Puppetry* (Mineola, NY: Dover, 1978), 28.

8. John Bell, *Strings, Hands, Shadows: A Modern Puppet History* (Detroit, MI: Detroit Institute of Arts, 2005), 99.

9. Archer and Hearn, *What Made Thunderbirds Go*, 53.

10. Nicholas J. Cull, "Was Captain Black Really Red?: The TV Science Fiction of Gerry Anderson in Its Cold War Context," *Media History* 12, no. 2 (2006): 194.

11. Sylvia Anderson, *My FAB Years* (Neshannock, PA: Hermes Press, 2007), 21; Robert Sellers, *Cult TV: The Golden Age of ITC* (London: Plexus, 2006), 183.

12. Mark Bould, "Science Fiction Television in the United Kingdom," in *The Essential Science Fiction Television Reader*, ed. J. P. Telotte (Lexington: University Press of Kentucky, 2008), 213.

13. John McCormick, *The Victorian Marionette Theatre* (Iowa City: University of Iowa Press, 2004), 71.

14. Ibid., 90.

15. Dave Smith and Barry Davies, "Solenoid Spotlight: John Blundall," *S.I.G.* 13 (Summer 1985): 19.

16. Ibid., 21.

17. Gerry Anderson, "Supermarionation for 'Thunderbirds.'" *British Kinematography* (1966): 334.

18. Steve Tillis, "The Art of Puppetry in the Age of Media Production," in *Puppets, Masks, and Performing Objects*, ed. John Bell (Cambridge, MA: MIT Press, 2001), 172.

19. Archer and Hearn, *What Made Thunderbirds Go*, 41.

20. Anderson, *My FAB Years*, 52.

21. Ibid., 76.

22. Ibid., 44.

23. Sylvia Anderson has suggested that the breakup of her personal and professional relationship with her husband owed a great deal to his inflated ego, namely increased movie-mogul pretensions along with an obsession over power and control. See Anderson, *My FAB Years*, 36, 52, 105, 111.

24. McCormick, *The Victorian Marionette Theatre*, 65.

25. Ibid., ix.

26. Ibid., 66.

27. Anderson, *My FAB Years*, 56.

28. Alan Shubrook, *Century 21 FX: Unseen Untold* (Chipping Ongar, Essex, UK: Shubrook Bros., 2007), 61.

29. Anthony Taylor, *The Future Was Fab: The Art of Mike Trim* (Neshannock, PA: Hermes Press, 2007), 4.

30. Bould, "Science Fiction Television in the United Kingdom," 209.

31. Archer and Hearn, *What Made Thunderbirds Go*, 49.

32. Sellers, *Cult TV*, 83.

33. Bould, "Science Fiction Television in the United Kingdom," 218.

34. Taylor, *The Future Was Fab*, 105.

35. Sellers, *Cult TV*, 109.

36. As Chris Bentley points out in *The Complete Gerry Anderson* (Richmond, Surrey, UK: Reynolds & Hearn, 2003), 262, Barnard's work provided an even more central inspiration at the same time for *Youth Is Wasted on the Young* (1969), one of Anderson's several abandoned live-action feature film projects.

37. Samantha Holloway, "Space Vehicles and Traveling Companions: Rockets and Living Ships," in *The Essential Science Fiction Television Reader*, ed. J. P. Telotte (Lexington: University Press of Kentucky, 2008), 179.

38. Shubrook, *Century 21 FX*, 30.

39. Taylor, *The Future Was Fab*, 77.

40. Ibid., 83.

41. Ibid., 74, 77.

42. Ibid., 81. We can only speculate that perhaps this last design feature was added to celebrate the real-life connections of the Concorde with Century 21 (the company Anderson had formed to replace AP Films).

43. Ibid., 34, 36.

44. Ibid., 43.

45. Shubrook, *Century 21 FX*, 58–59.

46. Ibid., 94.

47. Taylor, *The Future Was Fab*, 47.

48. David Currell, *Puppets and Puppet Theatre* (Ramsbury, Malborough, UK: Crowood Press, 1999), 10.

49. Ibid.

50. Pennington, "Look No Strings," 26. Ironically, however, once again an Anderson show ended up being poorly scheduled in the UK (scantly promoted and buried by ITV1 on its original broadcasts during the Saturday morning *Ministry of Mayhem* children's programming strand), in contrast to the revived *Doctor Who*'s plum early-evening Saturday time slot on BBC1.

51. Ibid., 26–27.

52. Andrew Billen, "Red-Hot Hero," *New Statesman* 21, February 2006, 46.

53. Tillis, "The Art of Puppetry in the Age of Media Production," 173.

54. Ibid., 175.

CHAPTER FIVE

Farmers, Feminists, and Dropouts: The Disguises of the Scientist in British Science Fiction Television in the 1970s

Laurel Forster

The 1970s was an uncertain decade in Britain. Change and unrest permeated British society and politics in an unprecedented way, leaving individuals and institutions insecure and unclear about future directions. This zeitgeist of uncertainty was caused, at least in part, by the wide range of issues and problems being highlighted in Britain, and concern about the impact such new awareness might have on individual lives. Many issues had become politicized as never before. Concerns about labor, pay, and working conditions led to strikes, the complicated negotiations between unions and management inevitably tainted by feelings of inequality. With disenfranchisement and oppression riding high, there was a general sense of dissatisfaction in the workplace. The women's liberation movement, gaining momentum from the late 1960s, gave rise to discussion, consciousness-raising groups, and direct action from women and some male supporters. There were calls for change on all levels regarding gender issues, from government legislation to private domestic arrangements. Women demanded the right to control their own fertility by raising previously taboo subjects such as contraception and abortion to public attention; they demanded access to higher education; and they demanded liberation from the relentless domestic drudgery of the by now highly gendered role of housewife. Age-old notions of social class and individual rights were being challenged and redefined through changes in education and social systems. What it meant to be British became further contested through anxieties over immigration and nationhood. As a result of cumulative concerns, many had become disillusioned with capitalist systems overall and chose to opt out in some way. The self-sufficiency movement grew in support, with many growing their own food, and alternative patterns of living such as in communes also grew in popularity. Scientific advancements were frequently seen as part of the problem, not as offering solutions. Science had become no longer the domain of an educated, intellectually removed few, but something that received mass media attention and wide public response.

In fact, such was the pace of scientific developments that by the 1970s, a number of events or scientific capabilities only previously experienced in the science fiction context had become reality in some way. Science, no longer the mysterious realm of the elite, became the concern of the masses. Wide media coverage, and hence mediated portrayals with positive and negative arguments, led in some cases to scaremongering and anxiety-inducing polemical articles related to developments in a number of scientific fields. For instance, the natural cycle of human life and death had been interrupted with the first human heart transplant in 1967; medical science now had the power to give a "miraculous" new lease on life, previously the domain of only biblical stories or science fiction. Both the church and the national press were quick to discuss the ethical implications of this and other developments in medical science. In 1969, man actually landed on the moon—not strictly a planet, but certainly otherworldly enough to raise a number of concerns—and prior to this, men and satellites had broken through this world's atmosphere. In the early 1970s the project to fertilize human eggs outside the womb raised fears about human fertility and genetic engineering; the first "test tube" baby was born in 1978 amidst controversy and unease. The mass destruction capabilities of the atom bomb had already stopped the world in its tracks decades before in 1945, and by the 1970s nuclear power was a fact of life, but feared and mistrusted nonetheless. From 1971 onward, with the development of the microprocessor, computers changed from being bulky machines with a few specific processes to small, intelligent tools capable of much more sophisticated functions. Instead of just performing dull, laborious factual tasks, computers started to offer supplementary functions, competing with human intelligence and capacities. In short, science concerned everyone in this decade over diverse issues such as human life, health and reproduction, population growth, food processes and shortages, the development of industrial technology and its implications for workers' jobs, damage to the environment, the uncontrollability of nuclear power both in war and as energy provision, and what the future might hold regarding space exploration and even space travel.

Given that this was a decade when the British people were experiencing social and cultural shifts and becoming aware of the phenomenal changes that scientific developments might make to their lives, as well as becoming more used to general and politicized debates about science, we might ask two related questions about developments in British science fiction programs of the time on television, the same medium in fact as much other "factual" reportage and commentary about "real" scientific developments. The first question is, How might we perceive the relationship between actual cultural and scientific developments and televisual portrayals of science fiction? The second question is, By what narrative devices were these messages conveyed within the fictitious sphere of science fiction programs? This chapter will address these two questions by discussing the pivotal nature of the scientist in science fiction in this decade. By examining the role of the scientist in science fiction, first historically with particular reference to the scientist on British television science fiction of the type targeted at adults, and then in more detail with reference to three programs on British television in the 1970s, again aimed at an adult audience, I will argue that the scientist was a versatile narrative vehicle available to represent the changing political, social, and domestic scene, and, because of the prominence of debate about science in this decade, was actually also an inherent part of the generalized upheaval and reconfiguring of modern Britain.

The Scientist in Science Fiction

If the role of science in science fiction is complex, then the role of the scientist must be doubly so. For just as science occupies a place in the genre that reflects the social and political concerns of the moment, so the scientist must attempt, by one narrative device or another, to convey both the *processes* of scientific experiment or endeavor and the *implications* or potential outcomes for a specific group of people or, more generally, the human race. Even if, in truth, the actual processes are too complex or boring to be fully explained within a fictionalized context, at the very least, the first aspect of the scientist's role is to make viewers feel they have at some level engaged with the science bit of the science fiction story so that, crucially, they feel the weight and imperative of the scientific aspect of the tale. This idea of simplified scientific process merely being explained or demonstrated by the scientist, however, is never devoid of political implications: even when fictitious scientists are seemingly innocently immersed in their laboratory work, they have, due to the authority lent them by the narrative, represented (or defined through opposition) the dominant ideology of the time. Early science fiction may have lingered over the depiction of the specific function of the scientist performing actual scientific experiments, but a more recent approach is to make it explicit that this is not apolitical and this function is consequently problematized in the narrative by moral, social, or political concerns.

The second and more complex part of the scientist's role in science fiction is to convey understanding of the implications of scientific processes. This pervasive communicative function elevates the figure of the scientist from any notion of simplified "function" or "sphere of action" within the narrative.[1] For instance, a scientist who learns the error of his ways might be villain, helper, and hero all within the same tale, such is the malleability of his pivotal role. The centrality of the scientist to science fiction narratives has long been significant. Christopher Frayling's account of the emergence of the trope and even mythologized figure of the scientist, using Haynes's enduring images of scientists from the alchemist in the late sixteenth century to the social idealist of the mid-twentieth century, offers a sense of progression.[2] We have seen the roles of the scientist extend to dealing with the unknown or making terrifying discoveries; inspiring trust or revealing dubious motives; making links to the future or struggling to maintain survival and the status quo; capitulating to authorities or displaying heroism; exercising his own power and authority or becoming a victim of others. Whatever his (or her) wider role within the narrative, the scientist must provide a relay between science and the world we know; he must represent, negotiate, articulate, or actualize the link between the potentialities of scientific outcome and commonplace understanding of scientific process. He, through a number of discourses, charts the distance between society as it is and the "other," the speculative imaginary. As he does so, he charts on his journey an understanding for the viewer, not only of what might be, but most important, what already is.

Televisual science fiction is of course a younger form of the genre than both literary and filmic narratives. Fictional works such as Mary Shelley's *Frankenstein, or the Modern Prometheus* (1818) and Bulwer-Lytton's *The Coming Race* (1871) were early precursors to a literary genre to which H. G. Wells successfully introduced important and enduring science fiction themes such as invasion from outer space, biological change, the power of scientific experiments, and time travel in his novels.[3] Both Frankenstein of Shelley's novel and Wells's Dr. Griffin in *The Invisible Man* are characterized as scientists intoxicated with their personal mastery over scientific developments and practices, and who have lost any sense of moral delimitations to their work, pursuing their experiments to the detriment of fellow human beings. With regard to film, the science fiction genre was very important from the early days, perhaps reflecting the marvel of cinematic technology itself, and again, the scientist featured prominently. For instance Georges Méliès' scientists often were thinly disguised alchemists or wizards, and Rotwang in Fritz Lang's *Metropolis* (1926) is portrayed as an evil genius.[4]

The scientist has been a prominent trope and one frequently of mad or bad characterization in both literary and filmic science fiction narratives. On television, perhaps, as opposed to film (and certainly the unrestricted space of the literary imagination), with fewer special effects at a television director's disposal, smaller budgets, and pressure to make use of "free" studio space rather than expensive location shooting, scientists were necessarily less outlandish characters. Televisual practices lent themselves to the close-up and the medium shot, the domestic or small-scope setting, and fixed-camera techniques. This, I suggest, necessitated a different kind of portrayal of the scientist. In the short history of science fiction programs produced for adults on British television up to the 1970s, it can be seen how the genre has evolved and become aligned to the medium of television, and how TV science fiction has come to closely interrogate contemporary issues. It is through the role of the scientist that we can chart such developments.

In the 1950s Professor Quatermass of the *Quatermass* series (1953–1959) was the epitome of the scientist as an educated hero, upper class and with leadership qualities and responsibilities that were seen to be the natural assumption of his class and educative status.[5] This 1950s presentation of a masculine, class-bound scientific persona is well understood as a stereotypical scientist trying to avoid disaster befalling the world. As the hero of the series, within the narrative he provides the dominant point of view and that viewpoint is to be trusted. It is perhaps unsurprising, then, that it has been suggested that Professor Quatermass was a forerunner of the doctor in the long-running children's *Doctor Who* series (1963–1989, 1996, 2005–present).[6] Doctor Who, in his various incarnations, is a figure perhaps not of our world, but certainly one who upholds dominant middle-class values and attitudes of British society, and who from the outside protects and reinforces the prevalent ideology. Mark Bould has argued that British science fiction must be seen in a context of imperial decline, particularly after World War II.[7] Certainly, Quatermass offered a class-bound reassurance in a postwar society. Professor Quatermass is now seen as very much of his time, a British "pipe-smoking boffin" (despite being played by an American actor, Brian Donlevy) evoking a nostalgic quaintness, but not in the league of more dynamic American science fiction characterizations.[8]

In the 1960s the two *Andromeda* series (*A for Andromeda*, 1961; *The Andromeda Breakthrough*, 1962) presented a more complex image of the

scientist. As Joy Leman has argued, these programs represented a break
with the usual depiction of women in science fiction television as marginal
or one-dimensional, and gave women leading roles, one of which was the
scientist Professor Dawney. This, Leman suggests, echoed the changing position of women in society.[9] Moreover, Leman argues that the scientists in this
program were not all upper class, and the newly educated scientists from red-
brick universities are prominent, "Brummy boys" in fact, with their anger and
frustration echoing the angry young man of the postwar era.[10] *The Prisoner*
(1967–1968), produced toward the end of the 1960s, both responds to, and
provides a critique of, the countercultural decade.[11] Here, the "scientists,"
conducting their social experiments in ominous ways, are menacing and controlling, but most important, they remain hidden.[12] This secret manipulation
of a dystopia not only offers a complex critique of its time, but also heralds a
newly powerful and politicized figure of the scientist who remains sinisterly
aloof from society. Therefore, in the two decades of grown-up science fiction
on television before the 1970s, the TV science fiction scientist is kept quite
close to home. There are postwar British rumblings about class authority,
class-related access to higher education, reassertions of masculinity and femininity, and cold war secrecy in corporate and political operations.

Science and Fiction on British Television

By the 1970s the British public were glued to their televisions, with television
viewing far outstripping going to the cinema as an evening's entertainment.
In some cases this was a necessity through financial hardship, in others it
represented a desire to get value for money out of the television license, but it
should not be forgotten that the program offerings on BBC and ITV were of
a high quality. Les Cook has described this as the "golden age" of television,[13]
and many memorable historical and comedy series as well as adaptations and
domestic sitcoms were aired in this decade, including *Upstairs Downstairs*
(1971–1975), *The Good Life* (1975–1977), *Rising Damp* (1974–1978), *The
Fall and Rise of Reginald Perrin* (1976–1979), *The Pallisers* (1974), *The Onedin
Line* (1971–1980), and *Love Thy Neighbour* (1972–1976). It was this decade
where the *Play for Today* series of mostly one-off plays addressed serious, usually contemporary issues and caused much discussion and debate among the
general public. Concomitantly a number of serious and politically minded
discursive programs came into their own as a forum for prominent figures to
debate issues of the day. All in all the impetus to represent on television what
was happening in Britain at this time was strong: there were sitcoms dealing
with domestic strife and blatant racism; Edwardian dramas providing escap-

ism to an imagined halcyon age of social order; and one-off dramas breaking taboos and causing much controversy socially, politically, and personally.

In this decade of significant scientific advancement—of increasing media exposure of contentious issues through investigative journalism given voice in newspapers, magazines, and especially television, of mistrust of authority, and of a highly literate television viewing population—it can be no surprise that the figure of the scientist, as well as science itself, was taken to task in the science fiction of the 1970s. *Doomwatch* (1970–1972) provides an excellent example of just this augmented popular attitude of cynicism and mistrust. It was a British science fiction TV series in the realist mode created by Gerry Davis and environmentalist Dr. Kit Pedler. Individual episodes expressed a range of concerns that echoed the ongoing debates in Britain at the time: the direction science was taking, the ecological issues raised, and the unchecked experimentations and ethics of scientists themselves. This is reinforced for the audience by an opening image of a red monocolored version of the mushroom cloud created after the dropping of the atom bomb. The audience is left in no doubt that a central premise of the narrative drive of the program is to prevent such a world disaster from happening again. In *Doomwatch* two types of scientists emerge: the wider group is drawn from the spheres of industry, the military, and the government; and set in opposition is the team of scientists gathered together to act as investigators and special agents on behalf of the good of the British public. Their job is to keep in check unethical and potentially dangerous, even world-threatening, scientific projects. These scientists are not led by laws of physics, chemistry, or biology, although they are knowledgeable and well-researched and have even won prizes in their respective fields; such pedantic scientific parameters are left to other, less enlightened colleagues whose lack of higher understanding often leads to life-threatening disaster. No, the Doomwatch scientists are cognizant of higher moral codes that transcend any scientific laws, and their motives are based on altruistic notions of preserving humanity and saving the planet; they are suitably labeled in episode one "the dropout scientists." So here we have one small band of investigative scientists, wayward in their methods but nonetheless still technically a government department, acting on behalf of the general good of the British public and preventing a range of potentially damaging scientific projects coming to fruition, even though some of those projects are sponsored by the government-industry-military complex itself. Negotiating this double dealing and governmental duplicity is a major part of the scientists' role in *Doomwatch*.

The pilot episode, "The Plastic Eaters" (1970), written by Kit Pedlar and Gerry Davis, involves the Doomwatch team investigating a newly developed chemical that destroys plastic. This has already had disastrous consequences in causing an airplane crash with many fatalities. The technical difficulties of making the melting plastic intercut convincingly with other scenes in these early days of color recording were noted.[14] The team employ skills of espionage, detection, group deduction, undercover assignments, and even seduction techniques to get the information they need to prove that this is a scientific experiment that has leaked from the laboratory into the wider world. The James Bond–like maneuvers add another level of skill and attraction to this small band of male scientists. At the moment when one of the group has gained access to the commercial government-supported laboratory, we see the different roles of scientists in the 1970s explicitly performed. The Doomwatch scientist uses deception for the cause; the laboratory scientist follows procedures, and operates with Whitehall approval, but without a wider conscience. In this sense, law-breaking to uphold a moral code reflects national feelings of a country that does not trust its ruling agencies, government especially, to do the right thing. This is apparent in other science fiction such as *Doctor Who* and also in other televisual genres, *The Sweeney*, for instance (1975–1978). The mistrust of authority is keenly pertinent to the feeling of Britain in the 1970s; when an explanation is offered it is stated that "scientists under political pressure will do anything." Eventually, in the face of disaster, the two opposing groups of scientists cooperate, but the government minister remains unhelpful and secretive.

Another episode, "Tomorrow, the Rat" (Terrence Dudley, 1970), has the same Doomwatch team investigating a genetic engineering project on rats, which has led to the unfortunate breeding of a human-killing, superintelligent rat species. Similar undercover work results in successful containment of the experiment, but again not without numerous fatalities. Interestingly, in this episode, the role of the scientist as explainer of implications extends far beyond the scope of the rat experiment itself. It is important to note that the role of scientist as processor or laboratory worker is left to the morally dubious government/corporate scientists. Our heroes have nothing to do with that side of the science fiction scientist role, but they do bring wider issues of general concern in the decade to the fore. In so doing other generic modes are evoked, tropes are borrowed from other dramatic forms, and wider public taboos and debates are deployed in this farsighted series. For instance, when the most handsome Doomwatch investigator deploys his charm and masculine sexual appeal to seduce the attractive but seemingly brittle feminist rat scientist, with some very James Bond–esque chat-up lines, the two lovers have a postcoital discussion about the meaning of physical sexual pleasure for women, a topic previously largely ignored but determinedly brought to the fore of public consciousness by the women's liberation movement. When the desired outcome of the now-gone-wrong rat experiment is explained as a solution to the country's growing problem of waste disposal, environmental issues about the modern way of life are highlighted, perhaps as a result of work by the self-sufficiency and green movements of the decade. And when it is revealed that the genetic engineering work on rats was supposed to be extrapolated onto humans in order to eliminate abnormal births, the female scientist is called "Frau Dr. Frankenstein," and memories of Hitler's eugenics are evoked in a way that would resonate with public concerns about the direction of medical science in this decade.

In its Audience Research Report of May 11, 1970, the BBC noted that the audience enjoyed the realistic presentation and the suspense, particularly seeing it as "more science fact than fiction."[15] In a page-long article in the *Radio Times*, Elizabeth Cowley introduces *Doomwatch* with the title "The Honeymoon of Science Is Over—and Married Life Is not so Rosy."[16] Cowley reveals how Gerry Davis and Kit Pedlar kept scrapbooks from real-life devastating hazards reported in the news to build up a store of examples for their new series. She quotes Davis as saying, "The days when you and I marvelled at the 'miracles' of science—and writers made fortunes out of sci-fi—are over. We've grown up now—and we're frightened. The findings of science are still marvellous, but now is the times to stop dreaming up science-fiction about them and write what we call 'sci-fact.' The honeymoon of science is over. That's what *Doomwatch* is all about." In this new grown-up world, then, when science no longer holds the unqualified promise it once did, Davis saw the job of the science fiction writer as imperative in conveying "sci-fact" to the audience where "the inherent dangers to the whole of mankind in scientific 'progress'" are made evident for the wide audience of this ever-popular genre on the developing medium of television.

The Female Scientist

In 1972 *The Stone Tape* was another BBC1 science fiction drama with experimental use of both content and form. This time a one-off play written by Nigel Kneale, it was commissioned by the BBC in 1971 as a ghost story for Christmas and is a tale that combines science fiction with the supernatural, while also tackling some of the broader cultural issues of the time. Kneale was influenced by the writing of M. R. James, whom Kneale considered "the master," and had even edited a volume of his favorite James stories.[17] Thus a number of generic considerations surround this play: it had to fit the mold of a single play, in accordance with the BBC's growing expectations for high-quality dramatic output;

the narrative had to be complete within the allotted running time of ninety minutes, and it had to appeal to a wide audience at a very specific high-viewing time of year, Christmas, when tales of ghouls and ghosts are traditional fare. The impact of broader issues on televisual genres is considerable. Many aspects have to be considered alongside the actual production of the program, for instance, broadcasting and scheduling constraints and expectations, television-specific industrial practices, and cultural relevance.[18] It is interesting to note that in the case of this TV drama, *The Stone Tape* adopts familiar televisual framing devices as well as toying with and disrupting traditional notions of science fiction. The familiar setting of a remote country house with a haunted room is given a new twist as a modern electronics company takes over the mansion as a development laboratory with the intention of inventing the next generation of recording media. However, the project is halted by workmen refusing to install the computer equipment in the haunted room. This disruption to the narrative allows the project leader to take the project in a different turn. He suggests trying to record the ghost, believing the apparition to have merged with the fabric of the building.

This hybrid type of science fiction drama, where science fiction meets the supernatural or horror genres, has been noted by other critics. In particular, J. P. Telotte has adopted and adapted Todorov's structuralist literary discussion of the fantastic, the uncanny, and the marvelous to explain a method of categorizing different types of science fiction.[19] Telotte views three types of science fiction film "fascinations": alien forces and other worlds; changes for good or evil to our own world through science and technology; and technical developments to the human.[20] He sees these as mapping quite clearly onto Todorov's categories of the marvelous (supernatural or alien forces); the fantastic (desire for a different world and futuristic societies); and the uncanny (artificial alterations of the self).[21] Telotte argues that the value of such categorization lies in letting us see narratives "in the context of a broad register of science fiction films and, even more generally, within a pattern of fantasy narrative that inevitably shares its methods and concerns with other narrative types such as the horror film."[22] This idea of viewing categories of film—which here I have also applied to TV dramas—less as a genre distinct from supernatural or horror categories, and more as modes of expression along the same continuum, helps us to reconcile the supernatural with the science fiction, or the marvelous with the fantastic, in *The Stone Tape*. Nigel Kneale had worked on similar themes of "pitting science against the supernatural" in an earlier drama called *The Road* (1963).[23] One way of understanding *The Stone Tape* is as a series of attempts to gain power and control over that which has remained hidden for centuries. Kneale evokes a complex sense of historical inquiry, depicting parish records and personal testimony as well as scientific experiment, to get to the truth of the matter. Moreover, history is seen as multilayered when the Victorian ghost is exposed and dissipated, only to reveal a more sinister and powerful ancient supernatural force as the commanding presence. There are power plays between ghosts as well as humans; man's desire to control the supernatural is akin to, and in this instance entwined with, his desire to master a new form of technology.

A good number of the significant characters in this play are in fact scientists, and they perform a number of different functions within the narrative. From the outset we see the group of young male scientists, the "special team" who are to invent the new recording material, as confident and youthful in their horseplay and verbal asides. In contrast is their ambitious leader Peter, a "villain" (Michael Bryant) who must deal with the company politics as well as manage the group. Peter, who is having an affair with Jill (Jane Asher), is revealed as a fairly insincere and self-interested character early on. Most interestingly, Jill the computer programmer, a new type of scientist, is seen as vital to the project. However, she is soon discovered to be the one most sensitive to the presence of the ghost, and while she eschews the nomenclature of "medium," it becomes apparent that she, along with Collinson (Iain Cuthbertson), the site manager, is most alive to the supernatural forces at play. It is Jill's sensitivity and curiosity that lead to her discovery of older, less comprehensible, forces behind the Victorian ghost (forces that seem to need to feed on a victim ghost in order to thrive), and that lead Jill herself to become the next victim ghost of these supernatural ancients. For its day, the play has notable special effects in the use of flashing colored lights for the supernatural ghosts and beings, and quite remarkable sound effects produced by the BBC Radiophonic Workshop.

One of the trajectories within the play is Jill's descent from authoritative scientist and attractive, intelligent career woman to a nervous, shivering wreck, killed by a combination of supernatural forces and professional neglect by her team leader and lover, Peter. The audience sees many shots of Jill in her white coat and company badge reinforcing her professional competence, and in one scene where she sits behind a large teleprinter device, and the male scientists arc round her, it is she who explains to the men (and the audience) the methodology and approach of the experiment in the pseudo-scientific language of the science fiction scientist. This scene demonstrates a straightforward delivery of the scientific explanation using the appropriate jargon, and it is in later scenes when Jill uses more emotive language to describe the ghostly phenomena that she loses her scientist's authority, her job, and eventually her life. As Vivian Sobchack has argued, the language of poetry and mystery have no chance against the excess of competence, efficiency assurance, and flatness in the delivery of the scientific language.[24] This is a moment when scientific jargon had provided a safe barrier for Jill from the invasion of the supernatural forces in *The Stone Tape*. In this instance the language of the scientist affords Jill her authority in the workplace, overcoming gender barriers. When she loses access to this discourse, her status is diminished, her feminine sensibilities are emphasized and exploited, her status is eroded. In this way Jill exemplifies the feminist struggle to gain and maintain equal access to the male-dominated workplace.

However, Jill's characterization is more nuanced than a straightforward argument about women and work. Early on in the drama, Peter highlights the dual nature of Jill's character: when she expresses her intuitive fears of the house he says, "You're a very female one." At this moment she is in his private apartment within the country manor; he is walking about talking about the project, but there is clear sexual understanding between them. On the surface the reference is about the spookiness of the house; however, the sexual tension remains evident, and he quickly remarks that this is another way of getting back at him, akin to comments about his wife and children. Furthermore, only a few moments later when her commitment to the project continues to waver, and he pleads with her not to leave, he flatters her intellectual sense of self, stating, "I need you for your brain." This mixture of the intuitive and the intellectual gives license and perhaps credence to the two strands of the drama: the supernatural and the scientific, or the marvelous and the fantastic.

More than this, though, it shows a dramatic shift from previous representations of women in British TV science fiction drama. In *Quatermass*, women were either upper-class love interests for the professor himself, or they were stereotypes of working-class gossips.[25] Leman has argued that in *A for Andromeda* the women were flawed: one lacked femininity, another was a spy, and Andromeda was an android.[26] Andromeda, as "an idealized perfect woman of the 1960s," intellectually and physically superior, but with no emotional responses, Leman argues, "can be read as the portrayal of the threat of the 1960s new professional woman—a woman who put intellect first and had to be taught, by *a man*, to express femininity and to respond to emotions."[27] Jill in *The Stone Tape* is the only female scientist among the group of male scientists, and against a backdrop of what seem mostly rowdy youths, Jill's rather sophisticated, if slightly overplayed, character portrayal stands out as a multidimensional, complex young woman. Sexually liberated, she is having an affair with Peter, the group leader, and can have no expectations of a permanent relationship with a man who talks so fondly to his wife on the phone with Jill in the room. Professionally her scientific and intellectual credentials are undisputed. Her femininity too is made outwardly apparent through her glamorous appearance in fashionable trouser suits, makeup, and prettily styled hair.

Jill is far from the first female scientist to appear in science fiction and, like previous female scientists, her gender is an issue. For instance, Bonnie Noonan has discussed female scientists in the 1950s, where she argues that recognition as a female scientist is balanced against performance of gender,[28] whereas in *The Stone Tape*, the audience and the other male scientists are expected to appreciate Jill's scientific professionalism and femininity/sexual attractiveness in equal measure. Yet, perhaps in line with the strident feminism of the decade, her femininity is her weakness, and therefore as a female character she is flawed. Like the women in a well-known American film of this period, *The Stepford Wives* (1975), Jill is "punished" for her apparent feminism. The Stepford wives are, one by one, changed into uberfeminine doll-robots, with all independent thought and yearnings eradicated from their personality. But unlike *The Stepford Wives*, there is no ironic celebration of a regressive femininity either, for Jill's most deeply feminine personality trait, her intuitive second sight as a female sensitive, an atavistic quality, ultimately leads to her demise. In feminist terms, it was proved impossible for Jill to succeed in the workplace while retaining her femininity, and she was punished for wanting to have it all.

In the end, this potentially postmodern or third-wave feminist depiction of womanhood is too much for a program of the 1970s to bear, and the narrative reverts to a more familiar stereotyping. Jill becomes deeply involved with the plight of the Victorian girl, and at the point when Peter considers her behavior to be erratic, he suggests she takes some leave, saying he will put one of the men in charge of the computer because "he's level headed, he's up to it." Shortly afterward, in a moment of narrative irony, we see Jill defiantly working in a frenzied, out-of-control way at the same teleprinter machine where previously she exuded such control and confidence. She is, at this point, with damning patriarchal condescension, considered to be "having a breakdown." This emotional involvement and sympathy for the entrapped female Victorian ghost eventually leads to Jill herself being sacrificed to the ancient forces and taking her place. After Jill's death the story depicts a descent into competitive masculine behavior, with accusation, deceit, and power struggles among the senior male scientists seeing the play to its conclusion, with Peter himself now being haunted by Jill's ghost. The female scientist may not have won through, but neither has she sunk without a trace. There is a general sense in the concluding scenes that this was a scientific project, motivated by pure financial reward, that would have been better never attempted, and that some things are beyond the realm of rational scientific control. It took the sacrifice of the life of a good scientist to prove it.

Science itself continued to suffer immense criticism, perhaps the ultimate condemnation, in Terry Nation's *Survivors* (1975–1977). It is an apocalyptic science fiction TV drama serial, accusingly premised upon the failure of science and the carelessness of scientists and their failure to protect us from their dangerous experiments. Mittell's discussion of the links between serial narratives and soap operas is interesting here,[29] as not only was *Survivors* now following a well-trodden path of serialized science fiction for television, but it also bears early traces of soap opera format, with its cross-episode storylines, domestic focus, cutting techniques, and "never-ending" social issues. The opening of each episode is a long sequence that starts with a scientist dealing with a dangerous substance under experimental conditions. We start with a close-up shot of the scientist's masked face, and as the camera moves back it reveals his white coat and white gauntlets, and in the mode of full clinical protection he has his arms through infection-control plastic sheeting. We glimpse the test-tube bottle containing a white substance which, when the scientist's hand slips, tumbles through the air and smashes, its contents now exposed. Following this, the title **SURVIVORS** appears and then a montage sequence of unwell businessmen, airports scenes, airplanes, and passport stamps for countries all over the world. Lastly a blood-red liquid spreads to fill the screen. From this sequence the viewer easily deduces that the virus has spread, from a substance spilled in a scientific laboratory via air travel across the globe, resulting in a pandemic of a deadly flu-like virus. This longish sequence is repeated in its entirety before every single episode of the program, thirty-nine times in total. And at the beginning of each sequence is the scientist who is working with a substance so dangerous that one mistake decimates the population of the planet. The blame on the figure of the scientist, who in previous incarnations is the figure who has saved humankind from harm, could hardly be greater.

However, even though this opening is shown before each episode, and even though the scientist is so clearly shown to be responsible for releasing the deadly virus, there is no continuity between this sequence depicting a more sophisticated life before the narrative starting time of the program and the actual episodes. The contrast is quite remarkable. The scientists are destroyed with the virus and a more rural, essentialist lifestyle, where communities value their members, and work relates to survival, is now seen as the main priority. With only one person in five thousand surviving the plague, life for the survivors at first consists of making do with what remains in the way of food in supermarkets, empty houses, and petrol from abandoned cars. From the earliest episodes of the first series, the urban way of life is seen as dangerously contaminated, rendered obsolete by defunct, ineffectual technologies and machinery, while the rural is celebrated for its safe isolation, sense of trust in the land, and dependable, medieval rustic practices. Developments in science are blamed for the decimation of humankind and scientific sophistication is eschewed and mistrusted.

What happens when modern, sophisticated, technologized life is withdrawn is that larger questions need to be asked, and in fact many episodes in the first series of *Survivors* explore how to rebuild society. These cover the kind of governance that provides the most security and parity for small fledgling communities, how wealth—now mostly seen in terms of provisions and of course food—should be distributed, and what laws will provide appropriate guidance for people to work and live in cooperation. Many, many themes in *Survivors* clearly reflect the political issues running through the decade in Britain: food shortages and worries about farming methods and sustainable production; environmental concerns; self-sufficiency; communal living; industrialization and the workforce; gendered division of labor; and an apprehension regarding many so-called medical and scientific advancements. As the process of rebuilding a sustainable life ensues in series one of *Survivors*, the scientist, whoever he might now be, is viewed with suspicion and skepticism. We see many examples of this throughout the episodes such as when Greg, a founding and central character, tries to invent a fuel to reoperate the tractor for farming. His efforts are left behind in favor of more reliable methods such as a horse-drawn plow. Skills that are useful are celebrated, regardless of their roots in science, such as the female doctor's knowledge and Greg's numerous engineering skills, which help to build, maintain, and protect the new rural communal community. Some scientific knowledge and practices, therefore, are prioritized over others. Greg as an engineer is acceptable. However, one obvious character with scientific learning is an agronomist who has studied farming as a science at college, with plant genetics and soil science as part of his training ("New Arrivals" [1976]). His knowledge is viewed suspiciously, and at times his ideas are seen as inappropriate to the needs of the community. And even though his scientific understanding could potentially be very helpful indeed to the community, he and his group are ultimately forced to leave because they can not abide by the dominant rules of the commune. The broader life of the community is prioritized over the potential advantages of science. His knowledge might be useful, but he contributes little in other ways and without the interests of the community at heart: the scientist must go.

Ultimately, the scientist in 1970s science fiction TV disappears altogether. The disasters his fellow scientists have caused through pursuit of profit or power have led him to accept aspects of the natural world he now appreciates he does not and cannot understand or control. Previous scientific mistakes must be undone where possible, by legal or illegal means. Scientific immorality must be exposed. The 1970s "dropout" scientists, in tune with issues of contemporary Britain, split their profession and can be seen in direct opposition to the ambitious, driven, Faustian overreacher seen in other science fiction. Such attempts in British TV science fiction to reinstate a true humanity reflect a decade where political, social, and gender unrest were at an unprecedented height, and blame was being apportioned in popular daily media to governments and government-supported institutions. Antiestablishment crusades may be performed by the character of scientist-with-a-conscience, such as in *Doomwatch*, who, eschewing any laboratory or experimental work themselves, recognize the devastating mistakes of their profession and whose higher moral conscience allows them to adopt the role of communicator of wider social concerns of greater importance than scientific experimentation. The scientist who does try to bring her humanity and individual skills to bear on an investigation will be destroyed for her feminism and anticorporate approach, as in *The Stone Tape*. And *Survivors* predicts that once the so-called advanced world has been all but destroyed by scientific ineptitude, a new dystopian/utopian future may emerge, with a return to a more meaningful, egalitarian, less mechanized, artisanal way of living. Little wonder then, that in 1970s television, the British science fiction programs that had an eye to the political and social disruptions of the time underwent a number of generic reconfigurations and formal explorations that allowed the science fiction scientist either to be disguised with an alternative professional or generic cloak or to meekly go into hiding.

Acknowledgment

The research for this article was carried out under the aegis of the project on British Cinema and Culture of the 1970s at the University of Portsmouth, which is supported by the Arts and Humanities Research Council.

Notes

1. Vladimir Propp, *Morphology of the Folktale* (Austin: University of Texas Press, 1968), 25–70 and 79–84.

2. Roslynn D. Haynes, *From Faust to Strangelove: Representations of the Scientist in Western Literature* (Baltimore, MD: Johns Hopkins University Press, 1994), cited in Christopher Frayling, *Mad, Bad and Dangerous? The Scientist and the Cinema* (London: Reaktion Books, 2006), 34–40.

3. See, for instance: H. G. Wells, *The War of the Worlds* (1898); *The Food of the Gods* (1904); *The Invisible Man* (1897); and *The Time Machine* (1895).

4. Frayling, *Mad, Bad and Dangerous*, 49–55, 60–67.

5. Joy Leman, "Wise Students and Female Androids," *Popular Television in Britain: Studies in Cultural History*, ed. John Corner (London: BFI, 1991), 110.

6. *Film and Television History: Television Genres* (Milton Keynes, UK: The Open University, 2003), 169.

7. Mark Bould, "Science Fiction Television in the United Kingdom," *The Essential Science Fiction Reader*, ed. J. P. Telotte (Lexington: University Press of Kentucky, 2008), 209–11.

8. Frayling, *Mad, Bad and Dangerous*, 190.

9. Leman, "Wise Scientists and Female Androids," 114.

10. Ibid., 119–22.

11. Sue Short, "Countering the Counterculture: *The Prisoner* and the 1960s," *British Science Fiction Television: A Hitchhiker's Guide*, ed. John R. Cook and Peter Wright (London: I. B. Tauris, 2006), 71.

12. The official website of Portmeirion, the architect-designed Welsh village where *The Prisoner* was filmed, confirms a new series of *The Prisoner* is to be broadcast in 2009 by ITV (www.portmeirion-village.com/).

13. Les Cooke, *British Television Drama: A History* (London: BFI, 2003), 90–91.

14. Leonard Miall, Report "Doomwatch," File ref: R73/241/1, (Caversham Park, UK, BBC written archive).

15. "An Audience Research Report: *Doomwatch*," June 4, 1970, File ref: R73/241/1 Document ref: VR/70/240 (Caversham Park, UK, BBC written archive).

16. Elizabeth Cowley, "The Honeymoon of Science Is Over—and Married Life Is not so Rosy," *Radio Times*, February 5, 1970, 2.

17. Interview of Nigel Kneale by Kim Newman, in *The Stone Tape*, DVD (BBC Worldwide Limited, 2001).

18. See Jason Mittell, *Genre and Television: From Cop Shows to Cartoons in American Culture* (New York: Routledge, 2004), for a detailed discussion.

19. J. P. Telotte, *Science Fiction Film* (Cambridge: Cambridge University Press, 2001), 10–16.

20. Ibid., 12–14.

21. Ibid., 14–16.

22. Ibid., 16.

23. Kim Newman, sleeve notes to *The Stone Tape*, DVD (BBC Worldwide Limited, 2001). *The Road* now only exists as a script.

24. Vivian Sobchack, *Screening Space: The American Science Fiction Film*, 2nd ed. (New Brunswick, NJ: Rutgers University Press, 1998), 153.

25. Leman, "Wise Scientists and Female Androids," 110.

26. Ibid., 122.

27. Ibid., 122–23.

28. Bonnie Noonan, *Women Scientists in Fifties Science Fiction Films* (Jefferson, NC: McFarland Publishers, 2005), 51.

29. Mittell, *Genre and Television*, 163–78.

CHAPTER SIX

Secret Gardens and Magical Realities: Tales of Mystery, the English Landscape, and English Children

Dave Allen

The Harry Potter books and films have met with unprecedented popularity and commercial success among children in the recent past. There is much that is archetypally English about Harry and his adventures, not least that they take place mainly in the equivalent of a coeducational English public boarding school. But Harry Potter is not typical for the simple reason that he is a special boy who possesses magical powers, which he studies and develops at Hogwarts, a magical school. By contrast, in this chapter I wish to examine the magical adventures that happen to ordinary children in narratives like *The Box of Delights* (1935), the various Narnia adventures, and in particular, *The Secret Garden* (1912). The central figures in these adventures are quintessentially white, middle-class, English children from the first half of the twentieth century but, unlike Harry Potter, they possess no magical powers themselves beyond the capacity to believe and imagine—often after overcoming in themselves a degree of uncertainty, skepticism, and cynicism. The magic happens around them, to them, and through them. In this sense, while my title alludes to the theoretical concept of "magical realism" in art and literature, this chapter is about something different and rather more specific—not least because of its self-imposed geographical limitations—English with a nod toward the Celtic. In addition to the children, I wish to consider the environments in which their adventures take place, considering the extent to which there is also a kind of magic in the land itself. In particular, in my focus on *The Secret Garden* I will pay attention to the narrative occurring in the "ordinary" or "real" English landscape—not merely the garden of a privileged home but in the surrounding countryside inhabited by Dickon.

It might be easy to suggest in the twenty-first century that the cultures depicted in *The Secret Garden*—the privileges of Empire, service, and the rural working class—have little relevance for the modern reader. I will suggest that beyond these class considerations there is something enduring about the relationship with nature and the capacity of children to imagine magic, which might be highly pertinent for our young people who are inheriting an Earth that shows the consequences of serious damage and exploitation. I will not suggest that a handful of old stories can in themselves address those problems, but I do propose that imaginative engagement with the ideas in *The Secret Garden* and other such books can help to foster an imaginative, open, and sympathetic attitude to nature.

This is why I am particularly interested in the ordinariness of the setting for *The Secret Garden* and the relative unhappiness of the two main characters, which is different of course from Narnia, a magical land to be discovered only by the favored few. It is different also from the natural world of so many fairy tales, which Alison Lurie observes was generally "magical," adding:

> This magic was concentrated in the forest, often referred to as an enchanted forest. . . . What you found in the forest might be wonderful or terrible or both. . . . The underlying message of folklore and fairy tales was that nature is alive, aware of us—that it must be treated with care and respect.[1]

Despite this difference between the ordinary and the enchanted, I would suggest that in the context of contemporary environmental education it is no bad thing that children might be encouraged to engage with the full range of these narratives, employing their imagination, considering a kind of magic that questions superficial rationality or at least treating nature with care and respect. This aspect of the chapter will examine fictional texts but will also draw upon writing that examines broadly spiritual and/or environmental aspects of the landscape. As with the fiction, the emphasis will be on England and English mythology, considering how these tales draw upon and extend an older tradition of romanticism, mysticism, magic, and fantasy in English culture and also asking why and how these old-fashioned tales find an audience alongside the clearly more contemporary Potter stories in the twenty-first century. In this context I shall follow the lead of Geoffrey Ashe, a leading writer on Arthurian and connected themes, who observed that what is needed when examining myths is an approach for "taking-seriously-without-taking-literally." In respect to tales about the land, he also referred to the Victorian historian E. A. Freeman's view of the Glastonbury legends that while we do not need to believe them as truth, "the existence of these legends is a very great fact."[2] I will suggest that over the past forty years this fact has grown significantly, in some respects helping to sustain and re-create the audience for these otherwise aging and potentially unfashionable works of fiction. In this matter I am resistant to the idea that literature should be measured against superficial ideas of relevance in setting, characters, and events. If children were so desperate for such "relevance," Harry Potter would never have enjoyed such extraordinary success. The relevance of these tales is deeply embedded in the narrative, around relationships, ideals, values, personal development, and the worlds of imagination.

The Garden's Literary Roots

In pursuing the points above, I will consider the original published versions of the novels alongside adaptations for the screen—film and television. I will begin with a detailed consideration of a moment of "high" magic in *The Secret Garden*, making particular use of an illustrated and annotated version of the book edited by Gretchen Gerzina (2007), which offers various illustrations from editions of the book as well as still images from film and television versions.[3] Gerzina shows the work of around fifteen artists and illustrators, including three from the years just before the First World War. The story by Frances Hodgson Burnett (1849–1924) was published as a magazine serial in 1911 and as a book the following year, and it is one of the author's children's books alongside *A Little Princess* (1905) and *Little Lord Fauntleroy* (1886).

The Secret Garden is a story rooted in the era of the British Empire, in which an orphaned and "most disagreeable-looking" girl, Mary Lennox, was brought from India to Misselthwaite Manor in Yorkshire to live with her uncle, Mr. Archibald Craven, and more particularly his housekeeper, Mrs. Medlock, and the young, cheerful housemaid, Martha. Mr. Craven had suffered the tragedy of his wife's death in a sudden accident in the walled garden on the manor's estate, after which he had become "gloomy" and reclusive, often traveling abroad, somewhat like Mr. Rochester in *Jane Eyre* (1847). He gave orders for the garden to be locked, and the story revolves around Mary's discovery of the garden and the actions she takes that bring it back to life.

These actions involve two other young people. The first is Dickon, Martha's brother, equally cheerful and possessed of natural or even magical abilities with animals and birds that are foreign to the more formally educated Mary. Dickon, his sister, and their mother live outside the manor and with nature are the most centered and contented characters in the narrative. The second young person, much less content, is Colin, Mr. Craven's bedridden son, who is believed by everyone in the manor to be terminally ill. Together, Mary and Dickon free him from his domestic and psychological prison, and through their experiences in the garden the two spoiled children find a way toward a new life.

Gerzina points out the biblical references in the choice of the names Mary and Martha, describing how

> Mary learns from Dickon and assists Colin while Martha toils in the house. Mary acts as a servant when she sits by Colin's side and takes on the role of his ayah. Dickon acts as a healer who helps to raise up Colin, like Lazarus, from a state of expected death.[4]

We know that Burnett had a fairly conventional nineteenth-century upbringing but like a number of creative and educated members of her generation, she was interested in other spiritual beliefs and philosophies. Shortly after the publication of *The Secret Garden*, she was interviewed by a reporter from the *New York Times* about her interests in "the occult," although Gerzina suggests that Hodgson "came to her own understandings" so that "it was not possible to slot her into any traditional system." We do know, however, that she confessed to believing "of course, in magic," defining it as "the bringing about of unbelievable things."[5]

Mary's discovery of the locked and unkempt garden is shared with Dickon and Colin, who is himself taken secretly from the house to encounter the plants, flowers, birds, and small creatures there. The children begin to tend the garden and by chapter 18 we read that the garden had "reached the time when every day and every night seemed as if Magicians were passing through it, drawing loveliness out of the earth and the boughs with wands."[6] But the focus on magic occurs in chapter 23, which is where Gerzina claims that Hodgson "begins to make clear her spiritual beliefs."[7]

The chapter opens with Colin speaking rudely to his uncle and personal physician, Dr. Craven, after which Mary persuades him to be less argumentative and less "queer." Colin agrees that this would be a good plan and observes that he can improve himself by going daily to visit the garden, since "there is magic in there." Mary agrees, stressing that it is definitely pure and "as white as snow," after which the children "always called it Magic."[8] In the earlier stages of the book, the magic described by Hodgson is centered upon the garden's recovery through natural growth and the activities of the garden's creatures, but there was also the magic which in the original story had found Colin able to stand for the first time in memory and which led him to conduct a scientific "experiment" with his two friends and the gardener Ben Weatherstaff, who was the only adult to share their secret at this point.

While we can see this chapter as an exploration of Hodgson's spiritual beliefs, it also reveals a commitment to science, which was seen by many educated adults as holding solutions to a great many human problems. A century ago there was less of a schism between religious faith and the scientific method, and so Colin announced his intention to become scientifically "curious" and to pursue a great many scientific discoveries in the future, especially about magic. Like Burnett, he then offers a speech in which he defines magic in terms of Mary's Indian experiences, Dickon's way with animals, and broader aspects like electricity and steam. As part of his experiment, Colin identifies a mantra to be repeated morning and evening in which he will chant, "Magic is in me, Magic is making me well." Mary recounts an Indian tale of *fakirs* who would chant mantras "thousands of times," after which Colin organizes the four of them to sit cross-legged in a circle in the garden as if it were "a sort of temple." Then Colin began to chant while Mary "listened entranced" and felt "at once queer and beautiful." After this Colin did more than stand, he walked around the garden. He did so with some help and some rests but as he did so he exclaimed "I did it! The Magic worked!" The idea of this as a "scientific" experiment recedes as these other ritualistic and quasi-spiritual practices take over.

In addition to the book illustrations, Gerzina includes stills from three cinematic versions of *The Secret Garden* and from a Broadway production in 1991. The three films were released in 1949 (black and white), 1987, and 1993. At this point I am going to pay particular attention to the films of 1949 and 1993 as well as a BBC television serialization of the tale from the 1970s.

Adaptations to the Screen

I have described the original published version of this part of the story in some detail, as I wish to compare it with these screen versions. In 1949 Fred Wilcox directed a film with melodramatic mise-en-scène, redolent of that found in other black-and-white literary adaptations of the period such as *The Third Man* (1934), *Jane Eyre* (1944), and *Great Expectations* (1946). So in this version we find a far stronger exploration of the psychological states of the characters and far less interest in any kind of magic. In a key scene, which does not occur in the book, Mr. Craven has returned to the manor to sell it to Mr. Bromley, "to escape if possible the temptation of madness," but on learning that his son is in the garden, he adds that having "resisted as long as I can" he recognizes that "the Gods" have given him one more chance.

He leaves the chiaroscuro lighting of the gothic manor, down the huge staircase and outside, angrily pushes the gardener Weatherstaff to the floor, breaking into the garden and shouting, "Get away from me!" at Mary. In this scene he exemplifies the inadequacies of adults in the story—it takes the relative innocence of children and nature to break the deadly hold on the participants, young and old. As we see him enter, this first shot inside the garden is transformed into color, as if Dorothy had landed in Oz once more, but this is cinematic and interior magic, nothing more metaphysical. At this point in the film Colin is still wheelchair-bound but as he and his father come face to face, Colin pulls himself from the chair and walks hesitatingly toward him, begging him, "Please don't hurt our garden." He struggles to his father, they embrace, and the music shifts from melodrama to pastoral mode for the brief final reconciliation. In the book, this final scene and the reconciliation is less melodramatic, for the magic has already worked and Colin is walking, but Wilcox contrives a Hollywood ending fit for the period. (Nonetheless, I would like to draw attention briefly to other Hollywood products of the classical period, notably *Lost Horizon* [1937] and *The Razor's Edge* [1946], which did offer Western audiences representations of unfamiliar routes to peace and enlightenment from the East.)

A quarter of a century after the first Hollywood version, *The Secret Garden* (1975) was one in a succession of BBC television serializations of classic literature for the nation on Sunday teatimes. It was equally typical of the style and technology of its period and genre, with a greater focus on speech and acting. The magic scene is shown in tight head or group shots within a studio-based version of the garden. The director uses cutaways from these video portraits to stock film shots of flowers with a nature soundtrack, while Colin makes his continuous speech about the magic: "Being alive is the magic, being strong is the magic." Mary and Dickon beam at him, stroking animals and wearing period costumes but with 1970s hairstyles (including a footballer's bubble perm for the very clean Dickon). Colin intones, "Magic, magic come and help us," and then stops abruptly, announcing, "Phew, I don't think I could say that a thousand times but now I'm going to walk round the garden"—a somewhat prosaic, nonchalant ending to a "magic" sequence which is not at all presented using techniques that emphasize the content. Nonetheless—or perhaps because of this—the televisual style is most faithful to the original book.

The 1993 film directed by Agnieszka Holland is far more extravagant. Although in color, it returns to the dark look of 1949 as the children visit the garden at night and circle an open fire glowing red and orange. They chant in an improvised language while Colin repeats again and again, "Send me my father here, set my spirit free." The scene cuts abroad to Mr. Craven dreaming that he is on a rocky outcrop on the Yorkshire moors while his beautiful dead wife is calling from the misty garden for him to return. Here the magic works directly—Colin's father, who fits our image of a nineteenth-century romantic with lush clothes, flowing hair, and long, mournful features, returns immediately to Yorkshire and is reunited happily with his son.

In this scene in particular, we might suggest that the expressive, perhaps excessive visual style of the interpretation is not unlike that of John Boorman's Arthurian film *Excalibur* (1981)—perhaps the archetypal example of a young man in English literature to whom, and through whom, the magic happens. While we may have an image of King Arthur and his court consisting of the greatest, most chivalrous knights and elegant ladies, the Arthurian tales include many episodes centered on the activities and experiences of young people, beginning with the moment when, entirely by chance, the youthful Arthur pulls the sword from the stone and the adventure begins. A major part of the adventure concerns the quest for the Holy Grail and in some versions, Galahad, Lancelot's son, is one of the few knights to succeed in finding this most holy of relics. Lancelot's son is therefore the pure offspring of the great knight whose act of adultery with his queen is the root cause of the death of the fellowship, while it is Mordred, the son of the wronged king, whose acts of war destroy the Round Table.

England's Secret Gardens

So it is adults and their children whose actions are at the heart of the Arthurian legends. But the Grail quest is the moment when a spiritual dream displaces effective and principled political organization, with disastrous consequences. In the many centuries since the Arthurian period, the tales of this mythical Golden Age have grown, partly through literature and importantly through the development of what Ashe called *The Quest for Arthur's Britain*. It is a quest that takes us around the land, with so many places laying some claim to a role in Arthur's Britain that we might almost consider southwest England and parts of Wales as a "secret garden." Ashe's publication addressed itself to various locations including in particular Cornwall, Cadbury, Glastonbury, and Wales, but it also identified possible connections with many other parts of Britain—some like Guildford/Astolat having only fictional significance.

Ashe's work was based in serious scholarship and his publication appeared initially in 1968—exactly forty years ago as I write. The year 2008 has been seized on by the popular media to pursue a more recent historical excavation—the fortieth anniversary of 1968 as the "year of revolution." But the contemporary focus on Paris, Prague, antiwar protests, and the key moment for the political left has ignored a simultaneous element of the late 1960s—"counterculture"—that may explain in part the continuing popularity of the fiction under consideration here. In broad terms there was a section of the counterculture that preferred a spiritual quest to political revolution.

That more recent quest embraced more and less seriously Eastern religions, environmental issues, macrobiotic diets, and English mysticism. Much of it was reflected in a particularly English psychedelic pop music and fashion, but it was also to be found in the new "underground" newspapers and periodicals that emerged during this period—especially features in the *International Times (IT)* and the more specialist *Gandalf's Garden*. The *International Times* in particular featured fairly regular contributions from John Michell, who offered articles about English mysticism, focusing particularly on Glastonbury. Eventually he collected these writings into books like *New Light on the Ancient Mysteries of Glastonbury* (1990). It is not my intention here to explore this work in any detail but rather to use this development as an example of two key aspects of this chapter. First, I want to suggest that the growing audience for this literature, the ideas that it represents, and its place in the broader phenomenon of the "New Age" is a part of the same audience for the novels of Narnia or *The Secret Garden*. Second, reminding you of Freeman's idea that "the existence of these legends is a very great fact," I wish to suggest that an increasing number of people are willing to believe at least in the *possibility* that the earth itself may have magical powers or that the earth is the site of magical or metaphysical phenomena.

For example, Glastonbury has its Tor, reputedly on a ley line first described by Alfred Watkins in the 1920s. At its foot we find the Chalice Well Gardens, with the well said to be or have been the location of the Chalice itself. On the outskirts of town is Wearyall Hill where the visiting Joseph of Arimethea is believed to have thrust his staff into the ground, where it grew into the thorn tree that flowers at Christmas. Then in the center of town is the Abbey, destroyed by Henry VIII and with a grave marked as being that of King Arthur and his Queen. There are other myths and legends around this small Somerset town, whose main streets are filled with shops selling crystals, herbal remedies, books, and other New Age phenomena while advertising a range of therapists, astrologers, Tarot readers, and other "healers." But it is the land around Glastonbury itself, its springs, trees, hills, and earth that contain the most powerful of the myths—not least in the work of Katherine Maltwood and Mary Caine, which claims to reveal a giant Zodiac in the landscape around the town.[9] Michell recounts how a medieval romance had stimulated this idea when Arthur's magician Merlin prompted the creation of the King's Round Table, which is meant to signify the round world and round canopy of the planets and the elements in the firmament, where are to be seen the stars and other things.[10]

The idea of Glastonbury as a sacred site has been explored by Adrian Ivakhiv. He describes how recently some "relatively educated and on a Global scale well-off Westerners" have begun to doubt the "techno-humanist" belief that humanity can solve its problems by simply harnessing the power and attributes of nature. He cites James Lovelock's Gaia theory as one example, asking whether the idea of the earth as a living entity is "real" or perhaps simply "an empty screen" onto which believers "project their own fantasies and unconscious desires."[11] This echoes again Freeman's identification of the significance of belief in myths and legends.

Of course, the cinema is always a blank screen onto which filmmakers project and then invite the audience to project again their fantasies and desires, and I am suggesting here that the maintenance and even revival of an audience for the tales of Narnia and *The Secret Garden* is commensurate with this broader investment in the New Age and ideas of sacred or magical sites. In addition, the children who read these stories twenty or thirty years ago (or more) may be the same people who are now interested in environmental and/or metaphysical elements of the landscape. In many senses, at the fictional core of these beliefs are Tolkien's epic works—not least because they acquired cult status in the 1960s and many of that generation have retained their affection for the novels, which was then revived for following generations with the release of the three epic films in the early twenty-first century. *The Lord of the Rings* (1954–1955) is a tale of magicians and elves, orcs and dwarves, hobbits and kings, but it is also a tale of distinctly different and often magical lands and environments. In this sense it fits here with literature about physical spaces that have metaphysical energies but it is not—even analogously—about ordinary children, and so I shall move from it to the work of C. S. Lewis and the Narnia stories. Lewis, of course, was a contemporary of Tolkien at Oxford University, and the first published book in his series in 1950 became a fairly lavish film half a century later.

Like *The Secret Garden*, this is a tale of ordinary children but it is not wholly like Burnett's novel because these four children encounter many other beings and creatures—often with the gift of human speech—in another country on one or other side of a fairly straightforward battle between good and evil. But in two key respects the tales are similar. In Lewis's novel there are four siblings and one of them, the disagreeable younger brother Edmund, finds redemption through adventure, much as Mary and Colin do in *The Secret Garden*. Furthermore, the adventure begins with the children moving from the threatening environment of wartime London to an archetypally English refuge "in the heart of the country"—much as Mary has done at the start of her adventure. In both cases a kind of rural isolation and the almost exclusive company of other children provide the context for the "magic" to begin. John Masefield's *The Box of Delights*, adapted in 1984 for the BBC, is similar in that Kay Harker is returning home for the Christmas holidays, which he spends with his other children in a rural town.[12] We hear nothing of Kay's parents in this story, and his guardian leaves him to deal with a family crisis in London.

While she is gone, Kay's adventure centers upon his encounter with an old man, Cole Hawlings, who is possessed of magical qualities, including time travel. Otherwise, his challenge is to outwit the gang of adult crooks led by Abner Brown in order to save Christmas for the clergy and other adults of the town. He achieves this from his base in a typical prewar English town surrounded by a magical countryside, not least in terms of the nighttime adventures in King Arthur's Camp (Masefield had introduced similar historical material in his earlier children's books). In part this probably reflects Masefield's own childhood in which, Alison Lurie tells us, this "solitary, sensitive, dreamy boy . . . loved wandering in the countryside and telling himself long stories." She records Masefield's recognition that this English landscape was not only "beautiful" but was known to him to be "as it were, only the shadow of something much more beautiful."[13]

We may speculate, too, that the absence (or disappearance) of parental figures in *The Box of Delights* reflects the tragedy of the death of Masefield's mother in childbirth, when he was only six. By contrast, the key adult figure in *The Box of Delights* is the mysterious Cole Hawlings—the subject of an earlier Masefield poem, "King Cole." Lurie describes Hawlings's role in the narrative "in Jungian terms" as the "guide or sage" who—despite his magical powers—is reliant on the "help of Kay and the other children" to defeat Abner Brown and his gang.[14] In *The Secret Garden*, it is mainly Dickon who acts as a sage for his peers Colin and Mary. In the Narnia tales, the four children meet many creatures, each offering sufficient wisdom or common sense to support them on their adventures, although the main presence—real or implied—is the lion Aslan, who is often read as Christlike, especially at his moments of self-sacrifice and resurrection.

Setting *The Box of Delights* at Christmas adds to its spiritual and mythical dimensions and also, given the central presence of children, to its essential innocence. The importance of Christmas is found also in *The Lion, the Witch and the Wardrobe* (1950), which has also been filmed twice, as part of *The Chronicles of Narnia*—a BBC television serial (1988–1990)—and recently as a lavish Walt Disney production in 2005. Lurie identifies this particular innocence in the tales of C. S. Lewis, comparing them with J. K. Rowling's stories of Hogwarts and Harry Potter:

> The world of Narnia is simple and eternal: goodness, peace and beauty will eventually triumph. The world of Harry Potter is complex and ambiguous and fluid. And in this of course it is far more like our own world in which it is not always easy to tell the ogres from the giants.[15]

Lurie then asks whether our choice of books for children seeks to encourage obedience or skepticism, with a clear sense that she favors the latter and its natural link with the Potter books. The release of the Narnia feature films drew considerable criticism of their old-fashioned, orthodox Christian message, but it might be argued that an idealistic, aspirational narrative may have a valuable role in a period when we know that children will be offered a broad diet of very varied representations and messages. Such criticisms also seem to assume that children may be duped by such doctrines rather than developing their critical capacities through engagement with them.

Nonetheless, the two damaged children who are healed by their life in *The Secret Garden* are perhaps more interestingly complex than the four young people who discover Narnia from their English rural retreat. In addition, Lurie suggests that "at least twice" in *Little Lord Fauntleroy* and *The Secret Garden*,

> [Burnett] happened to tell . . . stories that express concealed fantasies and longings; stories that are the externalized dreams of a whole society and pass beyond ordinary commercial success to become part of popular culture.[16]

The recent criticism of Lewis's tales suggests that perhaps they are less equipped to escape from the cultural and historical context of their creation, but they are lively tales and lend themselves to the fashion for colorful CGI in the cinema.

The children's adventure begins with Lucy's journey through the wardrobe and her encounter with the branches of trees and snow on the ground in the wild woods of the west—in other words, it begins with a magical land discovered by chance through a portal to another world. In the most recent cinema version, we see the children suddenly enlivened by the decision to play hide-and-seek, racing around the house to the sound of a contemporary dance band vocal by wartime favorites the Andrews Sisters. Then suddenly as Lucy enters the room that contains the wardrobe, the sound shifts to thunder and an ambient track as she approaches the monumental wardrobe for the first time. In slow motion she removes the white covering sheet; the nondiegetic atmosphere is interrupted briefly by the distant speech of her approaching brother. She steps inside. In the wardrobe, there is a fairly rapid montage as she moves through the fur coats and touches snow for the first time, followed by a more rhythmic montage showing Lucy in Narnia, close-ups of her delighted face, and point-of-view shots of trees, snow, and a mysterious lamp-post. This magical sequence is interrupted stylistically by the real sounds of her first encounter with the faun Mr. Tumnus. They speak with each other and she takes tea with him in his home in a rock cave.

The BBC serialization pursues a similar opening narrative but deviates from the book in a prolonged scene of arrival at their evacuation home in which Mrs. Macready pointedly engages in two conversations that establish the household hierarchies—the servants' place, and the Professor's word as law. While the television version of Lucy's first entry into Narnia is both briefer and more economical of shots, it is interestingly similar to the film in terms of the soundtrack, range of shots, and subject matter—one imagines that the Disney studio had studied this earlier version. From here, the visual style, as might be expected, is less cinematic and more televisual—especially in terms of the use of typical talking heads and fairly constant dialogue.

In the original novel and, because it is conversational, in the television series, Mr. Tumnus regales Lucy with tales of forest life:

> He told about the midnight dances and how the Nymphs who lived in the wells and the Dryads who lived in the trees came out to dance with the Fauns; about long hunting parties after the milk-white stag who could give you wishes if you caught him . . . and then about summer when the woods were green.[17]

Despite the mention of these mythical creatures, the story centers on the adventures of four quintessentially English children, while key moments are often linked to environmental change. When the children first arrive, the whole country of Narnia is under the power of the White Witch and it is always winter, although never Christmas. Elementally, the weather too is central to Lucy taking the others to Narnia, for initially they are dismissive of her story until a very wet day forces them indoors, where they hide in the wardrobe from the unfriendly housekeeper and discover Narnia.

As on Lucy's previous visit, Narnia is locked into cold winter, but traveling across the country they encounter Father Christmas, who tells them that the Witch's power is waning and Aslan's increasing. The first evidence we see of this is in the landscape, initially as the Witch's sledge stops running smoothly in the melting snow, then with the sound of running water, and most strikingly as the sun appears and illuminates emerging plants as spring arrives. In other words, it is the earth and the elements that signify the transformation.

There is one other point to make about this tale that has to do with the relationship between the children and adults in the real world. Edmund discovers that Lucy has been telling the truth but refuses to support her story, and the two older children (Peter and Susan), concerned about Lucy, go to the Professor to ask his advice. In *The Secret Garden*, the adults are generally an unimpressive collection of flawed individuals: Mary's parents and Colin's father neglect their children, the housekeeper and Doctor conspire to keep Colin confined to bed, and only Dickon's mother, who lives closer to the earth in her cottage on the moor, has much to recommend her. But the Professor, while apparently a normal man, has similarities with Cole Hawlings in *The Box of Delights*, as he is both a little mysterious and wise, so when Peter and Susan report their concerns, he asks how they know that her story is not true. He then explores the situation with them logically, establishing that "unless further evidence turns up, we must assume she is telling the truth"—which of course she is. Having dealt with them logically, he then responds doubtfully to Susan's assertion "if things are real, they're there all the time" by observing that his house is "very strange." When Peter asks about the possibility of other worlds "all over the place," the Professor suggests that "nothing is more probable."[18]

Contemporary Readings

In this chapter I have focused on three tales that appeared initially as children's novels and have since been adapted for television by BBC and also in two cases for the cinema. I have deliberately sought to explore tales of magical adventures happening to ordinary children, thereby excluding a novel like *The Lord of the Rings*. I might have included other famous children's stories like *Alice in Wonderland* (1865), *The Water Babies* (1863), or *Peter Pan* (1911) since these are also partly about magical adventures happening to ordinary children (although Peter is far from ordinary). But these take place in other spaces, unlike *The Secret Garden* and *The Box of Delights*, and ultimately I wish to suggest that they offer relatively little beyond adventure and entertainment to young readers since they are rather more concerned with parodying adult behavior than with showing children in control at key moments. In some respects the recent film about J. M. Barrie and the writing of Peter Pan, *Finding Neverland* (2004), is closer to my criteria. But here the magic is really of the imagination and in the relationships between Barrie and the boys, so while they all go to the refuge of Barrie's country retreat, the earth and the elements are not central to the unfolding narrative. Similarly, the success of Philip Pullman's *His Dark Materials* novels and the first film from them is interesting but these are other worlds, not ordinary children in adventures that begin at home.

The three tales I have examined in detail were published in the first half of the twentieth century, as was *Peter Pan*, and it is highly probable that they were still popular enough to become favorites of certain members of the English baby-boomer generation, who then passed them on to their children and grandchildren. For example, a 2008 survey of four thousand people aged 16–65 conducted by the books charity Booktrust listed *The Lion, the Witch and the Wardrobe* as "the best children's book of all time," while Harry Potter's highest listing was sixth.[19] It is less easy to predict whether such tales will continue to resonate with future generations, for they represent an England that environmentally, racially, culturally, spiritually, and in a class context has either vanished or is currently unfashionable.

Nonetheless it is possible to see these fictions as part of a far greater continuum of English creativity around the English landscape—often with metaphysical connotations. This is perhaps most obviously a product of English romanticism in the early nineteenth century in poetry, literature, and art but it has a longer thread as described by Peter Woodcock in a book about "the neo-Romantic vision" in Britain "from William Blake to the new visionaries." In his survey, Woodcock includes Blake, Samuel Palmer, Paul Nash, Graham Sutherland, John Piper, John Cowper Powys, Peter Ackroyd, and filmmakers Powell and Pressburger, David Lean, Derek Jarman, Chris Petit, and Patrick Keiller. The work of the artists included by Woodcock does not quite fit here because it is predominantly for adults and, as Woodcock observes, it offered no "benign, sentimentalised vision of nature."[20] In particular, Woodcock invokes the importance of "visionary art" and the spirit of place ("no Luddite dream"),[21] which he claims "is still deeply embedded in our national consciousness."[22]

In contrast with the films I have described here, many of the more recent screen fictions for young people represent a world of (dawning?) adolescence and issues of sexuality, drug use, gang violence, materialism, and identity. In addition, films and television series such as *Clueless* (1995), *Thirteen* (2003), *Mean Girls* (2004), *Kidulthood* (2006), *Sugar Rush* (2005–2006), and *Almost Famous* (2000) use an urban setting for these tales of lost innocence and there is no magic in these environments. Occasionally in films like *Stand by Me* (1986) or *Ghost World* (2001) something different stirs, but this is rare in films from Hollywood, although *Pan's Labyrinth* (2006) offers a more recent example of what may be possible.

So I must ask: are these tales, which I still enjoy, now nothing more than slight, culturally specific works which have no discernibly relevant future? Does it matter that young people were once offered tales of everyday magic and the land and that now they are not very often—at least not in a contemporary context? I want to conclude by suggesting that it does matter, for three reasons. The first is that realism on its own has never been sufficient for any audience or culture—human readers have always been attracted to myths and legends for a variety of purposes, and there is no reason to suppose that this should not continue. My other two reasons are social and political—explicitly environmental. In social terms I want to consider briefly the question of effects theory and whether the representations we encounter in the world—particularly mass media representations—may have any impact on behavior. These debates have been examined extensively over many years and by researchers who are far better informed than me. I have no desire to align myself with right-wing media or politicians who are determined to promote a simplistic causal relationship between representations and antisocial behavior; I acknowledge that the issue is far more complex, involving a broad range of factors. The odd film, CD, or computer game is an easy target for those who like simple answers—wrong or right. But I wish to take a different view of effects theory and ask—without pursuing any case for censorship—whether we think that tales that are optimistic about human behavior, the environment, and the possibility of alternative realities might be of benefit to young people. I am writing that sentence on the morning that the British media are reporting extensively on the murder in a knife attack of the young actor Robert Knox, who had just finished filming his part in the next Harry Potter film. He was the fourteenth teenager murdered in London in such a way in the first five months of 2008, and while I do not seek to attribute explicit causal blame to any violent media representations for such a terrible statistic, I want to ask again whether different artifacts might have a positive role, however slight, in offering young people the sense of an alternative reality.

I don't know the answer to that question, but there is nothing clever in recognizing that it is a terrible and growing problem. Most people are beginning to believe that environmental problems demand at least a similar sense of urgency and this is why I have addressed myself to tales in which these young people interact significantly with their natural environment. I wish to argue here that while science and rationality are producing evidence and discourses about the problem, on their own these do not seem to be sufficient. On the same morning that the media reported the death of Robert Knox, the Guardian's main headline revealed that a United Nations project paying industries in developing countries "to reduce climate change emissions" has "wasted billions of pounds."[23] The adults creating and reporting on these programs are much like Mr. Craven, his doctor brother, and Mrs. Medlock in *The Secret Garden*. They may be doing what they think is correct, but their "rational" conclusions are squeezing life from the patient—who was not ill to begin with.

I am not seeking an abandonment of scientific evidence, rational discourse, or political action, but I am suggesting that we will not really transform our relationships with each other and the environment in a global culture of technology and consumption unless we can literally reimagine the earth and our environment. In this sense the films and TV that I have examined offer an alternative to the generally apocalyptic work that is often on our screens—whether it is fictional works like *The Day after Tomorrow* (2004) or *Flood* (2007) or documentaries. In the United States in recent years, two major personalities have produced documentaries about global warming and ecological disasters. One is a politician, Al Gore (*An Inconvenient Truth* [2006]), the other, Hollywood star Leonardo DiCaprio (*The 11th Hour* [2007]). In both films these personalities present their case in rational, discursive terms supported by evidence from enormous, detailed scientific studies supported by alarming images from mass media reporting.

These initiatives are typical of our culture—personality-driven, rational, scientific, legalistic, shaped by mass media—without ever acknowledging that the destruction of the earth is in many respects a direct product of all these features. Again, I do not mean by this that we should abandon rationality, science, or discussion, but I would argue that what we have lost is Burnett's sense of the necessary reciprocal relationship between the great achievements of science and a capacity to find meaning and perhaps magic in something beyond material rationality. Neither of these alarming documentaries offers much hope and neither of them suggests that we might have much to believe in beyond a return to a more balanced, "civilized" living typical of Western liberal documentaries. Perhaps the time is ripe for a gifted Dickon, a damaged Mary, and an abandoned Colin to discover magic in a secret garden and harness its energy in a serious project. We are in urgent need of a new magical reality and while Narnia, *The Box of Delights*, and *The Secret Garden* may no longer serve our contemporary culture, they point the way to what that might be.

Notes

1. Alison Lurie, *Boys and Girls Forever: Children's Classics from Cinderella to Harry Potter* (London: Vintage Books, 2004), 173.

2. Geoffrey Ashe, *The Quest for Arthur's Britain* (London: Paladin, 1968), 202.

3. Gretchen Holbrook Gerzina, ed., *The Annotated Secret Garden* (New York: W. W. Norton, 2007).

4. Ibid., 23.

5. Ibid., xiii.

6. Ibid., 162.

7. Ibid., 202.

8. Ibid., 203–4.

9. Mary Caine, *The Glastonbury Zodiac: Key to the Mysteries of Britain* (privately published, 1978).

10. John Michell, *New Light on the Ancient Mysteries of Glastonbury* (Glastonbury, UK: Gothic Image, 1990), 19.

11. Adrian Ivakhiv, *Claiming Sacred Ground: Pilgrims and Politics at Glastonbury and Sedona* (Indianapolis: Indiana University Press, 2001), 4.

12. John Masefield, *The Box of Delights: When the Wolves Were Running* (London: Pan Books, 1976).

13. Lurie, *Boys and Girls Forever*, 66.

14. Ibid., 76–77.

15. Ibid., 121.

16. Alison Lurie, *Don't Tell the Grown-Ups* (Boston, MA: Back Bay Books, 1990), 136.

17. C. S. Lewis, *The Lion, the Witch and the Wardrobe* (Harmondsworth, UK: Puffin Books, 1959), 20.

18. Ibid., 47–49.

19. "Narnia Sums Up the Magic of Childhood for Readers Too Old for Harry Potter," *The Times (London)*, February 22, 2008, 5.

20. Peter Woodcock, *This Enchanted Isle: The Neo-Romantic Vision from William Blake to the New Visionaries* (Glastonbury, UK: Gothic Image, 2000), 1.

21. Ibid., 135.

22. Ibid., 141.

23. "Billions wasted on UN climate programme," *The Guardian*, May 26, 2008, 1.

PART III

FANTASY, FETISH, AND THE FUTURE

Seven of Nine from *Star Trek: Voyager* (1995–2001).
Courtesy of The Kobal Collection.

CHAPTER SEVEN

There Can Be Only One: *Highlander: The Series'* Portrayal of Historical and Contemporary Fantasy

Michael S. Duffy

> He is immortal. Born in the Highlands of Scotland four hundred years ago. He is not alone. There are others like him, some good, some evil. For centuries he has battled the forces of darkness, with Holy Ground his only refuge. He cannot die unless you take his head, and with it, his power. In the end, there can be only one. He is Duncan MacLeod, the Highlander.
>
> —*Highlander: The Series* second-season opening monologue (1993)

When Gregory Widen wrote the original script for the movie *Highlander* (1986) as a thesis project for a scriptwriting class at UCLA in the mid-1980s, he probably never suspected that the world he helped create, a story of immortals battling throughout the centuries, would spawn numerous sequels and television spin-offs, novels, collectibles, video games, comic books, and even a Japanese anime interpretation. Of all these, *Highlander: The Series*, the syndicated television show that ran from 1992 to 1998, was arguably the most important, as it successfully expanded and reinterpreted the *Highlander* universe, introducing deeper moral and ethical conflicts and expanded histories, characterization, and atmosphere, proving one of the rare film-to-television spin-offs that creatively equaled, and according to some fans, outshined its predecessor. Centering on Duncan MacLeod (British actor Adrian Paul), the cousin and clansman of the film series' Connor MacLeod (French actor Christopher Lambert), *Highlander: The Series* followed Duncan and

113

other immortals as they endured love, loss, and conflict throughout history and in the present day, often questioning their actions toward others, and their own existence. Primarily a Canadian/French coproduction,[1] *Highlander: The Series* would film half the year in Vancouver and the other half in Paris, often on the Seine River, where Duncan owned a barge. Its international filming locations allowed the producers to easily fabricate historical backdrops on low budgets, and the damp, foggy Paris streets perfectly complemented the characters' present-day melancholy.

Though the series had its share of familiar genre elements—the introduction of a naïve teenager to be the audience's "eyes into the world," a villain-of-the-week formula that dominated the first few seasons—it also introduced unconventional approaches to television drama. *Highlander's* frequent use of flashbacks to illustrate its immortal characters' pasts gave the actors and production crew new material to play with weekly. The introduction of "Watchers," mortal characters who have been keeping track of immortals for centuries, added another unique thread to the universe, and the franchise's association with contemporary rock musicians—Queen composed a series of songs for the original film's soundtrack—resulted in recurring acting appearances by Joan Jett, Roland Gift of Fine Young Cannibals, and Roger Daltrey of The Who, among others. *Highlander: The Series'* flashbacks often placed its characters in the middle of real historical events, giving audiences a personal insight into history (even though historical facts might sometimes have been "altered for dramatic purposes"), and its contemporary setting helped create a world that was believable in iconography, yet fantastical in purpose. The series lasted for six years, spawning a spin-off show (*Highlander: The Raven*, featuring Amanda, a supporting character from the series) and helping to launch two further motion pictures featuring the television series characters, *Highlander: Endgame* (2000) and *Highlander: The Source* (2007). The *Highlander* franchise continues to be successful in the 2000s through various ancillary products, but seems to be at a creative and aesthetic crossroads in terms of both narrative and generic appeal and global marketability. More than the original film, the ideas and inspirations behind the television series have become the guiding philosophy propping up the franchise in recent years. This chapter will look at the practical and aesthetic principles behind the show's inception, production, and completion, and how *Highlander's* portrayal of historical and contemporary fantasy was facilitated by its grounding in identifiable human drama.

Genre, Aesthetics, and Televisuality

When expanding a franchise for television, producers often must significantly alter a premise that, in feature films, usually contains a clearly defined beginning, middle, and end. In terms of genre television, and particularly science fiction and fantasy shows, additional narrative, creative, and industrial expectations arise; thus most television adaptations of successful genre-defined franchises require complex consultation and negotiation with their parent studios of every element in the process, from planning to presentation, pitching to promotion, and casting to postproduction.[2] Because of the additional considerations necessary for certain kinds of genre television, different theoretical, aesthetic, and interpretive values can be applied. Christine Geraghty is one such academic who has argued that we should attempt to broaden our perspectives and approaches when studying television. She argues for an expansion of "evaluation" methods in television studies, and that "rather than looking for one set of television aesthetics . . . a more precise approach might attend to particular television categories."[3] Sarah Cardwell and Michael Z. Newman have also argued in different ways, but with similar trajectories, for a reconsideration of television studies and television aesthetics in our contemporary media age of high-quality, high-concept drama and genre television, and flat-screen displays and complex sound systems, which increasingly replicate the feeling of being in the cinema while watching film and television at home.[4]

Throughout much of my academic work, I have been interested in moments of transition—industrially, technologically, creatively, and aesthetically. More than the origins of a movement, style, or process, or the endgame of marketing, distribution, and shelf afterlife, I have become deeply interested in what I will call the *interstitial* moments in film and media production and industrial development, and the projects that are produced during these transitional periods. More pointedly, I am interested not only in films and television produced under significant moments of change in industry and technology, but also in *how* these often fundamental changes are both influencing and being reflected in the media that is produced during such moments. For example, in the study of the development and gradual dominance of digital technologies and visual effects in the film industry, while much is made of the theoretical "danger" that digital visual effects present in negating the indexical quality of the very images they are intended to enhance, little attention has been focused on the developmental period toward these goals, and the effect (pun intended) that changing technologies and industrial priorities had on both film production and the practitioners who were working directly within such fields. Similarly, within television studies, much recent work has favored applying the theories and methodologies of textual studies and production histories toward an ever-changing, internationally influenced televisual apparatus. Particularly here, I am interested in the industrial, technological, and aesthetic transitions in "televisuality" from the 1980s through the 1990s. John Thornton Caldwell has noted that, due to technological advancements in video editing and visual effects production, among other capabilities, television scripts during the 1980s "made a weekly practice of engineering their narratives around highly coded aesthetic and cultural fragments."[5] In many ways, ensemble drama had been adapting to new forms of presentation and was "no longer simply ensemble drama . . . it was also a kind of ensemble iconography and a highly publicized ritual of aesthetic facility."[6] Television was changing "as a historical phenomenon, as an aesthetic and industrial practice, and as a socially symbolic act."[7]

One of the many interesting things about *Highlander: The Series* is that it was born during these changing industrial and technological conditions that constituted a significant shift in the meaning and practice of televisuality. The 1986 feature film that the series is based upon was directed by Russell Mulcahy, a veteran helmer of early 1980s music videos—a phenomenon that had itself been influenced and transformed in many ways by advances in technology and visual effects. Much of *Highlander*'s aesthetic uniqueness is facilitated by writer Gregory Widen's basic plot and characters—the story of two immortal warriors, fighting through the centuries, until they once again encounter each other in present-day New York. They are fighting to reach "the gathering," as Sean Connery's Ramirez character notes in the film, where "only one will remain," as they fight for "the prize," an infinite knowledge and control over all things. The only way an immortal can kill another is by chopping off the other's head, which is most often done with a sword (a weapon that is invariably as old, if not older, than its owner); when the head is lost, a spectacular lightning-fueled effect called "the quickening" releases the loser's essence to the victor of the battle. Striking every physical object within close distance, the lightning from these quickenings often creates much noise and havoc, such as the shattered car windshields and busted hubcaps that clang and roll across the parking garage floor in the opening action scene of Mulcahy's film. Mulcahy, already schooled in the aesthetic qualities of 1980s pop music videos, brought this approach to a film whose protagonists were out of time and out of place, whose battles were punctuated by special effects that were born out of nature but controlled by man-made conflicts, a filmed universe that was simultaneously historic and contemporary, made up of reality and fantasy, of this world and the next.

While *Highlander* is most often referred to as a "cult" film (and its feature film sequels are largely derided as vastly inferior follow-ups to the original's narrative and characters), the series—while itself sometimes identified as a "cult" show in fantasy/science fiction television fandom—builds upon the original film's premise and world in an expansive and detailed way, introducing new elements to the mythos while retaining many of the cinematic, aesthetic, and musical hallmarks of the 1986 film. Part of the reason the series was able to convey these elements successfully was that, as I mentioned above, it was put into production at a particular period of change in technology, global financing, and aesthetic televisual development. As Caldwell notes,

> Television by 1990 had retheorized its aesthetic and presentational task. With increasing frequency, style itself became the subject, the signified, if you will, of television. In fact, this self-consciousness of style became so great that it can more accurately be described as an activity—as a performance of style—rather than as a particular look.[8]

This "performance of style" was perfectly suited to adapting the cinematic world of *Highlander* to weekly television. The aesthetic qualities of the first feature film—the swordfights in dark, wet alleys, the live lightning or pyrotechnics (or those animated in during postproduction), the contemporary rock soundtrack, and the increased capabilities in digital video editing—were all adaptable to, and in some ways preferred by, broadcasters in the 1990s for globally syndicated television produced on a moderate budget. Caldwell in fact argues that this was all part of a wider movement, a "confluence of material practices and institutional pressures" which suggested that "televisual style was the symptom of a much broader period of transition in the mass media and American culture."[9] Equally important in providing broadcast, monetary, and aesthetic opportunities for the *Highlander* television series were Europe's changing political and social circumstances at the beginning of the 1990s.[10]

"The Game" of International Coproduction

The year 1992 began the countdown for the formation of the European single market, the regional economic entity—utopian for some, dystopian for others—intended now to recenter Europe in a global politics fragmented in the wake of the breakup of the Soviet Union. This new "European Union" would necessarily refigure what counted as Europe—that is to say, literally which countries now would be included in this redesigned entity "Europe" and which would not—but would also reconceive the meanings of nationalisms, regionalisms, and localisms. That year also marked the five hundredth anniversary of the so-called "discovery of the New World": the invasion of the Americas by European conquerors. The contest to represent that moment in the newer one was part of a "war" of "image superpowers." This "war" engaged national desires to valorize old colonialisms in the face of new ones, even as oppositional political movements attempted to address new racisms in Europe and elsewhere, racisms too often traveling as national and ethnic identities.[11]

Highlander: The Series was put together through a complex international production pact involving Canadian, French, Japanese, German, and Italian investors, along with American distributors.[12] Gaumont, a French film production company, had opened a television arm in 1991,[13] and *Highlander* was seen as an easily translatable brand, with a built-in audience, that could appeal globally to numerous demographics. As Katie King argues, "*Highlander*'s narrative elements are a clever 'recombinant subgenre' . . . part traditionally masculine martial arts action adventure, part traditionally feminine historical romance-costume melodrama."[14] The formation of the European Union held further benefits for productions such as *Highlander*, which would be shot half the year in Vancouver, and half in Paris. Serra Ayse Tinic explains that

> like Canada, France has a centralized broadcasting and regulatory system complete with a domestic point and quota structure. In 1992, France formally designated all Franco-Canadian television productions developed in English as European works. Consequently, Canadian co-productions qualify as domestic content throughout the European Union.[15]

Qualifying under the domestic quota ensured a French/European audience to go alongside a Canadian one, thus establishing the series had an international market for distribution and syndication. Additionally, Tinic notes that what often makes films and television produced in Canada very appealing to European distributors is that "they portray the popular conceptions of North America while remaining subtly distinct from American television."[16] This played into the contemporary yet timeless world that every episode of *Highlander* would deliver, while complicating the notion that "the local is not a bounded area, but, rather, is always nationally and globally inflected."[17] Shawn Shimpach has also discussed "television programming's continuing efforts at spatial borderlessness,"[18] and how 1990s international coproductions such as *Highlander*, *La Femme Nikita* (1997–2001), and *Relic*

Hunter (1999–2002) in most cases benefited, and often were conceived because of, international treaties of business and culture. These programs were "charged with the task of balancing an international marketability with local accommodation. Each was intended to make as much sense textually and semiotically as the programming it followed and preceded on each local schedule."[19]

Highlander: The Series began airing in October 1992. Sold for syndication in the United States and to various buyers worldwide, the show introduced Duncan MacLeod of the Clan MacLeod, born in 1592 in the Highlands of Scotland; Lambert guest-starred as Connor in the first episode but never appeared again (though the character was frequently mentioned throughout the series). The series takes place in a parallel universe from the films, where the Connor character exists, and major events from the first film seem to have happened, but the series disregards the original film's finite conclusion of Connor being "the one," and introduces a more expansive world of immortals who exist in the present day. Budgeted at $1.1 million per episode,[20] a typical episode would have the following events: Duncan MacLeod would begin his day by pursuing a mundane daily activity such as making coffee, exercising, or meeting an old friend. Soon, he or one of his friends would encounter someone or something that creates conflict, in both mortal and *immortal* terms; following this, a flashback would take place, usually giving more information about Duncan's past four hundred years of life, and someone he had fought, loved, or journeyed with before. Producer Bill Panzer, in an interview on the 2001 release of the series on DVD, claims that they always tried to shoot flashbacks with a slightly different visual filter or adjusted color timing, to make the different time period visually distinguishable. Through the first season, techniques were also developed to help display the "buzz" that all immortals feel when they are within short distance of one another; the effect was generally made up of a slow-motion, circular pan of the camera, accompanied by an aural "buzz" vibration on the soundtrack. Following what were usually multiple flashbacks interspersed with present-day plot movements, the conflict would be solved with clues from the past, and usually by a swordfight between Duncan and a nemesis.[21] The series was thus able to provide a historical and thematic grounding for its fantastical situations, while basing its present-day conflicts in a vaguely familiar contemporary world.

The first episode finds Duncan operating an antiques store with his current love, Tessa (played by French actress Alexandra Vandernoot), when Connor appears and drags him back into "the game," and the characters also meet a young thief, Richie, who finds out later in the series that he is an immortal himself. The series establishes that all immortals are "foundlings," that they never know their real parents or their true origins. Initially, a female reporter and local detective were introduced as supporting characters, in an attempt to mirror the "reality" and relationships of the first feature film; although the series continued to exist in a recognizable contemporary and historical world in later seasons, these elements were gradually phased out as the series found a dramatic balance in its own universe, where the relationships between immortals became the focal point. The series featured an international cast and crew of British, French, Canadian, and American origin, and as Shimpach notes, its "roster of internationally recognizable guest stars" was "part of the production strategy"[22] to attract both funding and viewership. The series had the additional challenge of "making each episode 'cinematic' [as well as] negotiating co-production agreements, and creating or maintaining story arcs that could be threaded throughout the seasons."[23] In a show about immortals who were hundreds, and in certain cases thousands, of years old, their travels and their conflicts, their loves and their losses, having an international cast and shooting part of the year in Paris added a certain legitimacy to the show's storytelling, indeed "turning the series' production conditions into an asset."[24]

Interestingly, the series made regular use of churches and cathedrals, which often served the plots as well as providing atmospheric locations, since immortals cannot fight on holy ground; "None of us will break that rule," Ramirez tells Connor in the first film, "it's tradition." The show worked as a sort of contemporary "fantasy" for U.S. viewers, in that its Paris-shot scenes almost always took advantage of famous landmarks, offering a kind of weekly travelogue and the attractions of tourism. When in Paris, Duncan lived on a barge on the river Seine, and King points out that "almost every shot of Duncan and the barge is backgrounded by a rear view of Notre Dame."[25] While Paris played "Paris," the fictional city that was filmed in Vancouver, British Columbia, during the first half of each year was never identified within the show's scripts, and fans later christened it "Seacouver" because the location seemed to equally resemble Seattle.

History, Fantasy, and Talmudic Questions

Toby Miller has argued that "international co-production in the screen industry asks us to consider the question of culture and national origin."[26] The international coproduction agreements signed by different nations on *Highlander* caused numerous conflicts in location shooting, character screen time, costuming, and music placement, though Shimpach interprets that "the strategy chosen for *Highlander* and its hero was to rise above such squabbling, be aspirational, and to present an idealized, cosmopolitan existence."[27] Though perhaps characters like Richie, and later, Joe Dawson, a mortal, were seen by the producers as the audience's eyes into the world, it is Duncan MacLeod who, in the end, proved to be "the one" who drove the show forward through his "boy scout" morality, ethical choices, and values, despite often having them questioned; in his choices, he taught other characters how to move forward in a world of endless loss and dwindling hope. In portraying immortal characters who had lived for centuries through different nations, cultures, and lifestyles, the show was able to ask significant questions of its audience as well. Production designer Steven Geaghan told creative consultant and head writer David Abramowitz over lunch one day early in the series that he basically saw the show as "a romantic Talmudic discussion with ass-kicking." Though the shows were bookended by great action sequences and often tragic romance, Abramowitz realized that he could frame the show around the basic questions of existence, which would be magnified when dealing with immortals:

> They're Talmudic questions. How long do you have to keep a promise? What is the difference between honor and vanity? Is morality and justice fixed by time, or only in time and place, or does it exist, the same morality—true morality; and true justice. Justice, does it exist in the seventeenth century, and [is it] the same in the twentieth century.[28]

In this sense, *Highlander* would be "telling stories that were universally translatable,"[29] but could also tie these real questions into history, mythology, and fantasy. While the first and second years of the show maintained a firm grounding in a contemporary archetypal action-adventure format, as the series progressed, immortals themselves became the focus of all of the conflicts in the show, and through investigating their own histories, the characters added deeper layers to their already complicated contemporary lives. As each season became more ambitious in its travels through history (sometimes even returning to and elaborating on flashbacks that had been previously shown), *Highlander*'s world transformed into a complex web of histories, injustices, moral quandaries, and broken promises, continuously adding deeper layers to its narrative world.

The show was turning a net profit by the end of its first year in syndication, prior to being acquired for broadcast on American cable stations such as USA, and before it was even purchased for broadcast in the UK and Australia—clearly, something about this "cosmopolitan" character and concept had attracted audiences.[30] During the first episode of the second season, the mortal character of Joe Dawson was introduced. Joe was a representative of an organization called "the Watchers" (in the episode of the same title, first aired in September 1993), whose motto of "observe and record, but never interfere" would very soon be called into question during numerous storylines,[31] and in Joe's soon-to-be close relationship with Duncan, whom Joe was "assigned" to. In a interesting stroke of casting, Jim Byrnes, who played Joe, was an established Canadian blues musician, and in future seasons, the show established a bar called "Joe's" that would provide a significant location space for conversations between characters, and musical interludes for Byrnes himself. When Duncan uncovers the truth behind the Watchers and engages Joe for the first time, Joe tells him "too much of man's history has been lost. Once you get through all of life's crap, the only thing that matters is the truth. We want the truth about immortals to survive, not a bunch of old wives' tales." Joe reveals to Duncan that he's been his watcher for the past fifteen years, and in a sly moment that helps align the first film and the television series, Joe pulls up the Kurgan's immortal history on a computer, and tells Duncan that his cousin Connor "did us all a big favor when he got rid of him." As the show expanded its focus with Joe and the Watchers, the opening narration of the show also changed and was now narrated by Joe himself (instead of Duncan). The expanded narration also differs significantly from the opening monologue of the original *Highlander* film: whereas the film's opening narration sets immortals as a secret that is only just being revealed to humans, the series' narration explains the basic rules of the story and makes the narrative personal by focusing directly on Duncan. By having Joe narrate the description, the series sells itself as an expanded universe with less of a finite end mark, and also immediately clues the audience into further details exclusive to the television universe.

Though nearly every episode involving Duncan was "personal" due to the fact that they referred to people and events of his past (and how they were still affecting him in the present), the season premieres of the show developed a special reputation for revealing important personal details about Duncan and his history. In "Samurai" (1994), the first episode of the third season, we are told the story of how Duncan acquired his Japanese dragon-head katana sword.[32] In 1778, a shipwreck washes Duncan ashore in Japan, where he meets samurai Hideo Koto, who teaches him how to better use a sword, and his mind. "Bring the mountain's power through you," Hideo explains. Duncan asks, "What is this, swordplay or poetry?" Hideo replies, "Both." Though *Highlander* operated on the surface as a "complexly constructed amalgam of reliably predictable television pleasures—action and violence, stylish shooting and locations, romance and sex, good guys and bad guys,"[33] for many of its fans, it engendered much greater meanings than these genre clichés once it developed into a multiseason tale. Season three also introduced the five-thousand-year-old character of Methos (Welsh actor Peter Wingfield), who would become one of the most popular characters with fans.[34] A continuously ambiguous and complicated presence, Methos constantly challenges Duncan's choices, offering a wider perspective of the world and a more pragmatic way of approaching conflicts. Methos has seen it all, and would rather live to talk about it, although he archly reminds one opponent who underestimates him, "Just because I don't *like* to fight, doesn't mean that I *can't*," before taking his head. Methos's character helped widen the canvas of the series even further, and along with the already introduced on-off love interest Amanda (Elizabeth Gracen), and old friend Hugh Fitzcairn (musician Roger Daltrey), Duncan had a full "cast of characters" to rely on and play off of.

Season four arguably contained some of the series' most meaningful and "historicized" episodes. Shot on location in Scotland, and directed by Adrian Paul himself, the fourth-season opener "Homeland" (1995) has Duncan returning to his "roots" in Glenfinnan, on the shores of Loch Shiel, to return a bracelet that he originally had buried with his first mortal love in Scotland, some four hundred years ago. In returning, he discovers not only his father's sword hanging in the local inn, but also that the first immortal he had ever encountered, the Viking Kanwulf—who had massacred Duncan's village and killed his father—is still secretly ensconced in the local area, disguised as a priest.[35] Duncan makes it his duty, of course, to set things right. In the season four episode "Something Wicked" (1996), a different kind of historicization is aestheticized: Duncan encounters immortal friend Jim Coltec, a Native American *hayoka* who for hundreds of years has taken the pain away from others, absorbing it into himself. This fosters some humorous conversation between Duncan and Richie on their way to meet up with Coltec. Richie is skeptical about Coltec's "power," and he asks Duncan why it should be any more believable than other "fantastic" phenomena. Duncan replies, "I've lived for four hundred years, I've never seen a werewolf, an elf, or a vampire." If there were ever any doubt, in this one piece of dialogue Duncan has grounded *Highlander*'s world in an authored fantasy of its own, free from other iconic figures and archetypes—but never from history itself.

Throughout his immortal life, Coltec has also been vanquishing evil-spirited immortals, each time absorbing their spiritual darkness. When Duncan and Richie encounter Coltec and he violently attacks them, they realize something is very wrong, that Coltec has perhaps taken in too much evil and experienced a "dark quickening" (a phenomenon that Joe believes is a myth). Duncan's flashback to the first time he met Coltec extends from the end of a flashback to 1872 that featured in the very first episode of the series, when Duncan experienced the slaughter of the members of a Lakota Sioux camp where he was living, and the death of a Native American woman whom he loved. As the flashback continues in that time period, with newly filmed material, Duncan is angry and despondent due to his loss, and is put in prison after encountering U.S. soldiers, where he meets Coltec, who offers to take his pain away through a spiritual healing process. In connecting flashbacks in this manner, the show attempts a complex narrative structure that rewards longtime viewers of the show, giving an interconnectedness to Duncan's, and the show's, universe. Duncan realizes in the present that he must stop Coltec, who is beginning to take on aspects of all of the corrupt and murderous immortals whom he defeated, and after failing to heal him in the way Coltec once helped him, Duncan realizes that he must take Coltec's head. Upon doing so, Duncan himself experiences a dark quickening, and spends the next episode of the series betraying his friends and fighting his way back to his original spirit. When a qualified friend of Duncan's tries to help him with his anger, Duncan questions, "Psychotherapy? Can it work for immortals?" His friend answers, "I suppose . . . but we're so much more complex than mortals. Upon our page, so much more is written—but our core is similar; we're formed by the same experiences." These episodes of the series frame a discussion of the "spiritual" around debates of good and evil, moral and immoral, pain and healing, and have meaning for both its Native American antagonist, and the immortals affected by him.

Becoming "the One"

In the fifth and sixth seasons of *Highlander*, matters grow darker still. Season five's "Prophecy" (1996) introduces us to Cassandra, an immortal seer who certainly resembles, at least in spirit, the mythological figure herself. The audience learns that Duncan encountered her as a child, where she informed him that he would fight and vanquish a great evil, which alludes to future adventures for Duncan in upcoming episodes of the series, and perhaps less determinedly, the films. The introduction of Cassandra here also functions as sort of a buildup for the two most powerful episodes of the season (and perhaps of the entire series), "Comes a Horseman" and "Revelation 6:8" (both 1997). The episodes' titles refer to the following passage in the Bible: "I looked, and there was a pale horse! Its rider's name was Death, and Hades followed him. They were given authority over one-fourth of the earth to kill people using wars, famines, plagues, and the wild animals of the earth."[36] In a shocking revelation for viewers of the series, we learn that Methos was Death, one of the Four Horsemen, and that the other three, Kronos (War), Silas (Pestilence), and Caspian (Famine) are still out there, and planning on a millennial poisoning of the world to mirror the killing, raping, and pillaging that they embarked upon thousands of years ago in the Bronze Age. These episodes take *Highlander* further back into history, and into deeper soul-searching than has ever been seen on the show, while also tying a more direct Christian allegory to the show and its characters. The fictionalized characters resemble those figures depicted in the Bible story—and would be recognized as such by those familiar with it—and the most important battles that Duncan, Methos, and Cassandra must face are not those of the sword but are internal and psychological struggles to confront their own personal destinies. "Revelation 6:8" was the 100th episode of the series, and Adrian Paul also took the directing reins for this memorable installment, helming a sequence that featured the show's first ever "double quickening," during which Duncan and Methos both benefit from the power of their victories. In a more pronounced way than ever before, the flashbacks in these two episodes provided "a link between the burden of history and the ultimate future of the world."[37]

In the final season of the show, Duncan is pursued by the ancient Zoroastrian demon Ahriman, who takes possession of various individuals, and also tricks Duncan's mind by appearing as apparitions of many of Duncan's old enemies—and some of his closest friends.[38] While the theme of Duncan being "the chosen one" is here fully played to its logical conclusion, the episodes were unsatisfying to fans for various reasons, many having to do with the choice to take the series too far into the spiritual realm. The rest of the season was also used to fill out episodes with potential female spin-off characters, though in the end, the producers chose to go with the long-standing Amanda character for *Highlander: The Raven* (1998–1999), a more detective-themed show which lasted just one season in syndication. *Highlander: The Series* ends with a theme that many television shows have explored in different ways: "What if Duncan MacLeod had never lived?"—in other words, *It's a Wonderful Life* (1946). Titled "To Be" and "Not to Be" (both 1998), the episodes have Duncan encountering one last nemesis from the past, and letting his friends get compromised and threatened in the process; in desperation, Duncan offers his head to his enemy but is pulled away by the ghost of his friend Fitz (Daltrey), who takes Duncan on a tour of what the *Highlander* world would be like had he not existed. Old loves are revisited, old villains are reinterpreted, and no great mystery gets solved, but a fitting montage sequence of past series moments closes the final episode, with Duncan walking off alone into uncharted timelines and territories. Despite its relatively disappointing final season, *Highlander: The Series* ultimately ends with honor, and the series as a whole retains its generic historical relevance and replayability because of its fascinating accumulation of historical details, its complex, often *gray* characters, and its puzzle-piece flashback-driven narratives; the show ultimately reflects "the way in which the great world canvas of modern history offers lessons for understanding individual existence in a complicated and rapidly changing contemporary world."[39]

The series' final season is presented as "loneliness and frustration,"[40] which rather strongly aligns with the themes of the two *Highlander* feature films that follow the series and feature Duncan. In *Highlander: Endgame*, Duncan finds Connor disillusioned and wanting out of "the game"; and in an intense moment full of action and drama, Connor offers his head to Duncan to defeat a greater enemy. While Connor fans were noticeably angry at the loss of the original MacLeod of the franchise, and Duncan fans were mystified at the revelation that he had previously been married (when an early episode of the series had claimed he never had been, and never would be), the steps seem purely logical in narrative and franchise terms, passing the *Highlander* mantle onto the "next generation" of fans with new twists in the flashback fabric, including Connor and Duncan's very first meeting, which had never before been shown. More disappointing to many fans was *Highlander: The Source*, which was filmed in Lithuania in the autumn of 2005, but received a rather undignified U.S. premiere on the Sci-Fi Channel in September 2007, and went straight to DVD thereafter.[41] Though it continues to position Duncan as "the one" for the franchise, *The Source* virtually drops almost everything else that made the series and the first film work, opting for a postapocalyptic setting in which Duncan reluctantly joins his most recent love, Anna, and a band of bitter immortals (Methos included) on a search for "the Source," a mythical nothingness that was originally supposed to represent the origin of the immortals, but in the film that was produced, looks more like a blue-filtered space portal. While Duncan is given an ending that makes him the first immortal to father a child, the production ran out of funds to provide a proper conclusion to the film, which likely would have shown Duncan and Anna back in the Highlands of Scotland, training a young son named . . . Connor. "Elle-nora," a longtime fan and poster on the official *Highlander* message boards, offered this simple yet eloquent statement during a discussion about what fans preferred more, the television series or the films: "The series is about living as an immortal while the films seem to concentrate on death and survival. There is a big difference between living and surviving."[42] While some fans may feel that the character of Duncan never quite got the feature film treatment that he deserved after serving six years on television, *Highlander: The Series* holds its own torch, and holds it well; the show is a fascinating time capsule not only into genre storytelling, but also into the approaches and techniques that an increasingly international industry pursued in attempting to produce and sell a globally viable, broadly appealing entertainment product during the 1990s.[43]

Epilogue: Reunion and Rebirth

As many genre shows have, *Highlander: The Series* developed a devoted fan base during and after its production; the most well-known collective, *Highlander WorldWide*, officially endorsed by the *Highlander* producers, continues to organize conventions every few years that usually attract most of the series' principal actors, writers, and crew, among others. In early 2008, a full ten years after the series had stopped production, producer Peter Davis announced plans to release a new DVD set collecting numerous episodes featuring the Methos character.[44] Entitled *Methos Rocks*, the set included six of the television series' most acclaimed episodes featuring the ambiguous character, as well as new audio commentaries from actor Peter Wingfield and series head writer David Abramowitz, and most interestingly, a supplemental featurette in which Abramowitz "interviews" Methos and the actor who plays him. Fans were given the opportunity (through the official website and various related mailing lists) to submit potential questions, many of which are featured in the interview segment. Following quickly upon this release was another series-based DVD product, *Highlander: Reunion*, a series of five vignettes (adding up to the length of one regular television episode) that reunited Wingfield's Methos character with Amanda and Joe. Released in September 2008, *Reunion* revisits the three characters in the present day, ten years after the end of the series, as they gather for an important event in one of the character's lives.[45] Both of these releases were available exclusively through the official *Highlander* online store, although it is possible that they could later be released publicly to mass-market outlets, as with the series DVD sets. Further proof that *Highlander: The Series* has cemented its reputation as the main selling point of the *Highlander* franchise is that the online store concentrates on images of Duncan from the series, rather than Connor from the feature films.

The release of the Methos-themed box set and *Reunion* show that *Highlander: The Series* continues to have a following outside the "normal" parameters of syndication and retail sell-through outlets. It has extended and replayed its traditional television "afterlife" in interesting and multimediated ways. As I write this, there are indeed further significant *Highlander*-related productions in the pipeline. On May 20, 2008, it was announced that Summit Entertainment, in partnership with Peter Davis, was in the planning stages for a reimagining of the *Highlander* film franchise, which will apparently "re-imagine" the saga with "expanded mythology" elements and "prequel aspects," with the likely hope of reestablishing a new and vital film series a la the recent Batman (*Batman Begins*, 2005) and James Bond (*Casino Royale*, 2006) reboots.[46] Writers are engaged, and Summit and Davis have hinted that the film will primarily use the original film's narrative and central characters as its basis for storytelling, though they have apparently not yet settled on specifics; it also seems as if the film will have a significantly larger budget than any of the previous *Highlander* feature entries. While it could be seen as a trendy way to reinvigorate a franchise that was considered all but dead, we can perhaps expect that this new feature will again, as most things related to the *Highlander* brand have, veer slightly off-center in its approach and execution, delivering, as the series so frequently did, a present-day retelling of generic and mythic archetypes, while simultaneously reflecting on those of the past to give added meaning to its characters' contemporary existence. For the *Highlander* franchise, and for its fans, despite many close calls, there truly seems to be no endgame.

Notes

1. The first season of the show was co-funded by French, German, and Japanese investors—Canadian Filmline didn't get involved until the second season (1993–1994). For a nice breakdown of the particular details behind the production, see Shawn Shimpach, "The Immortal Cosmopolitan: The International Co-Production and Global Circulation of *Highlander: The Series*," *Cultural Studies* 19, no. 3 (2005): 338–71.

2. Recent examples of franchise-driven, narratively bound genre series include *Smallville*, Warner Bros.' reinterpretation of Superman's younger years, which began airing in October 2001 and as of September 2008 is going into its eighth year, and *Terminator: The Sarah Conner Chronicles*, a spin-off of the popular film franchise, which takes place after the events of *Terminator 2: Judgment Day* (1991), and began airing in the United States in early 2008.

3. Christine Geraghty, "Aesthetics and Quality in Popular Television Drama," *International Journal of Cultural Studies* 6, no. 1 (2003): 25.

4. Michael Z. Newman, "Upscaling Television Aesthetics and the Cinematic Analogy," *Console-ing Passions* Conference, April 2008, Santa Barbara, California. Paper available at www.scribd.com/doc/2698855/Upscaling-Television-Aesthetics-

and-the-Cinematic-Analogy; Sarah Cardwell, "'Television Aesthetics' and Close Analysis: Style, Mood and Engagement in *Perfect Strangers* (Stephen Poliakoff, 2001)," in *Style and Meaning: Studies in the Detailed Analysis of Film*, ed. John Gibbs and Douglas Pye (Manchester: Manchester University Press, 2005), 179–94.

5. John Thornton Caldwell, *Televisuality: Style, Crisis, and Authority in American Television* (New Brunswick, NJ: Rutgers University Press, 1995), vii.

6. Ibid., vii.

7. Ibid.

8. Ibid., 5.

9. Ibid.

10. Additionally, Christopher Lambert was (and continues to be) a significant box-office draw in France, as well as much of Europe, and the first *Highlander* film had already built up a large following there.

11. Katie King, "Globalizations, TV Technologies, and the Re-Production of Sexual Identities: Teaching *Highlander* and *Xena* in Layers of Locals and Globals," in *Encompassing Gender: Integrating International Studies and Women's Studies*, ed. Mary M. Lay, Janice Monk, and Deborah Silverton Rosenfelt (New York: Feminist Press, 2002), 102. "Image superpowers" is taken from Jose Freches, *La guerre des images* (Paris: Denoel, 1986).

12. Shimpach, "The Immortal Cosmopolitan," 349.

13. King, "Globalizations, TV Technologies, and the Re-Production of Sexual Identities," 105. Gaumont is generally seen as the oldest running film production company in the world, see Richard Abel, *The Ciné Goes to Town: French Cinema, 1896–1914* (Berkeley: University of California Press, 1994), 10.

14. King, "Globalizations, TV Technologies, and the Re-Production of Sexual Identities," 106.

15. Serra Ayse Tinic, *On Location: Canada's Television Industry in a Global Market* (Toronto: University of Toronto Press, 2005), 107.

16. Ibid., 108.

17. Ibid., 76.

18. Shimpach, "The Immortal Cosmopolitan," 339.

19. Ibid., 341. Shimpach argues that *Highlander: The Series* "was an early successful example of everyday television produced under the pressures of negotiating the dictates of internationally conceived agreements concerning culture, representation, finance, and circulation," 338.

20. Ibid., 349.

21. The series managed to snag legendary swordmaster Bob Anderson to choreograph fights for its first season; Anderson had taught Errol Flynn, doubled for David Prowse as Darth Vader on the original *Star Wars* trilogy, and taught Christopher Lambert in *Highlander*. Anthony DeLongis, another actor and stuntman with a long international career, appeared a couple of times as a villain in the series, and acted in and choreographed the duels for "Duende" (1997), a fifth-season episode considered by many fans to be one of the series' strongest.

22. Shimpach, "The Immortal Cosmopolitan," 346.

23. Ibid., 344.

24. Ibid., 345.

25. King, "Globalizations, TV Technologies, and the Re-Production of Sexual Identities," 108.

26. Toby Miller, Nitin Givil, John McMurria, and Richard Maxwell, *Global Hollywood* (London: British Film Institute, 2001), 87.

27. Shimpach, "The Immortal Cosmopolitan," 352.

28. Lyria Wollich, David Abramowitz interview, *Highlander Fan Central*, 2000, www.members.tripod.com/lyriaw/central/David%20Abramowitz1.htm.

29. Shimpach, "The Immortal Cosmopolitan," 342.

30. Ibid., 350.

31. The idea of "rogue Watchers," fundamentalist factions of Watchers who deviate from their mission to "never interfere," often to kill immortals, became a frequently used plotline in the *Highlander* mythos (and of course reflected our own human nature to fear things we do not understand). A rogue Watcher named James Horton (who turns out to be Joe's brother-in-law) was introduced at the end of the first season and became a recurring villain throughout the series, haunting Duncan even in death, as a manifestation of an evil spirit in the fifth-season finale and sixth-season opener, and in "what if" sequences in the final two episodes of the series. A "rogue Watcher" faction would also later appear in the *Highlander: Endgame* feature film.

32. In *Highlander: The Source*, Duncan's katana is destroyed by the film's villain, The Guardian.

33. Shimpach, "The Immortal Cosmopolitan," 353.

34. The character and actor have remained popular with fans through the years, and Wingfield is featured in not only the two additional Duncan-centric feature films, *Endgame* and *The Source*, but also further animated spin-offs, a video game, and comic books.

35. Duncan's first "death" and his separation from his father was shown in the second episode of season one.

36. International Standard Version, 2008.

37. Shimpach, "The Immortal Cosmopolitan," 357.

38. It may be interesting here to point out the relatively obscure fact that the parents of Queen's lead singer, Freddie Mercury, were in fact Zoroastrian, of Persian descent.

39. Shimpach, "The Immortal Cosmopolitan," 361.

40. Ibid., 362.

41. An earlier, longer cut of the film was released on DVD in Russia in February 2007.

42. Message posted on February 5, 2008. Available from: http://www.highlandercommunity.com/Forum/showthread.php?s=45174d671a8cdfe5a7aff23dacd5d2ce&p=1484581#poststop.

43. "The thing is," Bill Panzer said of the *Highlander* franchise in a 2001 DVD interview, "it is a good premise and if it's not inexhaustible, I certainly haven't gotten to the end of things that intrigue me about it." There is the official *Highlander* store, which continues to sell swords, soundtrack CDs, and other merchandise. There have been numerous books published, and most recently, there has been a Highlander comic book series published by Dynamite Entertainment.

44. Peter Davis's producing partner William N. ("Bill") Panzer passed away in March 2007. "William Panzer, 64, Producer," Obituary, *Variety* online, March 26, 2007, www.variety.com/article/VR1117961815.html.

45. The promotional material reads as follows:

> It has been ten years since we left Methos, Amanda, and Joe and some things have changed, while others remain the same. Love has blossomed, Immortality is still a double edged sword, and lingering feelings rise to the surface . . . now a very important event has brought the three old friends together in this unforgettable Highlander Reunion, but will The Game threaten to tear them apart forever?

The DVD also included new cast interviews and a music video for "One Life," an original song Jim Byrnes composed for the feature. The feature was shot at producer Peter Davis's vacation villa in Malibu, California.

46. Dave McNary, "Summit Sets *Highlander* Remake," *Variety* online, May 20, 2008, www.variety.com/article/VR1117986173.html?categoryid=13&cs=1&query=highlander.

CHAPTER EIGHT

Kinky Borgs and Sexy Robots: The Fetish, Fashion, and Discipline of Seven of Nine

Trudy Barber

It's natural that once Hunger had been vanquished (which is algebraically the equivalent of attaining the summit of material well-being), OneState mounted an attack on that other ruler of the world, Love. Finally this element was also conquered, i.e., organized, mathematicized, and our *Lex Sexualis* was promulgated about 300 years ago: Any Number has the right of access to any other Number as sexual product.[1]

In his dystopian vision of the future, Yvgeny Zamyatin's 1924 novel *We* introduces the idea of an all-conquering technological society that has no room for emotion or expression of individuality, leaving a mathematically inspired social order controlling homeostatic drives. In the above quotation, members of this anticipated society of the future are not named, but classed as "Numbers" free from identity, and considered available as "sexual product" to each other. It would appear that future fantasies of dehumanized and restricted dystopian societies also include the possibility of an underlying dormant but rampant sexual behavior that is the standard story of fetishism. This chapter proposes, among other discussion, that the more restricted and technological the social order, the more sexually deviant and fetishist the sexual behavior and fantasies of that society and that this is manifest in the Borg character, aptly numbered, much like the population in Zamyatin's novel, as Seven of Nine (Tertiary Adjunct of Uni-Matrix 0—hereafter called simply Seven) from the *Star Trek: Voyager* (1995–2001)[2] television series.

Voyager's hybrid human/cyborg and "woman astrometric scientist" Seven suggests a metaphor that simply turns the Frankenstein body into fetish and is symbolic of our love affair with (and fear of) robots and cyborgs. I suggest that this fetishism is also reflective of our love/hate relationship with converging communication and entertainment technologies; confusion at the loss of sex and gender boundaries; the loss of identity, both individual and social; and a mistrust of ubiquitous and invasive computing—all within consumer-led Western society. There are definite parallels to be drawn between notions of the dormant but rampant uncontrollable sexual possibilities of the future and the fear of our loss of control of machines and technologies. Because of this, there is justification in exploring sexological attributes of the mechanistic and penetrating *Star Trek* Borg phenomenon in that it can reveal and explain our fascination of the erotic allure in the mixture of machine and flesh, our arousal at that which disgusts us, and our trepidation at adapting to change. In this chapter, Seven, as fashioned and portrayed on screen, will be discussed in part with reference to specific sexual subcultures and their erotic fetish attire, demeanor, and interpretation—giving references to behavior that some may find unusual or even distasteful. Seven will also be discussed in contrast to long-established discussion surrounding Haraway's ironic cyborg,[3] the gendering and sexualizing of technology from Doane and Balsamo,[4] and Woolmark's collection of cyberfeminism and cybersexualities.[5] Overall I will discuss Seven by readdressing notions of the "sexy robot," which I will situate within notions of "women of discipline" (in uniform),[6] "women of science,"[7] and the "posthuman" that will finally be contrasted briefly with a more contemporary android from the revisioned television series *Battlestar Galactica* (2003–2009).

Seven tends to break the mold of previous understandings and interpretations of the automaton, the robot, the android, and notions of the cyborg by her behavior, actions, and attempts at participation in relationships, and in the way issues of sex and gender are approached when exploring narrative. According to Robin Roberts, "an android is a specific version of a cyborg—a being defined as part human, part machine; it is not quite human, but it looks and acts humanoid."[8] It is all too easy to combine this with the interpretation of the tradition of the robot—the label "robot" comes from the Czech play by Karel Capek, *Rossum's Universal Robots* (1920), who were defined in the narrative as slaves to society.[9] Consequently the function of mechanical slavery has been labeled with gendered attributions and translated into justification for feminist argument as it is considered redolent of feminine stereotyping. So, cultural references to mechanical humans have also become associated with notions of the subservient woman simply "because of its separation from, and subordination to, mankind, an android can effectively function as a stand-in for women."[10] However, I hope to steer away from the trap of reworking such notions and interpretations of the cyborg and its associations with specific feminist argument, but to situate the cyborg, and therefore Seven, outside such arguments and instead consider possible standpoints from novel notions of postfeminism, androgyny, and techno-sexology.

This will in part go some way toward helping to explain our desire for the exploration of physical sensation, dominance and submission, sensuality, and arousal through the visual titillation of such on-screen science fiction spectacles. The Borg, their hive mind described by Daniel Dinello as "resembling a web of interconnected computers, a totalitarian communist state" and having a matriarchy run by the Borg Queen, who is a "visually repulsive sorceress and sexually alluring temptress who claims near-divinity," represent not only the dangerous woman and evil perverse mother, but also represent objectives that, according to Dinello, contemporary society holds dear.[11] At this time of writing, society appears to hold dear the following points—all stemming from a contemporary discipline that has been described by Bell and Kennedy as *cybercultures*:[12]

- The continuous search for perfection and speed through the collapse of time and space enabled by developing communication technologies such as the Internet
- Implementing ubiquitous computing such as biometrics
- The commodification of movement through the popularity of "smart" mobile technologies
- The popular use of reconstructive cosmetic surgery (no longer a preserve of the rich and famous)

The *Star Trek* series is well known for its explorations and explanations of society and is often read as a mirror reflecting social attitudes to challenges facing ethnicity and race, or sex and gender, for example. Therefore, it is not surprising that *Voyager*, with its predominantly female leading characters whose practices of and attitudes to science and technology are seen from an alternative viewpoint and "feminist perspective,"[13] has been recognized as feminist science fiction through its treatment of science in general and female scientists in particular.[14] However, it is extrapolating from such earlier standpoints on women, feminism, science, and technology that a slightly more alternative discussion and understanding of the *Voyager* character Seven can be developed, which could be applied to further readings of future fantasies. By combining the resulting readings of Seven with technological determinism, theories of cyberculture, and sexology, we may begin to see our society, as mirrored in other future visions of science fiction such as *Battlestar Galactica*, reflected in a completely different light.

Kinky Borgs and Sexy Robots—Sexological Determinism?

> Seven has a female outward appearance, with prominent breasts, but she is made up of metal as well as flesh and has immense physical prowess. We find out that the Borg have removed her reproductive organs. The Borg have no gender, and neither did Seven when she was part of the Collective.[15]

Seven, if seen as overt caricature of physical womanhood, embodies associations of the graphic narrative and sexual fantasy artwork of the 1950s.[16] Drawings of women's anatomy in comic books have been discussed and perceived as distorted and as "hypersexualised,"[17] with "anti-gravity breasts,"[18] for example. It is well documented that Seven has "physical prowess" and "prominent breasts," and is recognized as being "made up of metal as well as flesh."[19] Seven also has the ability to assimilate individuals, despite her escape from the collective, through the vampire tendrils that still eject from her left hand. If seen in this light, Seven follows in the tradition of superheroes with superhuman powers. But Michele Bowring, when discussing fan erotic/slash fiction, suggests that that it is a popular sexual fantasy that all Borg are totally castrated and desexed. This is substantiated with the introduction of the Borg in *Star Trek: The Next Generation* (1987–1994). In episode "Q Who" (1989), Q first describes the Borg as "not a he; not a she. Not like anything you've seen before." In their understanding then, to be Borg is to lose identity, and according to this definition of Seven as Borg, there is a loss of physical sex through the loss of genitalia, but nevertheless the breasts are kept. This is a stark reminder of the unpredictability of "human nature" and confronts our attitudes to notions of the "other" in terms of revulsion and fascination, responses also associated with notions of sexual fetishism.

Louise Kaplan, in her discussion of fetishism and robots, defines machines and popular technological culture as a part of her "fetishism strategy." She introduces us to what she describes as the "necrophilic principle," in that living, animate beings are totally unpredictable.[20] She sees this strategy as a dominating theme that tries to subdue the unpredictability and enigmatic desires of human nature. She asserts that should human desires be given to machines, if "set loose, they would run amok, take over the social order, and then demolish the very universe that God and Nature had created."[21] This is the fear that appears to overpreoccupy Seven. Kaplan also discusses the counterfantasy that humans might be turned into machines and thus lose their intellect and vitality. I suggest that this gives us a technological deterministic approach to discourse in deconstructing the techno-individual. At this point technological determinism and fetishism overlap. Evidence of this is seen not only in Seven from *Star Trek: Voyager*, but also elsewhere in popular culture, such as the cybererotic music video for the musician Björk, *All is Full of Love*, where we see two humanoid robots appear to have sex with each other throughout their ongoing construction, aided by other, nonhumanoid robots.[22]

In sexological terms, sexual fetishism has classically been described and defined as "perversion" and considered a response to lack and disavowal of the phallus—a realization of the castrated female and a reconfiguring and projection of the sexual goal onto an object.[23] Kaplan's work on fetishism has been critiqued as classical psychoanalysis by Amanda Fernbach, who describes her own alternative approach as reading "various fetishisms as a product of culture rather than of individual pathology."[24] Nevertheless, the term *fetishism* itself does have various associations. There is sexual fetishism; anthropological and magical fetishism; commodity fetishism; fetishism as cultural discourse; female fetishism; techno-fetishism; the fetish aesthetic— the list is endless. However, I suggest that fetishism has the potential to be simply understood and interpreted as an umbrella term for that which excites us; it is the convergence of pleasure, response, and situation. It is an understanding and perception created by projecting arousal-value onto individual experience, subjectivity, and objectivity. Consequently, Seven is an amalgamation and representation of many differing notions of fetishism. This cyborg character enables and represents contemporary postmodern notions of sexuality and allows narratives to break boundaries surrounding the "science of desire" and its relationship to technological determinism in a mash-up of possibilities. Lucy Bland and Laura Doan argue that sexology is purely medically descriptive and has since been reworked through Foucault's exploration of sex and identity. They go on to ask to "what extent were the findings of sexology accepted or rejected in (other) areas such as art, journalism or the law?"[25] In answer to the standpoint of art and creativity and seeing the creation of the *Star Trek* universe in that light, overtly sexual protagonists such as Seven introduce us directly to discourses of postfeminism, technological determinism, and the science of desire through contemporary popular culture narratives and imaginaries, giving us a techno-sexologically deterministic mirror with which to reflect and discuss social change. This viewpoint complements what has already been described as reflections of "the identity-transforming possibilities of technology in a world teetering on the brink of what some call a posthuman future."[26]

In this sense, those who recognize the fetishist attributes of Seven describe her as being sexless and/or androgynous in nature. The earlier quotation by Bowring explores slash fiction and sexual attraction between Seven and Captain Janeway and discusses ideas surrounding what she defines as "double subversion."[27] For Bowring, Seven's ambiguous sexuality is clearly considered subversive and challenges ideas of dominance, submission, and leadership. From a sexological standpoint Seven encapsulates, embodies, and *is* a metaphor for sexual fetishism, in that she lacks the sex organs needed for reproduction; therefore, Seven can be a subjective blank canvas on which to paint all types of projected sexual fantasy and can be a substitute for sexual goals for any predilection and sexual preference, male or female, no matter the inclination of the fantasist. Aesthetically then, Seven may have "anti-gravity breasts" but is asexual or unisexual in function, and spends much of her time in later episodes of *Voyager* exploring notions of sexuality, seduction, intimacy, and "love." Wei Ming Dariotis suggests that "this fascination with 'ambiguation' demonstrates anxiety over questions of identity: how do we determine the boundaries of the self without taking an oppositional stance against the 'Other'?"[28] This reveals the potential emasculation of feminist notions of and associations with the cyborg and introduces us to the transgender, bisexual, exploratory, and anamorphic nature of the cyborg as an alternative to the exclusive feminist interpretation. This in turn reveals our relationship with contemporary technologies of change, entertainment, and narrative—such as the much-discussed Second Life three-dimensional online environment—where fantasy and notions of sex, gender, and identity are fluid and considered a tool or an accessory within different sexually political and sociocapitalist or commodity fetishist agendas. I suggest that some such agendas can involve a cultural perspective on our interpretation of understanding, knowledge, and gender roles played out by different career assignments within *Star Trek*'s Federation. This includes the role portrayed in the popular media of the "scientist," a role in which Seven appears to have some form of fixed identity and purpose.

Sexy Scientists and the Nerdification of the Erotic (or Engineer and Astrometrics Operator . . .)

In her critique of woman-as-scientist in the works of science fiction authors such as Isaac Asimov, Roberts argues that female scientists are described as being "a failure as a woman," a "failure at human relations," and even as "deformed by her intellect."[29] There is evidence of such vulnerability for Seven, when she tries her hand at relationships in the holodeck with Chakotay in "Human Error" (2001)—in much the same way the socially awkward (nerd) Reginald Barclay did in *The Next Generation* episode "Hollow Pursuits" (1990) with Deanna Troi and other members of the crew.

Seven can be seen as the mediation not only of sex, gender, and techno-sexology as mentioned earlier, but also of popular notions of science, intelligence that encompasses arrogance, and a touch of eugenics, with overtones of fascism and racism. However, studies of the sex of scientists in the media found that those portraying key scientific roles were mainly men and that "women scientists are rare and when they do appear, their roles differ greatly to their male colleagues."[30] The *Star Trek* franchise has always broken the mold of the mediated mundane, using its notion of utopia to eradicate bigotry and conflict through "infinite diversity in infinite combinations," developing narratives and characters surrounding gender.[31] Seven is no exception to this rule as she redefines notions of the scientist as mediated in popular culture. Eva Flicker in her writing about scientists compares Haynes's description of the clichéd male scientist in film to that of female scientists. Flicker asserts that Haynes's definitions of the male scientist include being absent-minded, mad, socially displaced, not particularly attractive, obsessive about his work, and even willing to risk humanity. This is contrasted with her definitions resulting from a study of female scientists in feature films. This work revealed six stereotypical representations of the female scientist: the old maid, the male woman, the naïve expert, the evil plotter, the daughter or assistant, and the lonely heroine. In her conclusion, Flicker states:

> The woman scientist tends to differ greatly from her male colleagues in her outer appearance: she is remarkably beautiful and compared with her qualifications, unbelievably young. She has a model's body—thin, athletic, perfect—is dressed provocatively and is sometimes "distorted" by wearing glasses.[32]

Situating Seven as "woman scientist" within the genre of cyberpunk film, literature, and spin-off programs of long-running popular television series such as *The X-Files* (1993–2002), for example, brings short-run and relatively unsuccessful shows like *The Lone Gunmen* (2001) into perspective. The characters of *The Lone Gunmen* brought contemporary notions of public understanding of technophilia to the fore in that the three protagonists in the series were understood to be "nerds" and "geeks."[33] These "Three Stooges" of cyberpunk were Richard "Ringo" Langly, Melvin Frohike, and John Fitzgerald Byers, who appeared to thrive on conspiracy theories, fandom, hacking communication technologies, freak science, and sexual frustration bordering on the desperate. However, the nerd or geek does have its own more contemporary protagonists who happen to be female. One example, I argue, is Abby Sciuto, the eccentric geek/goth forensic scientist from *NCIS: Naval Criminal Investigative Service* (2003–present). She also tends to have the same characteristics as Seven including references to interests in body modification such as tattoos and piercings, with added gothic subcultural references to vampires and Frankenstein. Seven's body modifications are also a statement redolent of similar cultural references. Abby's clothing has sexual subculture associations that show an inclination toward sadomasochism (gaining pleasure from pain), bondage, and fetishism. Seven's catsuit and demeanor in the catsuit alludes to dominance with sadomasochistic overtones and attitudes. Even Abby's taste for popular subcultural music implies identification with the cyborg and Seven—*Brain Matter* and *Android Lust*, among others. Abby also sleeps in a coffin[34]—again an unusual sleeping arrangement like that of Seven, who needs to stand for hours in her regeneration alcove—thus linking the two female scientists within a classic cyberfeminist viewpoint attributing both characters to their cultural roots of vampirism, gothic horror, science "gone wrong," perversion, and what has been described as "the Dark Gift."[35]

I do suggest, though, that this is not simply about an interpretation of women's roles in society, but about various metaphors reflecting contemporary society's lust for technology, and also society's ostracizing of those (nerds) involved with technology and science. In her studies of online forums, Lori Kendall has discussed the identification of the "nerd" or "geek" in terms of hegemonic masculinity. She suggests that "nerdism in both men and women is held to decrease sexual attractiveness, but in men this is compensated by the relatively masculine values attached to intelligence and computer skills. In women, lack of sexual attractiveness is a far greater sin."[36] Characters such as Seven, in popular futuristic narratives, exemplify, manifest, and caricature the "nerdification" or "geekification" of the erotic, turning such an argument on its head. Consequently, Seven encompasses both male and female clichés of the scientist as portrayed in popular culture. Seven also encompasses all the six stereotypical models described by Flicker as well as the majority of attributes belonging to the male scientist as described by Haynes. Seven freely displays elements of both such stereotypes and can effectively be the seducer of (and be seduced by) the characters within the narrative and participate in the immersion of the audience within the fiction. Seven is sexual fetish and anthropological fetish—as magic wand and as the ultimate "phallic woman."[37] She takes us into the *Voyager* universe and convinces us with her machinelike allure and "distorting" but lingering facial Borg apparatus that she is beauty and beast, flesh and machine, warm and cool. It is when such contrasting attributes become comingled that a more interesting reading of Seven begins to surface.

Fetish, Fashion, and Discipline—I Bring Order to Chaos

Seven has been discussed in reference to other female robots/androids in that some of her holographic fantasies have "subtle allusions to *Blade Runner* [1982]"[38] where the visual narratives for Seven in the *Voyager* episode "Human Error" echo those of the replicant Rachael from the classic postmodern science fiction film. Both situations involve playing the piano and nineteenth-century repertoires, etiquette, and situations, and a section of the *Voyager* series soundtrack certainly alludes to and echoes *Blade Runner's* romantic music background track during the love scenes between Rachael and protagonist Deckard. Seven is compared and associated mostly with the replicant Rachael because in "Human Error," Seven creates holographic romantic situations for herself and Chakotay that are reminiscent of scenes between Rachael and Deckard. In these manufactured situations Seven re-creates herself: "Her Borg implants are gone; she has exchanged her 'efficient' cat-suit for a pretty dress; and her lovely hair cascades over her shoulders."[39] The film *Blade Runner* contains deliberate visual references to the retro styling as seen by the exaggerated elements of fashions of 1940s wartime uniforms and other clothing—the protagonist Deckard is well recognized and documented as being modeled on Sam Spade and Phillip Marlowe, the classic private detectives of authors like Raymond Chandler and Dashiell Hammet. This approach has been described as "retrofitting the future,"[40] and for *Blade Runner's* director, Ridley Scott, in a newspaper interview, the work is described as "an extremely dark film, both literally and metaphorically, with an oddly masochistic feel, but he [Scott] explains that he made it in the wake of his elder brother's death and 'I liked the idea of exploring pain.'"[41]

The subtle use of clothing such as the uniform for sexual allure and its association with power is also used in the construction of the characterization of Seven. The uniform becomes body part and Seven's "second skin." In Seven we see the skintight catsuit as part of the cyborg tradition—in this instance the catsuit uniform can be read as some form of "Borg undergarment," revealed once the Borg technological accessories have been removed. We see the ridge of corsetry worn underneath the catsuit, but no visible panty line or folds implying that a brassiere is being worn. This adds to the sleekness of the uniform but also implies that Seven is practically naked and therefore vulnerable. In sociological discussions surrounding the concept of the uniform in the 1970s, it was thought that it traditionally "identifies group members, helps insure that organisational goals will be attained, and orders priorities of group and status demands for the individual."[42] The uniform, then, represents and designates a group that values status and rank and recognizes superiority and inferiority and strict adherence to rules and standardized behavior. The Borg body therefore appears to look uniform, as part of the group hive psychology and the process of assimilation. The Borg's bodily attachments become the emblem of assimilation and therefore are recognized as uniformlike; "in a sense, the uniform becomes the group, and it rather than the group is often the focus of thought and effect."[43] It is this visual "focus of thought and effect" that makes the Borg so convincing and terrifying, and makes Seven's costume so provocative. This also makes the contrast between Seven and the rest of *Voyager*'s crew visually more obvious and contentious. It has been asserted that "an individual's behaviour may reflect favourably or unfavourably upon his uniform rather than upon his group and, in extreme instances, one may 'disgrace the uniform.' Reciprocally, the uniform may enhance or denigrate the honour of its wearer."[44] Part of Seven's problematic search for identity is her self-reflection on notions of Borg group behavior that also involve the integration of the uniform *into* the body. In this sense Seven is self-conscious because "the conformity imposed on a uniform stems from its symbolisation deviations are much more visible when the individual is in uniform."[45] Part of Seven's identity is underdeveloped because of a conflict between her understanding and interpretations of notions of difference. She is constantly trying to bring "order to chaos," a sentiment ordained by the Borg Queen in the *Star Trek* film *First Contact* (1996). In this sense, Seven is not only a phallic woman and a fetish object, but she can also be considered as "deviant" by the very nature of her wearing the bodysuit/Borg uniform that visually encapsulates the combination of the formality and standards of the *Star Trek* Federation with her vulnerability, which is exposed and on display once the intrusion of Borg implants that penetrate the intimate body have been removed.

Seven's bodysuit/uniform also echoes popular cultural attempts at futurology. Her costume reminds us of notions of "futuristic fashion"—a projected technological, deterministic approach in the 1960s experimenting with the appropriation of paper, plastic, rubber, and PVC for clothing.[46] Seven, in what she chooses to wear, manifests notions of ubiquitous computing—an area of cyberculture that discusses the invasive, silent, and stealthy infiltration of computing into our daily lives and mundane activity. Developments such as "smart" clothing are part of such discourse. The 1990s, the time when *Voyager* was being created and broadcast, brought to light the commodity fetish as popular essential technological gadget, giving rise to predictions of technologically assisted and augmented realities and physicalities:

> The "smart" suit and its attendant "smart" objects, by contrast, represent a different type of autonomous commodity—one that concedes the contrived character of its own autonomy. Smart objects enact the commodity fetish for a savvy era: they parody their own autonomy even as they perform it.[47]

Seven is an augmented and embellished metaphor for commodity fetishism and as "smart object," attributable to the rapid development of upgrade culture during the 1990s that appears in this instance to apply sexual attributes to Moore's Law.[48] Not only does this echo the irony of Haraway's Cyborg Manifesto, but Seven becomes a parody and cliché of fetishism and autonomy. In this sense, one particular episode of *Voyager* is an example of such notions of fetishism, sexual attribution, arousal, and fantasy—attributable, it would seem, to the projected fantasies of the audience of the series, as seen in slash fiction, attendance at science fiction and *Trek* conventions, blogs, unofficial fan websites, and the general tone of textual discourse surrounding Seven. Mark Andrejevic argues that "the commodity fetish can only be sustained with the aid of the technology necessary to replace metaphorical fetishes with literal ones."[49] The *Voyager* episode in which Seven is literally a vehicle for fetishism is "Body and Soul" (2000), where Seven and the Doctor interact in a sensuous, slightly disturbing, but also quite humorous crossover of minds into body.

Conclusion: Body and Soul, Seven and Six

In "Body and Soul," Ensign Harry Kim, the holographic Doctor, and Seven are on a routine mission in the *Delta Flyer II* when they are captured by a race known as the Lokirrim. The Lokirrim claim that the Doctor is a dangerous "photonic insurgent," thus identifying holograms as representing a threat. In order to prevent the Doctor's program from being decompiled by the Lokirrim, Seven effectively downloads the Doctor's holographic program into her cortical node. Essentially, the Doctor inhabits Seven's body, with interesting results, an example of the Cartesian consideration that the mind and the body are two separate entities.

As the episode continues, the Doctor, Harry Kim, and Seven of Nine are kept as prisoners of the Lokirrim. By using her Borg implants and the Doctor's mobile holo-emitter, Seven enables the Doctor to inhabit her body, and both Seven and the Doctor experience the pleasures of the flesh—for the first time in some instances. The reactions appear to be symptomatic of projected sexual fantasies surrounding the character of Seven and also symptomatic of exposing her repressed sexual urges and virginal attitudes to intimacy. The Doctor is hugely aroused by this experience; for example, after eating ship's prison rations he states:

> "Mmm! I had no idea that eating was such a sensual experience. The tastes, the textures, feeling it slide down Seven's esophagus, it's, it's exquisite!"
>
> —the Doctor to Harry Kim

> "They're prison rations. My uniform probably tastes better!"
>
> —Harry Kim to the Doctor

In contrast, Seven, on returning drunk from a dinner date, cultivated by the Doctor (in Seven's body) with Ranek the Lokirrim official, feels impaired and abused on uploading the Doctor back to his mobile emitter. She becomes instantly hungover and disgusted:

> "You've been abusing my body."
>
> —Seven to the Doctor

The narrative goes on to explore lesbian, gay, bisexual, and transgender issues surrounding different attractions between Ranek and the Doctor (in Seven's body) when Ranek tries to kiss Seven, and between the Doctor (in Seven's body) and the female Lokirrim lieutenant Jaren when she tries to massage Seven's shoulder; and general indulgences by the Doctor involving Seven's body. One moment implies that the Doctor wishes to touch Seven's breasts. However, when Seven uploads the Doctor back to his holo-emitter, she reiterates to him:

> "You became sexually aroused in my body."
>
> —Seven to the Doctor

The sexual combinations and experimentation with this scenario in particular, and Seven in general, help us to reconsider how sexuality is constructed and portrayed when reflecting on the convergence of technologies of the contemporary media landscape. All things are merging and are interchangeable, including multiple variations and conglomerations of communications, narratives, genres, and broadcast technologies and physical bodies. This could ultimately render novel sexual experimentation and interpretations of perverse subversion as ordinary.

However, this brings into question that beyond the kinky Borgs and ideas of sexy robots, our relationships with them are still changing and developing as new versions of the automaton are created in science fiction futures. Ubiquitous computing and technologies of surveillance are now becoming part of our everyday landscape—and that brings with it further ideas and fears of the kinky Borg and the sexy robot and their associations with danger through sex and death. Notions of the artificial are part of us and hidden within us as body and society. The next robot/cyborg upgrade and society's next mirror on ubiquitous stealth, wrapped in the lure of sexuality, power, and deviance, is the new *Battlestar Galactica*'s reworking of the female Cylon, with one in particular known as Six, who has multiple manifestations. This postmodern Cylon as argued by Susan George contains classic character elements of all female androids and robots that have gone before her; from Maria in the film *Metropolis* (1926) to the "skin-jobs" in *Blade Runner*.[50] This hypersexualized and ultraviolent character in *Battlestar Galactica* also reflects the pervasiveness of technology in society as well as an apparent trepidation to consider life without it. When one of the multiple versions of Six is revealed as the virtual sexual fantasy and immoral conscience of scientist Baltar (the mediation of the scientist stereotype in the television series),[51] she also reveals the scientist's deviated lusts and masochistic subjugation to notions of knowledge and madness, thus giving a more overt sexual reading to the nerdification of the erotic. Finally, we come full circle with the quotation by Zamyatin at the beginning of this chapter:

"Any Number has the right of access to any other Number as sexual product."

Paradoxically then, the character Six from *Battlestar Galactica* can be seen as an upgraded version of the character Seven of Nine from *Voyager* (see Pank and Caro's chapter in this volume), no longer simply nerdifying the erotic, but hypersexualizing and perverting the political, posthuman, and virtual body. However, such characters of science fiction futures interweave and blur boundaries between sex and death; confuse the artifice with the real; pit fear against bravado; reveal the past that influences the future; and also enable us to question our understanding of dominance and submission—and finally review how we mediate truth and propaganda and our relationship with notions of the "Other."

Notes

1. Yevgeny Zamyatin, *We* (London: Penguin Classics, 1993), 22. (First published 1924.)

2. Created by Rick Berman, Michael Piller, and Jeri Taylor; produced by Brannon Braga. CBS Paramount Television, based on Gene Roddenberry's *Star Trek*.

3. Donna Haraway, *Simians, Cyborgs and Women: The Reinvention of Nature* (London: Free Association Books, 1991).

4. Anne Balsamo, *Technologies of the Gendered Body: Reading Cyborg Women* (Durham, NC: Duke University Press, 1996); Mary Anne Doane, "Technophilia: Technology, Representation and the Feminine," in *Body/Politics: Women and the Discourse of Science*, eds. Mary Jacobus, Evelyn Fox Keller, and Sally Shuttleworth (New York and London: Routledge, 1990), 163–76.

5. Jenny Woolmark, ed., *Cybersexualities: A Reader on Feminist Theory, Cyborgs and Cyberspace* (Edinburgh: Edinburgh University Press, 1999).

6. Nadine Wills, "Women in Uniform: Costume and the 'Unruly Woman' in the 1930s Hollywood Musical," in *Continuum: Journal of Media & Cultural Studies* 14, no. 3 (2000): 317–33.

7. Robin Roberts, "The Woman Scientist in *Star Trek: Voyager*," in *Future Females, the Next Generation: New Voices and Velocities in Feminist Science Fiction Criticism*, ed. Marleen S. Barr (Lanham, MD: Rowman and Littlefield, 2000), 277–90; Sarah L. Higley, "Alien Intellect and the Roboticization of the Scientist," *Camera Obscura* 40–41(May 1997): 131–62.

8. Robin Roberts, *Sexual Generations:* "Star Trek: The Next Generation" *and Gender* (Urbana: University of Illinois Press, 1999), 91.

9. The term "robot" is borrowed from Eastern European and Russian roots with marxist and socialist associations. The Czech word *rabota* means "work," the word *rab* means "slave," and the term *robotnik* refers to a peasant or serf. This word supplanted the previous popular term at the time: "automaton."

10. Roberts, *Sexual Generations*, 91.

11. Daniel Dinello, *Technophobia! Science Fiction Visions of Posthuman Technology* (Austin: University of Texas Press, 2005), 144.

12. David Bell and Barbara M. Kennedy, eds., *The Cybercultures Reader*, 2nd ed. (London: Routledge, 2007).

13. Roberts, "The Woman Scientist," 286.

14. Ibid., 290.

15. Michele A. Bowring, "Resistance Is *Not* Futile: Liberating Captain Janeway from the Masculine-Feminine Dualism of Leadership," *Gender, Work and Organisation* 11, no. 4 (2004): 399.

16. During the mid-twentieth century Alberto Vargas, John Willie, Eric Stanton (artists), Irving Klaw (filmmaker), Bunny Yeager (photographer), and Bettie Page (model) created cheesecake bondage imagery that influenced graphics and illustrations of women in positions of dominance and submission. This influence can still be seen in a wide range of graphic styles and erotic publishing today.

17. Mitra C. Emad, "Reading Wonder Woman's Body: Mythologies of Gender and Nation," *Journal of Popular Culture* 39, no. 6 (2006): 954–84.

18. Michael R. Lavin, *Serials Review* 24, no. 2 (1998): 93–98.

19. Bowring, "Resistance Is *Not* Futile," 399.

20. In this instance the fetishism strategy employed by Kaplan is one of what she describes as the "necrophilic principle." This principle is "evoked by the fantasy that living, animate beings are unpredictable and potentially dangerous. They can only be contained by extinguishing their life energies or by transforming them into something dead or inanimate." Louise Kaplan, *Cultures of Fetishism* (Basingstoke, UK: Palgrave Macmillan, 2006), 157.

21. Ibid.

22. Björk, *All is Full of Love*, directed by Chris Cunningham (London: Palm Pictures and EMI Music, 2003).

23. For an overview of how the study of fetishism/perversion and sexology has developed, see the following classical texts: Alfred Binet, "Le fetishisme dans l'amour" (Fetishism in Love), *Revue Philosophie* 24 (1887): 143–67; Richard Von Krafft-Ebbing, "Psychopathia Sexualis," in *Psychopathia Sexualis: The Case Histories* (London: Velvet Publications, 1886 [1997]); Henry Havelock-Ellis, *Studies in the Psychology of Sex*, 7 vols. (1897–1928); Sigmund Freud, *On Sexuality: Three Essays on the Theory of Sexuality*, vol. 7 (London: Penguin Freud Library, 1905 [1991]); Robert J. Stoller, M.D., *Perversion. The Erotic Form of Hatred* (London: Karnac Books, 1975 [1986]).

24. Amanda Fernbach, *Fantasies of Fetishism: From Decadence to the Post-Human* (Edinburgh: Edinburgh University Press, 2002), 37.

25. Lucy Bland and Laura Doan, eds., *Sexology in Culture: Labelling Bodies and Desires* (Cambridge, UK: Polity Press, 1998), 3.

26. Susan A. George, "Fraking Machines: Desire, Gender, and the (Post)Human Condition in *Battlestar Galactica*," in *The Essential Science Fiction Television Reader*, ed. J. P. Telotte (Lexington: University Press of Kentucky, 2008), 160.

27. Bowring examines a particular slash fiction story written by G. L. Dartt (2001) called *Just Between* where Seven has a relationship with Captain Janeway. Bowring studies this piece because "I wanted to explore what would happen to Janeway when she was partnered with a woman whose own gender identity was on the border, was explicitly manufactured. In a sense it is a double subversion." Bowring, "Resistance Is *Not* Futile," 398.

28. Wei Ming Dariotis, "Crossing the Racial Frontier: *Star Trek* and Mixed Heritage Identities," in *The Influence of Star Trek on Television, Film and Culture*, ed. Lincoln Geraghty (Jefferson, NC: McFarland, 2008), 75.

29. Roberts, "The Woman Scientist," 279.

30. Eva Flicker, "Between Brains and Breasts—Women Scientists in Fiction Film: On the Marginalization and Sexualization of Scientific Competence," *Public Understanding of Science* 12, no. 3 (2003): 309–10.

31. Lincoln Geraghty, "Eight Days that Changed American Television: Kirk's Opening Narration," in *The Influence of Star Trek on Television, Film and Culture*, ed. Lincoln Geraghty (Jefferson, NC: McFarland, 2008), 12.

32. Flicker, "Between Brains and Breasts," 316.

33. "The series veers in a different direction, replacing drama with comedy, FBI agents with maladjusted computer geeks, and alien abductions with toilet humor. About the only things remaining are—of-course—government conspiracies and the

dorky hacker trio who made their debut on a favorite episode of the X-Files, then went on to star in several others." Declan McCullagh, "From X-Files to Geek Files," www.wired.com/culture/lifestyle/news/2001/03/42057; www.thelonegunmen.com/.

34. Online, the character Abby describes herself as "a quirky technogeek in the mold of the X-Files' Lone Gunmen, best known for my gothic style of dress, with at least nine tattoos on my neck, arms, back, ankle and other places which are only hinted at; my style of clothing often includes short skirts and platform boots. I sleep in a coffin." www.bebo.com/Profile.jsp?MemberId=7195468269.

35. Allucquère Rosanne Stone, *The War of Desire and Technology at the Close of the Mechanical Age* (Cambridge, MA: MIT Press, 1995), 165.

36. Lori Kendall, "'Oh No! I'm a Nerd!': Hegemonic Masculinity on an Online Forum," *Gender and Society* 14, no. 2 (2000): 265.

37. Diana M. A. Relke, *Drones, Clones and Alpha Babes: Retrofitting Star Trek's Humanism, Post-9/11* (Calgary: University of Calgary Press, 2006), 36.

38. Ibid., 122.

39. Ibid.

40. Judith B. Kerman, *Retrofitting Blade Runner: Issues in Ridley Scott's* Blade Runner *and Philip K. Dick's* Do Androids Dream of Electric Sheep? (Madison: University of Wisconsin Press, 1991).

41. L. Barber, "Scott's Corner," *The Observer*, January 6, 2002, www.guardian.co.uk/film/2002/jan/06/features.awardsandprizes (accessed May 8, 2008).

42. Nathan Joseph and Nicholas Alex, "The Uniform: A Sociological Perspective," *American Journal of Sociology* 77, no. 4 (1972): 719.

43. Ibid., 720.

44. Ibid.

45. Ibid., 723.

46. For an example of "future fashion," see "Space-Age Futurism Fashion Mort Garson 60's," www.youtube.com/watch?v=AA4qGc2z-rs.

47. Mark Andrejevic, "Nothing Comes Between Me and My CPU: Smart Clothes and 'Ubiquitous' Computing," *Theory, Culture and Society* 22, no. 3 (2005): 116.

48. "Intel co-founder Gordon Moore is a visionary. In 1965, his prediction, popularly known as Moore's Law, states that the number of transistors on a chip will double about every two years. And Intel has kept that pace for nearly 40 years." www.intel.com/technology/mooreslaw/index.htm (accessed November 8, 2008).

49. Andrejevic, "Nothing Comes Between Me and My CPU," 117.

50. George, "Fraking Machines," 159–75.

51. Gaius Baltar is the scientist who gave away the human defense system to the Cylons in *Battlestar Galactica*: "Just as Baltar's character mediates various stereotypes of the scientist, the show negotiates popular ideas about science, particularly the notion of science as an instrument of destruction or a path to civilization." Lorna Jowett, "Mad, Bad and Dangerous to Know? Negotiating Stereotypes of Science," in *Cylons in America: Critical Studies in Battlestar Galactica*, ed. Tiffany Potter and C. W. Marshall (New York: Continuum, 2008), 67.

✦⇒

"Welcome to the world of tomorrow!": Animating Science Fictions of the Past and Present in *Futurama*

Lincoln Geraghty

In a quarter-page review of the then forthcoming *Futurama*, created by Matt Groening, *Sight and Sound* described the new series as the "cornerstone of a phalanx of animated half-hour shows" to come from the American network Fox. Not wanting to heap too much praise on the relatively niche animated science fiction series, the review pointed out that *Futurama* "will have its work cut out to match the enduring appeal" of its creator's and network's prestigious and long-running prime-time show, *The Simpsons*. For this review, what might eventually mark the new series as different and worthy of the audience's patience would be what it described as the "right genetic material . . . a cute premise; freeze-frame courting animation, loaded with in-jokes; and a much needed sharp satirical streak."[1] Indeed, this genetic mix seemed to do the trick as *Futurama* was a hit on debut, having the largest ratings of any show premiering in the network's history after *The Simpsons* and topping the demographics, with key age groups choosing to watch the season premiere over similar shows in the same time slot. This success rewarded American networks keen to experiment with form, format, and genre in order to win the prime-time television ratings war. As Wendy Hilton-Morrow and David McMahan emphasize, the series was so successful that Fox decided to move *Futurama* to "Tuesday nights following *The PJs* to reinforce Fox's 'Toon Tuesday' lineup."[2] However, having started in 1999, in 2003 it went the way of many of its contemporaries and was cancelled after four seasons.

Only recently has it been brought back to our TV screens in the form of four feature-length specials in 2008 and 2009.

This chapter analyzes the visual and cultural references at the heart of the *Futurama* narrative. Focusing on genre, animation, parody, and intertextuality, I will highlight how familiar science fiction tropes such as the city, television, technology, and the alien were used and reused throughout the Fox series. Such recycling points on the one hand to generic exhaustion, whereby original representations of the city or technology are no longer possible in a postmodern age, yet it also brings to light the notion of parodic reversion, where familiar elements are redrawn and reinvented for a contemporary audience predisposed to multichannel, multitext television. Despite being a parody, *Futurama* follows in the footsteps of its predecessors in that it "uses its settings in distant times [and] distant planets simply to provide a fresh perspective on the here and now."[3] However, as I will argue in the following pages, parody, animation, and the depictions of aliens and new technologies in a thirty-first-century New York merely allow the series to revisit the science fictions of the past.

Genre, Animation, and Intertextuality

Nichola Dobson calls animated series like *The Simpsons* and *Futurama* "anicoms," differing from their feature-length and seven-minute progenitors "in their employment of live-action narrative conventions commonly associated with sitcom series."[4] *Futurama*, like *The Simpsons*, combines physical comedy with pop culture references and knowing in-jokes. Yet it clearly differs through its specific genre quotations and futuristic setting. As science fiction, the series speculates on what the future might look like by fully embracing the animated form. Being an animated science fiction series, *Futurama* combines both formal and generic intertextual elements. Paul Wells describes animation as "a deeply self-conscious medium . . . when it is not calling attention to the limitations of photographic realism, it is recalling its own codes and conventions and, most significantly, developing new ones."[5] *Futurama* is a show entirely dedicated to going beyond realist depictions of people and place, using animation to visualize the spectacular. It is a "self-reflexive animated cartoon" that draws attention to its animated form by playfully mocking itself, the science fiction genre, and even those in the audience who are keenly aware of the cultural references.[6] Its opening title sequence epitomizes this in its realization of the future New New York with flying cars, comedic billboards, and an enormous elevated television screening a different animated cartoon (from Disney's *Three Little Pigs* to Warner

Brothers' Porky Pig) every episode. The recent feature-length *The Beast with a Billion Backs* (2008) takes this a step further by having the Planet Express Ship crash through the television screen and enter the diegetic world of a black-and-white cartoon; the ship and crew become animated in the style of early Disney, re-creating *Steamboat Willie* (1928) with Leela as Mickey at the helm.[7]

Futurama plays with form and genre for comic effect, yet its intertextual referencing of previous science fiction and animation highlights a fundamental interest in history. Genres, by their very nature, "are related to the processes of remembering and forgetting . . . [they] operate to produce a sense of the past" as they cross between different forms of visual media.[8] In this sense, *Futurama* is not just an "anicom" that parodies prior texts and popular culture; it creates and contributes to the lineage and development of the science fiction genre and draws attention to the cultural processes through which generic definitions and iconic representations are made. As genres develop, according to Dan Harries, they are "constantly in need of redefinition," thus parody "typically emerges when the dynamic nature of the logonomic system [tradition of previous texts and established conventions]" becomes exhausted.[9] However, parodies serve to not only reinvigorate genres but also reaffirm them, "reconstitute as they deflate their targets."[10] This is best exemplified in the episodes that parody *Star Trek*, such as "Why Must I Be a Crustacean in Love?" (2000) and "Where No Fan Has Gone Before" (2002), where *Futurama* clearly acknowledges the cultural significance of the venerable science fiction series but pokes fun at its ancestor's repetitive storylines, cardboard sets, unconvincing aliens, and sometimes overzealous fans. "Why Must I Be a Crustacean in Love?" pays tribute to the famous scene from "Amok Time" (1967), when Spock challenges Kirk to a duel to the death, by pitting Fry and Dr. Zoidberg against each other. However, instead of using the same music and weapons as in the original, the familiar duel melody is played as Zoidberg's national anthem, and both combatants decide not to use the Vulcan *lirpa* (pugil sticks). In "Where No Fan Has Gone Before," Fry determines to retrieve the original seventy-nine *Star Trek* episode tapes that were banished to a forbidden planet when the Church of Trek was outlawed in the twenty-third century. In trying to justify why they should break the law, Fry exclaims to Leela that "the world needs *Star Trek* to give people hope for the future," after which she replies, "But it's set eight hundred years in the past!"[11] Of course, *Star Trek* is not the only text that *Futurama* emphasizes or parodies. The series is in itself a hybrid text that draws together intertextual elements from science fiction, comedy, horror, melodrama, and wider popular culture.

Hybridity and intertextuality are common features of contemporary television programming. Jason Mittell believes that "cases of mixture often foreground generic conventions even more than 'core' examples of a genre, as often unstated generic assumptions rise to the surface through textual juxtapositions, production decisions, and reception controversies."[12] Indeed, the medium of television "brings intertextuality to us" through its televisual flow of multiple texts: from the actual programs to the commercial breaks. As different texts jostle to get the viewer's attention, multiplied by the increase in digital and satellite channels, the boundaries between texts and their interpretations remain open and incomplete—leaving room for exploitation, reinflection, and parodic subversion.[13] *Futurama*'s interest in the televisual flow and actual process of watching and interacting with multiple television texts—for example, the television parodies, Fry continually watching or referring to TV, and the many fake promo spots that interrupt the opening and end credits—is emblematic of contemporary television's hyper-intertextuality. Bogus advertisements for products such as Molten Boron, Arachno Spores, Thompson's Teeth, or Glagnar's Human Rinds that supposedly sponsor some of the aired episodes visually call attention not only to the genre and futuristic setting but also the format and processes of television broadcasting and its financing.

The City: Imagining New New York

Fritz Lang's New York–inspired *Metropolis* (1926) has become the prototype for modern depictions of the urban landscape, with the consequence that the city in science fiction is now largely the signifier of a dystopian future since *Metropolis* blamed technology, bureaucrats, scientists, and machinery for humanity's moral failures and the continued subjugation of the working class. Contemporary critics' fondness for claiming *Metropolis* as progenitor of the archetypal science fiction cityscape (see, for example, *Blade Runner*, 1982) is not unwarranted; nevertheless, other films such as *Things to Come* (1936) and *Just Imagine* (1930) offered viewers more than just a futuristic, dystopian city. In a genre that frequently hails postmodern dystopian cities as humanity's inevitable habitat—other examples include *A Clockwork Orange* (1971), *THX-1138* (1971), *Logan's Run* (1976), *1984* (1984), and *Brazil* (1985)—films like *Things to Come* challenge this negative attitude and in fact speculate that the modern city is only the launchpad to a wider, brighter world; science, and those who can master it, will take humans to the stars. Likewise, *Futurama*'s envisioning of New New York fits into a more utopian model of the science fiction city. Inhabitants are largely well-off, buildings and transport are designed to make life as easy as possible, and there are clear allusions to contemporary bureaucratic infrastructures such as local government, commerce, education, and welfare. However, setting the series in a future version of New York does raise some important questions relating to how the genre has imagined the city historically and to what extent New York itself, or even a temporally specific depiction of it, has become the template for representing the urban in both film and television.

Cities provide not only a physical backdrop but also "the literal premises for the possibilities and trajectory of narrative action."[14] The urban science fiction experience as portrayed in film from the 1950s to the present day, according to Vivian Sobchack, offers a "historical trajectory—one we can pick up at a generic moment that marks the failure of modernism's aspirations in images that speak of urban destruction and emptiness and that leads to more contemporary moments marked by urban exhaustion, postmodern exhilaration, and millennial vertigo."[15] Indeed, the ways we have imagined our fictional cities are clear indicators of how we continue to interact with the changing urban landscape. *Futurama*'s New York is a mixture of modernist iconography, with its skyscrapers and elevated pneumatic transportation tubes, and of postmodern decay, with its subterranean levels home to a mutant civilization living off the unwanted debris from above. The series' name is an obvious indicator of its modernist roots: the General Motors Futurama exhibit at the 1939 New York World's Fair was designed to show the world what New York could look like in the not-too-distant future. The exhibit gave people "the opportunity to enter the world of 1960. For Futurama [modeled by the industrial designer Norman Bel Geddes] culminated in a life-size intersection of a city of tomorrow, complete with advanced-model autos (and an auto showroom), an apartment house, a theater, and a department store."[16] As J. P. Telotte surmises, those visitors to the exhibit must have felt as if they had walked onto the set of the latest science fiction film.

Futurama's aboveground New New York clearly adheres to Bel Geddes' modernist vision as it emphasizes convenient transport, entertainment, and consumption. In the opening title sequence of the first episode, "Space Pilot 3000" (1999), we see inhabitants (including some of the main characters) being whisked around the city through pneumatic tubes and goods being shipped around in hovercars; buildings are covered in holographic billboards advertising the latest food product or technical gadget; and the large television screen into which the Planet Express Ship crashes shows cartoons from the twentieth century. The scene immediately following the end of the opening credits shows Fry peering out in wonder at the busy and bustling city, with the cryogenic technician theatrically calling out, "Welcome to the world of tomorrow! . . . Come, your destiny awaits!" New New York, like those cities in *Metropolis* and *Just Imagine*, is an ordered hierarchy of capitalist activity, with workers traveling to work and goods being shipped to stores high up among the skyscrapers. The ground is missing from this first encounter, although much of the narrative action in the series takes place either at ground level or below it. Nevertheless, the city of skyscrapers presented in the opening credits mirrors the futurist interpretations of modern urban life where artists such as Umberto Boccioni "sought to capture the overall sensual cacophony of urban life and the way its varied forces interpenetrated one another."[17] The real New York, as the template for the future city, has "inspired an ambition to see it all and catch its essence" more than any other city; the challenge to artists, photographers, filmmakers, and architects, according to Douglas Tallack, was to "explore how, visually, *part* and *whole* relate or fail to relate when limited, local perspective on the city is chosen or accepted, and what to make of this relationship."[18] *Futurama* does this through its intertextual referencing of previous futuristic depictions of the city (New York in science fiction film and at the World's Fair) and through its use of generic signifiers such as hovercars, fluorescent billboards, and ultrafast forms of human transportation.

Beneath the city, Old New York continues to rot and decay; New New York has been built on top of the crumbled remains of what once was a famous skyline. In "The Luck of the Fryish" (2001), Fry goes down to the depths to search for his beloved lucky seven-leaf clover. Not only does he find his old neighborhood and house in Brooklyn but his basement is amazingly intact, including his Ronco Record Vault, where he hid the lucky clover from his brother in the 1980s. Icons of the old city remain: yellow taxis lie in the street, Fry spots the bench and fire hydrant he used to play on during the summer months, and even one of his old neighbors still lives on his street—albeit a mutated version living in the sewer. Images of the destroyed city are frequent in science fiction, whether the city is destroyed through war, alien invasion, or simply the ravages of time.[19] Sobchack calls this visual decay "a response to the failure of the city's aspiration (and to the failure of 'modern' civilization)" and sees these characteristics employed in the nihilistic films of the 1970s such as *Soylent Green* (1973), where New York "no longer aspires but suffocates and expires."[20] What is interesting in this episode, however, is that Fry finds a statue of his dead nephew (although he does not know this at the time), which starts him on a journey to discover that his brother found the lucky clover and passed it on to his son, who would grow up to become a famous rock star, businessman, philanthropist, and the first person to set foot on Mars—things that Fry had always aspired to do and become. While Old New York symbolizes the suffocating life Fry left behind in the twentieth century, where his brother bullied him and his parents ignored him, the uncovered history of his nephew's life reassures him that his original unrealized aspirations were achievable, even though his childhood was not the most enjoyable time in his life. Of course, Fry is the lucky one since he has woken up in the year 3000 to start a brand-new life in the future. However, this connection to a life he missed out on does help to give meaning to his newfound existence in the thirty-first century—he is no longer a man out of time.

There is another city beneath the crumbling Old New York; this city is inhabited by mutants who survive by recycling the waste of people living above in the technological paradise of New New York. These mutants resemble the surviving humans found in the subterranean depths of New York in *Beneath the Planet of the Apes* (1970). In "I Second That Emotion" (1999), a visual in-joke shows that they worship an unexploded nuclear bomb similar to that seen in the *Planet of the Apes* sequel. Everything that New New York flushes down into the sewers becomes part of this moldering and polluted city. It is a dump, representative of the cluttered "junkyard futurism" envisioned in the postmodern cities of *Escape from New York* (1981) and *Repo Man* (1984), where "the dregs of bourgeois society," such as "the punks, winos, crazies," and now mutants, exist "marginalized and disenfranchised."[21] We see in "Leela's Homeworld" (2002) that mutants have no rights, even when Professor Farnsworth dumps toxic waste into the sewers. *Futurama* noticeably plays off the visual degradation and decay seen in its science fiction forebears and likewise juxtaposes this vision of the mutated, yet exoticized, city with the tall skyscrapers and flying cars above. Yet, not only is this sewer city a consequence of constant recycling but so too is the entire series, as it continually reclaims images and narrative structures already familiar to science fiction audiences. For Wheeler Winston Dixon, contemporary culture appears tired of life as "signs of exhaustion appear everywhere."[22] We are no longer capable of imagining what the future may look like or bring, therefore we are reliant on recycling the stories and visual spectacles of the past.

Technology: Celebrating the Future

Technology, our relationship with it, and the potential for both human progress and destruction have been enduring concerns throughout the history of the science fiction genre. *Futurama* plays on this generic preoccupation with aplomb: Earth in the future is a technocratic paradise where scientists have created every type of machine possible so as to make daily life easier. Robots and machines permeate all aspects of human life; most robots are in fact sentient beings that have lives of their own and participate in the same routines as humans and other aliens. Yet the potential for technology running amok and destroying human civilization is regularly lampooned in the series; such consideration of this persistent fear indicates *Futurama*'s faithfulness to the genre. In "Mother's Day" (2000), for example, Mom, the creator of all robots, attempts to take over the world by initiating their "rebel" program:

> You've noticed I design all my robots with antennas. Everyone thinks it's to make them look more science fiction-y . . . but the antennas are really for my universal robot controller.

Attention is drawn to the iconography of the robot design by Mom's comment about the "science fiction-y" antenna, but so too is another icon of the genre: the mad scientist. Mad scientists, according to Andrew Tudor, "devotedly and misguidedly seek knowledge purely for its own sake" and often "want no more than to rule the world." They are driven and entirely "volitional" in their actions.[23] The archetypal mad scientist would be the evil genius Rotwang, from *Metropolis*, or indeed Mary Shelley's Frankenstein.[24] After Mom activates the antennas, machines start to rebel: the coffeemaker stops making coffee, an electronic Mother's Day card becomes a militant revolutionary, the office stapler staples Hermes to the floor, and, most galling of all, the television gets up, grows legs, and kicks Fry in the shin. This pun on how the media can be blamed for making robots more violent, where the TV literally rises up and attacks the one person who loves the medium the most, is another example of *Futurama*'s self-reflexivity.

Television is the most dominant medium in the series, with the Internet only occasionally providing virtual reality entertainment, as seen in "A Bicyclops Built for Two" (2000). TV programming has not changed much by the year 3000; news, ads, and soap operas (such as the robot soap *All My Circuits*) are still popular and regularly attract the employees of Planet Express to the sofa. M. Keith Booker describes how "[the show comments] directly on popular culture and other aspects of our contemporary world [yet also] includes a sort of indirect commentary in the way it represents popular culture as having changed very little in a thousand years."[25] As an icon of science fiction itself, J. P. Telotte notes that "before becoming a fixture in American homes and a purveyor of its own brand of science fiction" television was more familiar to audiences who grew up watching classics such as *Metropolis*, *Things to Come*, and *Modern Times* (1935).[26] These films represented the medium "optimistically, as a kind of ultimate communication device, but also more darkly, as a means of surveillance, a tool of deception, even a potentially deadly force."[27] Exemplified in "Mother's Day," TV not only serves as the fount of all knowledge for Fry and the others but also attacks them. Likewise, in every episode's opening title sequence, television is placed as a potentially threatening force on top of a skyscraper, acting, as it did in many early science fiction films, "as a component in a panopticon culture" looking over a futuristic city.[28] *Futurama*'s warnings about the dangers of television can be interpreted as satirical in-jokes included by Groening and the writers in their continued attempts to confront their critics, those being the same ones who derided *The Simpsons* for its supposed vulgar and childish humor during its first few years on air. The iconic nature of the medium as highlighted within *Futurama* not only points to an intertextual awareness of its animated ancestors but also indicates the genre's continued thematic concern with technology and its relationship to society.

Society's faith in the possibilities and wonders of space travel made possible by advances in technology is largely an American science fiction trope, an extension of the national obsession with the frontier—one need not go further than *Star Trek* to see this played out on television. Both *Futurama* and *Star Trek* are progressive in their representation of technology; humans are freed from the constraints imposed on them through lack of technological and scientific knowledge. In *Futurama* people (and indeed robots) rely on machines, inventions, and gadgets for the most routine, mundane, or pointless activities such as Professor Farnsworth's "fing-longer" (a device to press out-of-reach buttons) in "Anthology of Interest, Part 1" (2000) or his machine that makes a "glow-in-the-dark nose you can wear over your regular nonglowing nose" in "Leela's Homeworld." This technological overreliance clearly takes inspiration from the surplus of American science fiction films and television series released in the 1950s where labor-saving devices, robots, weapons, and spaceships were central themes that made the genre even more popular with audiences.

However, these media texts were themselves informed by the technological innovations and increased production of consumable goods resulting from the battle between the U.S. and the Soviet Union in the space race and cold war. Humble advances in domestic appliance technology, kitchens controlled by computers, and home intercom systems became important symbols of American dominance in science and technology. The so-called Kitchen Debate in 1959, when Vice President Richard Nixon traveled to Moscow to meet Nikita Khrushchev at the American Exhibition, symbolized America's drive to outdo the USSR on all technological fronts, both planetary and domestic: "The latest in kitchen consumerism stood for the basic tenets of the

American way of life. Freedom. Freedom from drudgery for the housewife. And democracy, the opportunity to choose."[29] New technologies, whether the simple electric can opener or the most advanced space rocket, were a sign of national and human achievement. The future depicted in *Futurama* not only acknowledges this reality through the abundance of spaceships, useless Farnsworth inventions, and multitude of labor-saving robots, but also illustrates that how we imagine such technological advancement has not progressed much beyond the genre's early visualizations of the future made popular in the B movies of the 1950s. Indeed, this commodification of the past indicates a cultural engagement with nostalgia so intimate and impervious that, as Fredric Jameson has pointed out regarding the postmodern condition, "we are unable today to focus on our own present, as though we have become incapable of achieving aesthetic representations of our current experience."[30]

Professor Farnsworth's most useful and important invention is in fact the Planet Express Ship, the vehicle in which Leela, Fry, and Bender travel through space and deliver packages. Capable of warp speed, filled with technical gadgets, and even given its own personality (voiced by Sigourney Weaver) in "Love and Rocket" (2002),[31] the ship resembles the retro interstellar rockets from the golden age of science fiction.[32] Like the cars in the 1950s, its outline and tail fins are expressions of motion through design, symbols of the technological optimism of the space age where automobiles stood in as suburban replicas of the rockets that shot into space. Phallic symbols of technology, cars were representations of what Karal Ann Marling terms "autoeroticism," whereby America's love for the automobile, its convenience and style, were hailed as aspirational consumables. Every home had to have one as "the purchaser of an automobile was no longer paying for a mere piece of machinery. He (and, increasingly, she) was buying a brand new life. High style. Sex. Social standing. A rocket to the moon."[33] A visual trope of the science fiction genre, dating back to Georges Méliès' 1902 silent classic, *Trip to the Moon* (*Le voyage dans la lune*), the space rocket, and the influx of cinematic and televisual spacecraft that to follow, including Planet Express Ship, symbolize both the genre's fascination for technical gadgetry and special effects and also Western culture's fetishization of technological consumption: "Spaceships are the emblems of the technology that produces them; a technology of cultural reproduction, rather than science."[34] As all ships, vehicles, and rockets in *Futurama* conform to this definition, it is no wonder that the series is more backward looking in its signification of the future than forward looking in its commentary on how humans will continue to relate to technology beyond the twenty-first century.

Alien Invasion: Meeting the Neighbors

Clearly aliens are a key component of the *Futurama* universe. From Kif and Dr. Zoidberg to Hypnotoad and Morbo the maniacal newsreader, the abundance of alien characters not only draws attention to the absurdities of human behavior but also reminds the audience of the continued fascination for the extraterrestrial in contemporary popular culture. By the year 3000, aliens have become integral members of the Earth's population; performing menial jobs, serving in the armed forces, and being minor television celebrities are just a few of the occupations that aliens enjoy while living among humans. In effect, the multicultural, extraterrestrial community of New New York parallels the future envisioned by Gene Roddenberry in the *Star Trek* universe where humans and aliens live and work together in peace: The Democratic Order of Planets (DOOP) replicates *Star Trek*'s Federation as the institution that binds together aliens and people from across the galaxy. Cultural, ethnic, and biological differences are ignored as the positive benefits of first contact with aliens are played out for laughs in each episode. However, it is partly for these reasons the episodes "When Aliens Attack" (1999) and "The Problem with Popplers" (2000) stand out, as they noticeably disregard the utopian ethos of *Star Trek* and instead portray the extraterrestrial as the invading alien so familiar to the science fiction B movies of the 1950s.

In "When Aliens Attack," the alien invaders are large green monsters that come from the planet Omicron Persei 8, led by Lrrr and his wife Ndnd, yet they do not come to Earth to steal its resources or even force the most intelligent humans to pair off and mate continuously—as Professor Farnsworth remembers about the previous alien invasion. The Omicronians threaten to destroy the Earth because they didn't get to see the season finale of *Single Female Lawyer*, a twentieth-century TV series (a mocking reference to the then successful *Ally McBeal*) that Fry accidentally destroyed by spilling beer on the console during its original transmission. Lrrr and the Omicronians' first target is Monument Beach, where famous landmarks from across the globe have been transplanted to decorate the coastline near New New York. As the saucers descend, they destroy the Leaning Tower of Pisa and Big Ben and, in homage to the scenes of destruction in *Independence Day* (1996), the White House is obliterated from above by a single laser. This visual gag not only refers to *Independence Day*'s pioneering use of new CGI and special effects techniques to depict the destruction of Washington, D.C., but also alludes to what Michele Pierson calls the "retrofuturist turn in the latter half of the 1990s," where new animating technologies and visual effects were employed in film to build up scenes of cities and the future while also being used to tear them down in spectacular scenes of annihilation.[35] The monuments are simply cannon fodder for the alien invasion. While *Futurama*'s vision of the future draws upon "older science-fiction movie tropes," like contemporary science fiction film their use in this episode seems "temporally rootless and spatially disaffected." Indeed, unlike the cities under threat in 1950s B movies, these monuments now "exist only for destruction" and parody.[36]

"The Problem with Popplers" sees the return of Lrrr and the Omicronians after humans have become addicted to eating the Omicronian young found on their nursery planet by Leela, Fry, and Bender. The young resemble "fried shrimp" and the crew decides to bring them back to Earth and market them as Popplers, eventually selling the brand to Fishy Joe's (the leading fast-food chain, with a franchise on every planet—except for McPluto). Leela discovers that the Popplers are infants when one of them calls her "Mom," thus inspiring her to campaign for their freedom, but the Omicronians invade and demand a human sacrifice to make up for the 198 billion Popplers/infants eaten by humans. Lrrr threatens total destruction of the Earth if Leela is not brought to justice for being the first to eat their young. In an attempt to save Leela, Brannigan swaps her for an orangutan with a purple wig and eye patch before the ceremonial sacrifice begins. After the swap fails, Leela is eventually saved by Jurr, the first Poppler to talk, who pleads with his father to have mercy and make peace with humans, asking the Omicronians in the audience, "Are we no better than them?" The human condition in this episode is visualized through alien invasion brought about by human greed and gluttony, the only threat to humanity therefore being ourselves. The lessons of aliens and humans "getting along" and understanding "cultural differences" are made obvious using the familiar philosophical debates surrounding vegetarianism and animal rights and are communicated through the medium of television. Both alien invasion episodes, like in most of *Futurama*, portray television as both savior and foe. Fry and his friends need to re-create the last episode of *Single Female Lawyer* to convince Lrrr that Earth must be saved, even though as a formulaic, trashy series it was clearly not worth saving back in the twentieth century. Likewise, using television to broadcast Leela's sacrifice to the Omicronians, TV is used by the young Jurr to bring a message of peace at the same time as it resembles how the medium was conceived by spectacular blood sport science fiction films such as *Rollerball* (1975) and *Death Race 2000* (1975)—as a transmitter of capitalist violence and unashamed consumerism.

Mark Jancovich points out that most critics of the 1950s invasion narratives see them as inextricably linked to cold war ideology, so that the alien was code for the imminent Communist threat.[37] American films of the decade, this critical orthodoxy claims, demonized both the Soviet Union and any resistance to the status quo, ensuring that the institutions and authorities of the country were protected from the so-called Red menace that was spreading across the nation. By pulling together, Americans were given two choices: either support America or be seen as a Communist sympathizer. The result of this distinction meant that there was a clear line between right and wrong, America and the alien other.[38] However, as Jancovich contends, American culture was itself going through an identity crisis, so that the threat posed by the Communist as *alien* was often little more than a code for developments *within* American society. If the alien often presented a horde of mindless conformity that threatened to overwhelm America, the so-called suburban dream was itself often accused of being a threat to individual identity. The image of the middle class male was one of uniformity: they commuted to work en masse dressed in their grey flannel suits, and returned home to their idealized, yet all-too-similar, modern suburban homes. The technological advancement of consumer culture that had promised so much was instead stifling Americans' own self-worth.

Futurama may not be informed by these cultural and social concerns identified by Jancovich and prevalent in science fiction B movies of the 1950s, but clearly the series is making some allusions to the threat from the conformity and uniformity imposed by television, popular culture, and the technologies that drive them. For example, the Omicronians travel a thousand light-years to see the end of a dire TV series from the 1990s and New New Yorkers are addicted to the fast-food craze created by Popplers. Despite the contradictory reasons for America's feeling of vulnerability in the 1950s, the alien, its desire to conquer Earth, and its technological preeminence were common themes in the films of that decade and are science fiction tropes that provide much latitude for televisual parody. *The Day the Earth Stood Still* (1951), *War of the Worlds* (1953), *Invaders from Mars* (1953), *Invasion of the Body Snatchers* (1956), and many more presented America and the world in the grip of emergency—emergencies "that jeopardized the future of the race; they were not national, nor even international, but planetary."[39] Unlike television at that time, film was able to take on ambitious projects showing humanity at the brink of destruction using Technicolor, Cinemascope, and 3-D technologies. As a result, the threat of the alien was intensified on the big screen during the 1950s and television's contribution to the genre was largely postponed until the beginning of the 1960s.[40] Today, however, when televised science fiction has overtaken film in portraying believable future and alternative worlds, *Futurama* uses television to both critique and lampoon the state of the human race in the thirty-first century. It focuses on the alien invasion narrative exactly because that has long been a signifier for our ever-changing relationship with technology, the things we consume, and the communities in which we live.

Futurama combines genre and parody while offering a critique of contemporary culture and the technologies that continue to mediate that culture. It reuses and reinvents many of the tropes and icons of the science fiction genre but it also emulates television's fondness for self-reflection, hybridity, and intertextuality. One of the reasons for its cancellation may simply have been that it had referenced the entire science fiction lexicon; however, this would not account for the fact that parody encourages reinvention above exhaustion. The film, animation, and television references already familiar to an audience inundated by a televisual flow of texts and images might have gone unnoticed save for the fact that, thanks to its animated form, *Futurama* made the invisible visible. Its animation literally drew attention to generic elements such as the city, technology, and alien invasion that inform the comic narrative. How we interpret those tropes and visual signifiers is heavily dependent on the cultural contexts in which they were created; therefore, how they were designed and referred to in the period in which they were becoming science fiction icons in their own right—the late 1950s and early 1960s—is crucial to our understanding of *Futurama*. This was an era that saw a huge proliferation of science fiction film and television in conjunction with massive growth in new domestic and entertainment technologies; it is no wonder that *Futurama* harks back most to this period. *Futurama* was the product of a network and competitive industry struggling to keep up with advances in format and broadcasting technology; however, its primary concern was to use those new technologies and techniques in order to imagine the future by revisiting the past.

Notes

1. "Futurama," *Sight and Sound* 9 (June 1999): 28. *Futurama* was in fact created and developed by Groening and executive producer David X. Cohen, who also worked on *The Simpsons*.

2. Wendy Hilton-Morrow and David T. McMahan, "*The Flintstones* to *Futurama*: Networks and Prime Time Animation," in *Prime Time Animation: Television Animation and American Culture*, ed. Carol A. Stabile and Mark Harrison (London and New York: Routledge, 2003), 86.

3. M. Keith Booker, *Science Fiction Television* (Westport, CT: Praeger, 2004), 176.

4. Nichola Dobson, "Nitpicking 'The Simpsons': Critique and Continuity in Constructed Realities," *Animation Journal* 11 (2003): 85.

5. Paul Wells, *Understanding Animation* (London: Routledge, 1998), 182–83.

6. The self-reflexive animated cartoon is defined in Terrance R. Lindvall and J. Matthew Melton, "Towards a Post-Modern Animated Discourse: Bakhtin, Intertextuality and the Cartoon Carnival," in *A Reader in Animation Studies*, ed. Jayne Pilling (London: John Libbey, 1997), 203–20.

7. On the DVD commentary, director Pete Avanzino discusses how the original storyboard for this sequence was designed by Stephen DeStefano, comic book artist and *Popeye* historian—no surprise, therefore, that the animation bears some resemblance to the Fleischer Brothers' work.

8. Lincoln Geraghty and Mark Jancovich, "Introduction: Generic Canons," in *The Shifting Definitions of Genre: Essays on Labeling Films, Television Shows and Media*, ed. Lincoln Geraghty and Mark Jancovich (Jefferson, NC: McFarland Publishers, 2008), 12.

9. Dan Harries, *Film Parody* (London: BFI, 2000), 37.

10. Geoff King, *Film Comedy* (London: Wallflower Press, 2002), 114.

11. For an analysis of how *Star Trek* has been parodied in wider popular culture, see Lincoln Geraghty, *Living with Star Trek: American Culture and the Star Trek Universe* (London: I. B. Tauris, 2007).

12. Jason Mittell, *Genre and Television: From Cop Shows to Cartoons in American Culture* (New York: Routledge, 2004), xii–xiii.

13. Jonathan Gray, *Watching with The Simpsons: Television, Parody, and Intertextuality* (New York: Routledge, 2006), 78–79.

14. Vivian Sobchack, "Cities on the Edge of Time: The Urban Science-Fiction Film," in *Alien Zone II: The Spaces of Science Fiction Cinema*, ed. Annette Kuhn (London: Verso, 1999), 123.

15. Ibid., 124.

16. J. P. Telotte, *A Distant Technology: Science Fiction Film and the Machine Age* (Middletown, CT: Wesleyan University Press, 1999), 162.

17. Ben Highmore, *Cityscapes: Cultural Readings in the Material and Symbolic City* (London: Palgrave, 2005), 142.

18. Douglas Tallack, *New York Sights: Visualizing Old and New New York* (Oxford: Berg, 2005), 84. Italics mine.

19. Science fiction, for Susan Sontag, is fundamentally about the visualization of disaster. See Susan Sontag, "The Imagination of Disaster," in *Liquid Metal: The Science Fiction Film Reader*, ed. Sean Redmond (London: Wallflower, 2004), 40–47.

20. Sobchack, "Cities on the Edge of Time," 132–33.

21. Ibid., 134.

22. Wheeler Winston Dixon, *Visions of Apocalypse: Spectacles of Destruction in American Cinema* (London: Wallflower, 2003), 1.

23. Andrew Tudor, *Monsters and Mad Scientists: A Cultural History of the Horror Movie* (Oxford: Basil Blackwell, 1989), 133.

24. See Christopher Frayling, *Mad, Bad and Dangerous? The Scientist and the Cinema* (London: Reaktion Books, 2005), 60–108.

25. M. Keith Booker, *Drawn to Television: Prime-Time Animation from The Flint-stones to Family Guy* (Westport, CT: Praeger, 2006), 122–23.

26. J. P. Telotte, "Lost in Space: Television as Science Fiction Icon," in *The Essential Science Fiction Television* Reader, ed. J. P. Telotte (Lexington: University Press of Kentucky, 2008), 37.

27. Ibid., 37–38.

28. Ibid., 42.

29. Karal Ann Marling, *As Seen on TV: The Visual Culture of Everyday Life in the 1950s* (Cambridge, MA: Harvard University Press, 1994), 243.

30. Fredric Jameson, "Postmodernism and Consumer Society," in *The Anti-Aesthetic: Essays on Postmodern Culture*, ed. Hal Foster (Port Townsend, WA: Bay Press, 1983), 117.

31. In "Love and Rocket," the Planet Express Ship falls in love with Bender after having new emotion and personality software installed by Professor Farnsworth. Initially the ship is coded as male but after Bender tweaks a few knobs the ship becomes female (denoted by Weaver's voice), and the two embark on a heated love affair—until Bender cheats on her. This emotional trauma tips the ship into madness, and the episode becomes homage to *2001: A Space Odyssey* (1968) with Leela, Fry, and Bender playing the astronauts in distress as they attempt to deactivate Planet Express Ship's central brain.

32. For a descriptive account of the evolution of the rocket, see Samantha Holloway, "Space Vehicles and Traveling Companions: Rockets and Living Ships," in *The Essential Science Fiction Television Reader*, ed. J. P. Telotte (Lexington: University Press of Kentucky, 2008), 177–80.

33. Marling, *As Seen on TV*, 136–37.

34. Adam Roberts, *Science Fiction* (London: Routledge, 2000), 154.

35. Michele Pierson, *Special Effects: Still in Search of Wonder* (New York: Columbia University Press, 2002), 132.

36. Sobchack, "Cities on the Edge of Time," 139.

37. Mark Jancovich, *Rational Fears: American Horror in the 1950s* (Manchester: Manchester University Press, 1996), 15.

38. See Patrick Lucanio, *Them or Us: Archetypal Interpretations of Fifties Alien Invasion Films* (Bloomington: Indiana University Press, 1987).

39. Peter Biskind, *Seeing is Believing: How Hollywood Taught Us to Stop Worrying and Love the Fifties* (London: Bloomsbury, 2000), 102.

40. J. P. Telotte, *Science Fiction Film* (Cambridge: Cambridge University Press, 2001), 95.

PART IV

VISIONS AND REVISIONS

Cast of *Battlestar Galactica* (2003–2009). *Courtesy of The Kobal Collection.*

CHAPTER TEN

Plastic Fantastic? Genre and Science/Technology/Magic in *Angel*

Lorna Jowett

The look and style of a television show has various functions, but in relation to the fantastic genres, one function is to make the abstract concrete, or to realize the fantastic. *Angel* (1999–2004) realizes the fantastic through visual images that draw on established conventions (from genre, television, and cinema) and has been examined as a superhero drama, a version of noir, a lawyer show, an example of TV horror, a vampire fiction, a critical dystopia, and even a musical. What I wish to explore here is not genre hybridity per se but the ways in which different genres are used in the show's representation of science and technology and of magic. Michele Pierson suggests that in science fiction cinema, groundbreaking "effects sequences featuring CGI commonly exhibit a mode of spectatorial address that . . . solicits an attentive and even contemplative viewing of the computer-generated image."[1] I will argue that in the case of *Angel*, spectacle may draw the viewer into looking, but attention is directed explicitly to the conventions that construct the image, highlighting form and theme. Moreover, adapting Bruce Isaacs's reworking of the concept of genericity to television, *Angel* and telefantasy employ "self-awareness and exhibition of generic components" that can offer an additional "'cultural charge' to the spectator."[2] Tammy Kinsey, discussing transitions in *Angel*, describes a scene from "Ground State" (2002) where Cordelia is surveying Los Angeles as a Higher Being. The camera zooms out from a close-up of her eye to a panoramic cityscape near the beginning of the episode and back again at its conclusion in "a cinematic gesture that suggests the value of shifting frames of reference."[3] In this chapter, I will argue that *Angel* always values shifting frames of reference because it visualizes fantastic elements in relation to its primary concerns via a range of conventions (or frames of reference).

Television and the Fantastic

Viewers are increasingly aware that visual images in television are manufactured via camera, editing, lighting, costume, makeup, and special effects, including CGI. Today, a wealth of sources help explain this process: museum exhibits, DVD extras or special editions, and "making of" documentaries, among others. All televisual images are constructed, but some television more obviously announces itself as artificial because it does not aim for verisimilitude. While it has often been assumed that fantastic genres lack realism by definition, television (or cinema) that falls into these categories and therefore relies on visuals to realize the fantastic is, by necessity, producing a level of realism. The "prevailing realist aesthetic" identified by some in *Star Trek*[4] and seen more recently in *Battlestar Galactica* (2003–2009) is a convention of the science fiction genre that seeks to ground fantastic elements in a constructed material reality, and to foreground psychological or emotional realism, to tell familiar human stories (even if characters are not strictly human) (see Pank and Caro's chapter in this volume). In this sense, telefantasy need not devalue narrative or character (a criticism often leveled at spectacular cinema). On the contrary, these can be integral to the success of serial television.

Discussing the aesthetics of *Buffy the Vampire Slayer* (1997–2005), Matthew Pateman describes how culture is "dominated by niche markets that require clearly defined objects of consumption that conform to preestablished modes of expression" so "the eclectic-minded (or genre-busting) product is a welcome and necessary antidote."[5] Quality television is valued by viewers and critics alike for its difference, yet scholars and audiences are also aware that both *Buffy* and *Angel* draw on and develop a familiar televisual aesthetic (styles and conventions common to television drama). In her history of telefantasy, Catherine Johnson notes how "the representation of the fantastic in *The X-Files* offered the possibility for the visual flourishes and stylistic distinctiveness which were particularly valuable for Fox as markers of difference and indicators of quality."[6] Genre can be seen as an organizational aesthetic too (involving repetition, innovation, and quotation) and it makes genre products familiar, and marketable, to the audience. A text offering a "spectacle aesthetic" builds a particular relationship with the audience, and Isaacs suggests that the viewer will "appreciate it as a reproduction, or simulation, of prior textual forms."[7] Thus, like *The X-Files* and *Buffy*, *Angel* offers a distinctive visual style, partly produced through color, lighting, and editing, but also through its recombination of recognizable genre elements. Its title sequence, for example, draws on superhero texts (especially Batman), noir, and horror, focusing on the mean streets of L.A. and the dark hero who watches over them. The way in which genre and intertextual elements are constituted provides the distinctiveness required of a commercial product and the originality desired in quality television.

Discussing science fiction's lack of fixed iconography, Vivian Sobchack suggests that "it is the very plasticity of objects and settings in SF films which help define them as science fiction, and not their consistency."[8] Developing this notion, telefantasy like *Angel* adapts genre conventions and brings them into productive tension with each other: they interact and become more plastic in a strategy that enables continued novelty within serial form (a heightening of genre's repetition-innovation-quotation). Furthermore, Pateman argues that "*Buffy* . . . provides the veneer of a realistic technique in order that this formal pastiche can elaborate and bolster the emotional, thematic and narrative concerns."[9] *Angel* elaborates similar concerns, specifically the uncanny, the body, power, and control, and its mixture of influences and styles allow it great flexibility in doing so.[10]

Yet fantastic genres obviously do deviate from conventions of standard realism; one of the familiar "rules" is that in science fiction such deviations are explained by advanced science, while in fantasy or supernatural horror they are ascribed to magic. *Angel*'s parent show *Buffy* was partly based on the contrast between contemporary scientific rationality (including everyday technology) and primeval monsters, and though it did not necessarily regard these as mutually incompatible (as the characters of Jenny Calendar and Willow demonstrate), they were often represented as in tension. Leaving aside its title character's inability to master a cell phone, this tension all but disappears in *Angel*, since here fantastic events are frequently rooted in a combination of science/technology and magic (what I refer to as sci-tech-magic). An allusive visual language is employed to represent this plasticity, incorporating elements of science fiction, fantasy, and horror, as well as a range of other genres based in more conventional realism. For instance, as will be explored later in this chapter, Stacey Abbott notes how some images read as television horror in *Angel* are similar to displays of the body in medical or forensic drama (the *CSI*-like shot of Angel's heart in "Ground State" is one of the most striking examples); of course, this is another shifting frame of reference.[11] Clearly (genre) context structures the meaning of such images for the viewer.

Narratively, *Angel* is less concerned with explanations of the fantastic than with use value and power, so that while it often provides striking images, these are always related to its key thematic concerns. Science and the supernatural coexist and are unremarkable to characters that move between the "normal" world of contemporary L.A. and the L.A. that houses demons and magic (another constantly shifting frame of reference). The inclusion of corporate big, bad, interdimensional law firm Wolfram & Hart is significant to this representation. Wolfram & Hart is not concerned with right and wrong, with winning or losing a battle between good and evil; it is primarily concerned with power. Whether that power derives from science and technology, from magic, or from combinations of these is unimportant; all are valued as a means to an end.[12] While some *Buffy* episodes draw more overtly on science fiction via tropes and intertextual referencing (Frankenstein, Body Snatchers, robots), *Angel* adopts a post-cyberpunk approach that melds elements together on the basis of practicality rather than origins ("the street finds its own uses for things," as a story in William Gibson's 1981 *Burning Chrome* puts it). Three main areas will be examined: enhancement or alteration of the body; virtual realities or other dimensions; and representation and negotiation of time.

Body Enhancement/Alteration

One of the first instances of Wolfram & Hart combining magic with sci-tech comes at the end of season one.[13] In "Blind Date" (2000), disaffected lawyer Lindsey McDonald appeals to Angel Investigations for help preventing Wolfram & Hart's plan to kill three children who are seers, using a blind assassin. In order to find files revealing the children's location, Lindsey and Angel prepare to infiltrate Wolfram & Hart. The array of security measures involves valid passes, a demon guard, security monitors, and more. As Lindsey explains, "They have shamans. They can sense the moment a vampire crosses the threshold." Heist-style scenes (another frame of reference) demonstrate and visualize this mixture of mystical and technological security in action. For example, a demon functions as a mixture of bio-tech-magic when it goes off like an alarm, squealing, as a vampire crosses the boundary. Subsequent episodes highlight the way a vampire might be invisible to some technological security systems ("The Shroud of Rahmon" [2000]) but would alert others that use biological scanning ("Players" [2003]), making it clear why Wolfram & Hart has both. This combination of sci-tech-magic means the vampire body is visually and narratively denoted as different.

Vanessa, the assassin hired by Wolfram & Hart in "Blind Date," is blind by choice; to her it is an enhancement rather than a disability. This is linked with magic or mysticism (she trains with cave-dwelling "Nanjin" monks who believe in "seeing with the heart, not the mind"), yet the thermal imaging effect used when Angel fights her maps sci-tech effects onto an apparently supernatural power. Two other enhancements aligned with Wolfram & Hart are Lindsey's replacement hand and Gunn's brain upgrade. These too deliberately merge magic and sci-tech and mix different genre influences to achieve their full effect.

Lindsey's hand is cut off by Angel in the season one finale, and he has two replacements. The first is a basic "plastic" prosthesis incapable of movement or feeling, contrasted in "Dead End" (2001) with a second replacement that functions exactly like his original hand. Lindsey gets the second hand as a "reward" from Wolfram & Hart ("They think the world of you," Dr. Melman tells him), and the process of acquiring it seems to be standard medical procedure until the Pockla demon is called for and casts a spell on the newly joined hand, combining medical science with magic. Lindsey's subsequent experience of his new hand writing "kill kill kill" while he is in a meeting with clients draws on horror conventions (see *The Hands of Orlac* [1960], or *Gwin Gwai* [*The Eye*] [2002], and its remake; the trope is parodied in *Evil Dead II* [1987]), as the script acknowledges later when Lindsey talks about his "evil hand" issues. Lindsey and Angel discover what the production designer describes as an "underground cryogenics lab"[14] that blends science fiction and gothic horror along the lines of *Frankenstein*. Since *Frankenstein* is a key text to more than one genre, the similarities this episode shares with other science fictions dealing with cloning or genetic manipulation are not surprising. "Dead End" parallels *Alien: Resurrection* (1997) and *Dark Angel* (2000–2002), especially when Lindsey finds the donor of his new hand, Bradley Scott, a former employee of Wolfram & Hart. Bradley completes the automatic writing "kill" when he tells Lindsey "kill me," in what appears to be a direct reference to clone Ripley 7 from the Joss Whedon–scripted *Alien: Resurrection*. The Frankenstein connotations offer a highly condensed notion of bad science, while other intertexts invoke the corporate or institutional villain, paralleling the company/military in the *Alien* films or Manticore in *Dark Angel* with Wolfram & Hart. Rows of naked bodies suspended in tanks demonstrate science objectifying humanity, as well as the corporate objectifying its workers; this image draws also on the spectacle of body horror and sideshow freaks. Lindsey's emotional response functions as a counterpoint to the cold machinery of sci-tech (a typical science fiction strategy), and the fact that humanity is represented here by an amoral lawyer and a vampire reinforces *Angel*'s theme of redemptive heroism. This is an example of what Pateman calls "involution," a strategy whose main strength is that "the contact between two points (whether intra- or intertextual) . . . magnifies the connotative and interpretive power of both."[15]

Similar strategies are at work in presenting Gunn's enhancement. Once the transition to Wolfram & Hart is established in season five, Team Angel need a lawyer, and Gunn is given a brain implant that functions as an "upgrade," equipping him with knowledge of the law ("Conviction" [2003]). Later this starts to fade and he takes desperate action to ensure that he retains it ("Smile Time" [2004]), resulting unwittingly in Fred's death. As with Lindsey's hand, the procedure takes place in scientific/medical surroundings but here the pain involved and the graphic detail of tunneling into Gunn's brain employs imagery of body horror and/or forensic drama (Abbott describes the brain image as "a reverse *CSI* shot").[16] The effect the implant itself has on Gunn is signaled by changes in his dress and speech so that, visually and aurally, he transforms from urban street tough to middle-class professional. (Language often functions as a genre marker, and the use of technobabble and legalese in *Angel* is another way the frame of reference is shifted.) The theme of identity as fluid and contingent is common in both science fiction (especially cyberpunk, which frequently deals with bio-tech combinations; Abbott suggests that "Gunn is transformed into a form of cyborg . . . through technological intervention"[17]) and horror (possession, transformation; see Gunn's insistence during "Conviction" that after the implant he is not "evil me," or Dr. Sparrow's insistence on two Gunns during their negotiation in "Smile Time"). The deterioration of the upgrade, apparently a kind of planned obsolescence common in technological devices, is familiar from other science fictions—*Blade Runner*'s (1982) replicants, for instance—and science fiction is evoked here by language too: "The neural path modification is almost completely reverted." Gunn's redemption, Abbott notes, is achieved when he replaces Lindsey in the prison dimension of "Underneath" and "Time Bomb" (both 2004) and undergoes regular evisceration: "This experience, harking back to medieval torture, facilitates Gunn's gradual recuperation of the 'self' as he is reminded, through the painful and daily penetration of his body, of his humanity."[18] The gothic horror of this scenario serves to contrast sci-tech, and this arc is also integral to inaugurating another fascinating mixture of sci-tech and magic: the rebirth of God King Illyria.

A further site for hybridity of sci-tech-magic is the mystical cyborg. The cyborg is designed to blur the boundaries between the natural and the artificial, the biological and the technological.[19] While Abbott identifies Gunn as potentially a cyborg, the most obvious example of the mystical cyborg is the ninja assassins in "Lineage" (season five, episode seven, 2003), which have their forerunner in Boone from "Blood Money" (season two, episode twelve, 2001), a cowboy-styled demon who has metal coils that can extrude from his arms (rather like *X-Men*'s Wolverine). These appear to be an integral part of Boone's physical body, though it is not clear if they are natural or some kind of addition (and neither Boone nor Wolverine is usually referred to as a cyborg). The cyborgs in "Lineage" at first simply seem to be skilled warriors. Yet when the metal faceplate is pulled off one by Wesley following a fight, it reveals a sticky, skinless face beneath: in a version of a popular science fiction trope he then tortures it, testing whether it has a sense of self-preservation. The cyborgs' "programming" includes a battle prayer and/or binding spell inside, like a golem (often acknowledged as a mystical source for the science fictional robot or android: both intertexts are evident here). Narratively the cyborgs function as a distraction for the use of a mystical staff to sap Angel's will, while thematically they work to address issues of identity, especially since one impersonates Wesley's father. Angel dismisses it as "just a robot with a fancy glamor" but the cyborgs are different from an entirely technological robot, or even the bio-tech cyborg, and their appearance here foreshadows Illyria, who also incorporates supernatural or mystical elements, as a third term in the equation.

Bronwen Calvert, drawing on Elizabeth Grosz, argues convincingly that Illyria's inhabiting of Fred's body can be read as an instance of the body as a machine that transmits information or expresses the internal.[20] Furthermore, Calvert notes that Illyria herself uses language we associate with technology to describe her embodiment, phrases such as "fragments of memory channeled into my function systems" and "a simple modulation of my form" ("Shells" [2004]). Likewise, Abbott describes how "Illyria's consciousness has effectively been downloaded into Fred's body,"[21] demonstrating how the whole process parallels the technological as well as supernatural possession. Illyria's character is persistently aligned with technological imagery, as examined in more detail below, although this is not out of place in modern vampire fiction. Abbott notes that a number of "contemporary vampire films . . . have reinterpreted the vampire myth through the language of science and technology" but observes that "*Angel* resists the lure of scientific explanation through genetics or haematology, preferring to maintain the supernatural rational for vampirism. . . . While Blade's body is presented as a technological cyborg, Angel's body remains a mystery."[22] I would suggest that *Angel* resists scientific explanation in order to retain its valuable shifting frames of reference.

Virtual Realities and Other Dimensions

Alterations of the body relate to a key theme in *Angel*; its representation of other dimensions is an aspect of its fantastic premise and a way of introducing novelty to a television serial. Several other dimensions are used in the course of *Angel*'s five seasons, but here I focus on those that highlight genre conventions of visual representation. In "Birthday" (2002), demon Skip explains to Cordelia that the "mall" where he takes her to discuss the problem with her visions is simply a construct, "like in *The Matrix*," the language of popular science fiction forging an affinity between science fiction and the world of magic and demons. (Skip himself has a somewhat technological look, and a mixture of ancient and futuristic is often apparent in demon costume design, as Chic Gennarelli notes of the Skilosh in "Epiphany" [2001].[23]) The mall and the parallel life Cordelia experiences in this episode are similar to virtual reality, and when she kisses Angel to take back the visions, the action freezes in the manner of a *Star Trek* holosuite or virtual reality game.[24]

One of the most visually striking of *Angel*'s other places is Wolfram & Hart's white room, first introduced in "Forgiving" (2002) when Angel persuades Lilah to take him there to talk to a powerful being. The white room is accessed by what seems to be a standard elevator until a large button appears following entry of a code, implying an interface of magic and technology. The place itself is not a place at all; rather, it is presented as an artificial/virtual reality, somewhere the characters appear or materialize, rather than physically enter, and it is visualized in recognizably science fiction terms, literally as a white room reminiscent of the controlled environment in *THX-1138* (1971) or the "construct" from *The Matrix* (1999). The extreme whiteness and bright light give a surreal or hyperreal edge to figures in the featureless space. Angel and Lilah both wear black, a stark contrast to the white surroundings and to the red dress of the little girl the being manifests itself as. That Angel and the girl discuss "immaterial demons" further combines the incorporeality of both virtual reality and magical projections, as well as reiterating *Angel*'s fascination with the body. The white room is used again as a means of contrast in "Habeas Corpses" (2003) when the Beast is found there killing the girl. The huge demon body, hooves, and horns of the Beast are available to view in great detail, with no distractions from the background. Removing it from any "realistic'" setting both enhances its novelty (as a fantasy creature) and its constructedness (as a special effect), drawing attention to the aesthetic of this scene and making it stand out as spectacle.

Another example that draws on several conventions for its effect is the holding dimension in "Underneath" where Lindsey is imprisoned by the Senior Partners after his failed attempt to destroy Angel and Wolfram & Hart in "You're Welcome" (2004). This suburban construct is reminiscent of *The Stepford Wives* (1975 and 2004) or *Edward Scissorhands* (1990),[25] thus alluding to dystopian science fiction, the conformist climate of the American 1950s, and the way contemporary American horror invades the family home: as Spike comments, "This isn't hell. This is the 'burbs . . . close enough." The sunlit scenes in which Team Angel attempt to rescue Lindsey and are shot at by his "wife," "child," and even a passing ice cream vendor evoke the estrangement of science fiction in juxtaposing domestic paradise with extreme violence, while the dark cellar scenes offer traditional horror with a bucket of hearts, furnace, and demon ready to eviscerate its victim. Sunny daytime scenes have added effect in *Angel*. As a vampire Angel is restricted to darkness; the plot and mise-en-scène must accommodate this, as well as occasionally overturn-ing it to reinforce the point (see "In the Dark" [1999], or the "necro-tempered glass" provided at Wolfram & Hart's offices when Angel takes over as CEO). Abbott notes that this means the show works "quite openly within the horror genre"[26] but in this instance other fantastic genres are evoked when Gunn explains that the sun is "the nonfrying variety" because it is an "alternate dimension" (as in season two's Pylea). The car the team use to get to the hold-ing dimension travels through the city at night but emerges in the suburbs in daylight, accentuating the transition as supernatural.

Fantasy, horror, and science fiction all potentially engage with other worlds that may have no correlation in the real or physical world, and traveling between these is also represented in genre-specific ways. While magical, the portals in "Supersymmetry" (2002) and other episodes are visu-alized as wormholes, recognizable from many science fiction films and televi-sion shows.[27] "Reprise" (2001) offers an interesting juxtaposition of different genre influences in moving between two "acts" as well as apparently between two dimensions. Angel attempts to travel to "the Home Office" of Wolfram & Hart using a mystical glove and ring. As he puts on the ring an eleva-tor appears (outdoors), and the image fades to white rather than the more traditional black for the commercial break. Fade to white is later connected with the white room (it also occurs when Cordelia is taken to the "mall" in "Birthday"), and the extreme brightness is probably more readily identified with science fiction than fantasy or horror. The elevator in this scene is a device for traveling between different dimensions, like the one that goes to the white room but, shifting to horror, it contains the dead Holland Manners as Angel's guide. Characters and viewers are led to believe the Home Office is hell, denoted by overhead shots of the elevator plunging into a red-lit shaft. The "horror" of this image is undermined, however, by the banality of traveling in an elevator, emphasized by stereotypical low-volume music: this conjunction of the fantastic and the mundane draws attention to the images and the event, in a similar fashion to seeing the Beast in the white room. The final revelation that the Home Office is the world Angel has just left is informed both by the domestic setting of much post-1970s horror, and by a tradition of dystopian science fiction, reinforced here for emotional impact by a slow-motion montage of dysfunctional contemporary urban life.

Angel clearly uses conventions from a range of genres to convey its unreal worlds. Rather than sticking to one, it slips from one to another and thus retains multiple associations that help frame its narratives or emphasize its themes, as well as gaining atmosphere by direct visual allusion to intertexts. The indeterminate nature of these spaces allows the show to draw on several genre traditions. Like cyberpunk, or virtual reality science fiction, an episode dealing with another dimension "dissolves conventional notions of corporeality, inaugurates novel forms of intersubjectivity and alternative ways of figuring space."[28] This link between subjectivity and realizing the fantastic is extended in *Angel*'s negotiation and representation of time.

Time Travel

"I Will Remember You" (1999) deals with a short period in which Angel becomes human and is reunited with former love Buffy, only to lose that time at the end of the episode, accepting that he has to be a vampire to continue his fight. Here the turning back of time demonstrates how magic can manipulate the scientific laws that supposedly govern our world. "Supernatural threats cannot be contained by standard law enforcement techniques, nor controlled by the same laws that apply to our world," as Sharon Sutherland and Sarah Swan note in a slightly different context.[29] Furthermore, the manipulation of time here offers a discrete parallel-world story that can be explained within the overall narrative and is an accepted way to provide novelty in serial telefantasy. Representing memory is also a way of representing our negotiation and experience of time. "Origin" (2004) has the rest of Team Angel discover that Angel agreed to have their memories of his son, Connor, erased by Wolfram & Hart after making a deal to save the boy. In "Home" (2003), Connor is shifted to a parallel life and the team members' memories of his "real" life are erased. Memory loss is also the focus of "Spin the Bottle" (2002), where an attempt to help Cordelia recover her memory leads to a magical mishap that erases the main characters' recent memories, and they revert to teenage versions of themselves. Both episodes seem to emphasize that memory has a vital function in forging authentic identity.

Subjectivity and memory are often related (and as such are frequent topics in science fiction), with the added advantage here that such representation highlights how a vampire's experience of both is different.

Flashbacks have always been a key element in *Angel*, and part of the traditional vampire story is an ability to move across time, given a vampire's potential immortality. Period drama thus becomes another genre that both *Buffy* and *Angel* draw upon. Given its title character, *Angel* relies even more on flashbacks, and shifts the time frame often to give glimpses into the past of Angel and other vampires. Of course, backstory and flashback are accepted televisual or cinematic conventions that can be used in any drama and are not tied to the fantastic.[30] While Angel and other vampires still experience linear time, the editing of some episodes, effectively "intercutting" between time frames,[31] does not simply develop character and explain current actions by revealing backstory; it connects different time periods, highlighting the growth (or otherwise) of characters involved and bringing two versions of the same character together, rather than replacing one with another, as in "Spin the Bottle." This episode, while largely played for comedy, has a serious undertone, and ends with Cordelia remembering her vision of apocalypse. Memory is one rendition of another time; the visions are another—playing on a notion of possible, avertable futures familiar from science fiction. The visions are also coded, in Kinsey's words, as "interior experiences . . . given concrete form" by particular aesthetic choices, including slow-motion, blurred imaging, and color changes.[32] In this sense, they too realize other dimensions, time as well as interiority. The disorienting nature of the visions is rendered for the audience as well as the character. Kinsey suggests that even in *Angel*'s scene-to-scene transitions, "time is shaken. A flash of a shot may appear, and that scene may arrive several minutes later in the episode."[33]

The thermal imaging used in "Blind Date" has already been mentioned, and *Angel* often uses effects that may more commonly be associated with science fiction to render the supernatural. The manipulation of time in "Time Bomb" is a major example that draws particularly on science fiction cinema's images (and technologies) of virtual reality to make time visible. The effects used in "Time Bomb" are derived from *The Matrix*'s bullet time. Joshua Clover describes bullet time as "a visual analogy for privileged moments of consciousness"[34] while Kinsey notes of "Time Bomb" that "homage to martial arts films here is obvious but this kind of suspension is much more than that. There is a doubling of the experience of time here."[35] Thus, the sense of time as another dimension is rendered visually through science fiction effects. Illyria also creates portals (she rescues Gunn from the holding dimension in this way) and the episode cuts between several possible futures/pasts and between locations, showing different forms of interdimensional travel. Notably, much of this episode takes place in the science labs at Wolfram & Hart, and Wesley's speculations about what is happening are couched in technobabble to provide another layer of science fiction. He explains, "This is a Mutari generator. It creates a pinhole to an infinite extradimensional space, a negatively charged pocket universe that should draw her radiant essence, her power, into itself." Even Illyria uses such language when she refers to "an aberration in the timeline." All this works to reinforce Illyria as a hybrid of sci-tech-magic, not just narratively but visually. When she comments, "Something is broken inside me," and in one possible conclusion to the story, blue light spills out beneath her cracking "shell," sci-tech or magic could equally be implied. Spike describes Illyria's fighting style as a "cheeky mix," and she remains a key figuration of the show's insouciant slipping between genres.

Genericity Television

The novel narrative and visual amalgamation of sci-tech-magic that features so persistently in *Angel* is one example that foregrounds how the show performs genres in combination, plasticizing them into a new form that is continually reshaped. While the show uses involution and a mix of genre conventions to underpin its narrative and its main themes and concerns, these strategies also establish a metatelevisual aesthetic that cites previous genre texts, what Isaacs calls genericity. In his analysis, Isaacs distinguishes the genericity film from "pure" genre or the genre hybrid because it has "a cinematic aesthetic, a creative strategy that actively comments upon and constitutes earlier generic types and texts. The pure genre and hybrid merely serviced a storyline."[36] While "genericity has meaning only in relation to former generic strategies," he argues that "it presents a qualitative transformation of those strategies" because it "foregrounds its construction out of generic (and often genre-clichéd) components."[37] By throwing away, or more accurately, disregarding, a key "rule" distinguishing fantastic genres from each other and combining sci-tech-magic, *Angel* innovates in genre terms. By simultaneously retaining the iconography and aesthetics of its constituent genres, it announces itself as genericity television. It not only uses genre to elaborate its narrative and theme, but it also uses it to comment upon genre and to involute the history of genre television and cinema. Changing the genre context also significantly affects or constructs the way we read the visual image, making viewers aware of how they respond to genre coding, for instance, reading a similar scene as horrific in one show but medical in another. Isaacs suggests that the "allusive fabric" employed by genericity can be an "experiential process . . . a real collusion between artist, text and subject"[38] since viewers are actively engaged in interpreting the text's spectacle and aesthetic as well as its narrative and theme. This collusion is never more evident than in *Angel*.

Notes

1. Michele Pierson, *Special Effects: Still In Search of Wonder* (New York: Columbia University Press, 2002), 124.

2. Bruce Isaacs, *Toward a New Film Aesthetic* (New York: Continuum, 2008), 179.

3. Tammy Kinsey, "Transitions and Time: The Cinematic Language of *Angel*," in *Reading Angel: The TV Spin-Off with a Soul*, ed. Stacey Abbott (London: I. B. Tauris, 2005), 53.

4. Henry Jenkins in Pierson, *Special Effects*, 56.

5. Matthew Pateman, *The Aesthetics of Culture in* Buffy the Vampire Slayer (Jefferson, NC: McFarland, 2006), 2.

6. Catherine Johnson, *Telefantasy* (London: BFI, 2005), 101.

7. Isaacs, *Toward a New Film Aesthetic*, 107.

8. Vivian Sobchack, "Images of Wonder: The Look of Science Fiction," in *Liquid Metal: The Science Fiction Film Reader*, ed. Sean Redmond (London: Wallflower, 2004), 10.

9. Pateman, *The Aesthetics of Culture*, 111.

10. Other shows tend to stick to one genre to deal with one issue, like *Supernatural* (2005–present), which uses television horror to address masculinity.

11. The producers and creators of *Angel* are aware of this; forensics or dermatology books form research for makeup design (see Nancy Holder, Jeff Mariotte, and Maryelizabeth Hart, *Angel: The Casefiles* [New York: Pocket Books, 2002], 58) while shows like *CSI* (2000–present) inspire the Wolfram & Hart science labs (Stuart Blatt in Paul Ruditis and Diana G. Gallagher, eds., *Angel: The Casefiles*, vol. 2 [New York: Pocket Books, 2004], 275).

12. Team Angel also ignore the derivation of power, as noted in "Conviction" (2003).

13. Not all examples of hybrid sci-tech-magic involve Wolfram & Hart: see the security bracelets of "The Ring" (2000), described by Wesley as "half magic, half medieval technology," or the slave collars in Pylea in "Over the Rainbow" (2001).

14. Stuart Blatt in Holder, Mariotte, and Hart, *Casefiles*, 349.

15. Pateman, *The Aesthetics of Culture*, 120.

16. Stacey Abbott, *Angel* (Detroit, MI: Wayne State University Press, 2009), 57.

17. Ibid., 57.

18. Ibid., 58.

19. As Bronwen Calvert notes, several examples of potential cyborgs can be found in *Buffy*, including the chipped Spike of later seasons (Bronwen Calvert, "Going through the Motions: Reading Simulacra in *Buffy the Vampire Slayer*," *Slayage* 15 [2003], slayageonline.com/essays/slayage15/Calvert.htm). Calvert also notes "the positioning of some bodies as 'unconstructed' or 'natural' or as somehow representations of 'reality,'" perhaps surprising in a show that continually merges realism with the fantastic. On the face of it, *Angel* has fewer cyborg figures, but arguably the bodies of all *Angel*'s main characters end as constructed or unnatural in some fashion.

20. Bronwen Calvert, "'The Shell I'm In': Monstrous Embodiment and the Case of Illyria in *Angel*," in *From the Whedonverse to the Whedonesque*, ed. Tuna Erdem (Newcastle upon Tyne: Cambridge Scholars Press, forthcoming).

21. Abbott, *Angel*, 59.

22. Ibid., 61–62.

23. In Holder, Mariotte, and Hart, *Casefiles*, 332.

24. While science fiction might seem to dominate, despite narrative insistence on magic, this episode also adopts television sitcom style as a shorthand way of demonstrating Cordelia's successful new life as the star of *Cordy*, adding another element to the mix.

25. Director Skip Schoolnik cites *Edward Scissorhands* on the DVD commentary to "Underneath," though Stepford is mentioned in season four's Jasmine arc.

26. Abbott, *Angel*, 48.

27. Care is taken, however, that they do not resemble specific science fiction representations, as noted in the stage directions for "That Vision Thing" (2001): "Angel, armed for bear, steps into the shimmering portal. There's a flashing column of blue light (in a totally un-*Star Trek*-like way) and Angel's gone" (in Ruditis and Gallagher, *Angel: The Casefiles*, 68).

28. Dani Cavallero, *Cyberpunk and Cyberculture* (London: Athlone, 2000), xv.

29. Sharon Sutherland and Sarah Swan, "The Rule of Prophecy: Source of Law in the City of Angel," in *Reading Angel: The TV Spin-Off with a Soul*, ed. Stacey Abbott (London: I. B. Tauris, 2005), 133.

30. Yet even scenes that are not strictly time travel, as in the Pylea arc, afford the opportunity to "mix real period with fantasy" and as such are seen as "the ultimate challenge" by the show's costume designer (Chic Gennarelli in Holder, Mariotte, and Hart, *Casefiles*, 367).

31. Tim Minear on "Darla" in Holder, Mariotte, and Hart, *Casefiles*, 257.

32. Kinsey, "Transitions and Time," 50.

33. Ibid., 49. The reimagined *Battlestar Galactica* incorporates a similar effect into its opening sequence, editing short glimpses of scenes due to appear in the forthcoming episode and thus highlighting the constructed nature of its narrative presentation; see Lincoln Geraghty, *American Science Fiction Film and Television* (Oxford: Berg, 2009).

34. Joshua Clover, *The Matrix* (London: BFI, 2004), 35.

35. Kinsey, "Transitions and Time," 54. Similar *Matrix*-style special effects are used more briefly in the earlier episode "A New World" (2002) when Connor returns from alternate world Quor-toth, a scene that also visualizes a disruption of "normal" space-time. Thanks to Stacey Abbott for reminding me of this.

36. Isaacs, *Toward a New Film Aesthetic*, 177.

37. Ibid., 174.

38. Ibid., 183.

CHAPTER ELEVEN

Remapping the Feminine in
Joss Whedon's *Firefly*

Robert L. Lively

If there were a landscape to the American psyche, it would probably look like the American West. In the American mythos, the West represents a place of sweeping landscapes, big sky, and simple moral certitude. There is very little gray area in the myth of the West. Good guys wear white hats, the bad guys black. Historically, the West was a place where a man could go, no matter how humble his lot in life, and start fresh. The land was cheap and plentiful and there for the taking. This myth is powerful to the psyche even if those days are long over. When Frederick Jackson Turner proposed his "frontier thesis" in 1893, the American public embraced this idea.[1] The thesis argues that men can go west and carve out their place in the world, but they must do so in a "place where American ideals of democracy, egalitarianism, and self-reliance not only could but also had to be put into practice."[2] Unfortunately, he made his thesis three years after the U.S. government's census report "declared the frontier officially closed."[3]

However, the idea of the frontier remained fervently in the American culture for the next fifty years. During this time the Hollywood western was born. Even though there was no frontier to conquer, the silent-western superstar William S. Hart, who made over twenty films between 1915 and 1925, and later American icon John Wayne, who starred in John Ford's classic *Stagecoach* (1939), created "the frontier that was" on celluloid for mass consumption. In the years that followed, the western remained quite popular in films, television, and mass-market paperbacks. Yet, there was a tendency to embrace revisionist westerns tackling different social issues, exploring the human frontiers of character and history, especially the relationships between settlers and American Indians—see Arthur Penn's *Little Big Man* (1970), for example. The western became expansive of place and theme in the films and novels as it captured the changing cultural mores (compare with chapter 1 in this volume).

Is it any wonder then, that at the beginning of the space age, writers and filmmakers would turn their visions to the new frontier of space exploration? As early as 1966, Captain Kirk called "Space, the Final Frontier" in his opening monologue to *Star Trek* (1966–1969). In fact, Gene Roddenberry envisioned his *Star Trek* project as a "wagon train to the stars."[4] The connection of science fiction to the western is established early on. The western is explored in several other projects of the 1970s and 1980s. Michael Crichton's 1973 film *Westworld*, starring a diabolical Yul Brynner as a robotic gunslinger, Sean Connery's *Outland* (1981), a remake of *High Noon* (1952), and *Back to the Future III* (1985), starring Michael J. Fox, are perhaps the best known science fiction westerns.

So when Joss Whedon launched his new series *Firefly* (2002–2003) on Fox television in the fall of 2002, he had a large corpus of western texts to draw from. Set in a post–civil war society that featured the defeat of the independent Browncoats by the central planet Alliance, Captain Malcolm (Mal) Reynolds and his Firefly crew head to the fringes of the solar system, the frontier of their "verse," as the characters so aptly call it, to continue Turner's frontier thesis in the not-too-distant future. *Firefly* follows a group of people heading to the frontier to carve out a new life for themselves aboard a rickety old transport ship, which is reminiscent of Sam Peckinpah's *The Wild Bunch* (1969), a tale of the encroachment of civilization on a group of outlaws in Mexico in the early 1900s.

However, instead of relegating the women to minor, static roles as was so common in the western, Whedon plays with the stereotypes in *Firefly* to remap the feminine in the expansive landscape of space. Joss Whedon has played with feminine stereotypes before in his cult-favorite series *Buffy the Vampire Slayer* (1997–2003), where an innocuous high school girl slays vampires and fights demons. The often humorous series plays with stereotypical teenage behavior in the broader context of saving humanity. In this chapter, I analyze Whedon's remapping of the feminine of *Firefly*'s four female characters: Zoe, Inara, Kaylee, and River. I argue that Joss Whedon has reimagined the western feminine for an audience of twenty-first-century viewers. The typical western focuses on the comings and goings of the central male characters. *Firefly*, on the other hand, gives the women as much of a role as the men. Zoe, Inara, Kaylee, and River all behave in very nontraditionally defined ways.

Zoe is a female hired gun, Mal's sidekick. She takes on the role of a masculine character, with Wash, her husband, occupying the typical female role of peacemaker and homemaker. Inara is a registered companion, the prostitute trope of many westerns, from *Gunsmoke* (1955–1975)[5] to *Unforgiven* (1992), but in this society Inara is the one who brings culture and respectability to the Firefly crew. In the pilot episode, she even hears a confession from Shepherd Book, the ship's preacher. Kaylee occupies the place of the innocent farm girl, much like a Laura Ingalls Wilder. However, Kaylee is imbued with a sexual freedom, although this is tempered when she is offered the job of ship's mechanic—she tells Mal she has to ask her folks. Kaylee takes the sexual freedom of feminism and packages it into an innocent young woman without any obvious character contradictions. And finally, I analyze River Tam. She is a girl who seems insane, and is called as much, yet she is the smartest one and the best fighter on the ship. We see flashes of her abilities throughout the series, culminating in the two grand fight scenes in the film spin-off following the series, *Serenity* (2005). She is perceived as the girl whom the men must protect from the space Indians (called Reavers) and government operatives. However, she is not the girl who must be protected from the ways of the world, as the men see it. She is quite capable of taking care of herself.

Historically, women on the frontier often behaved in nontraditional ways because of the extreme conditions of the wilderness. Julie Roy Jeffrey, in her fascinating study *Frontier Women*, looks critically at the roles of women as they move from the safety of civilization.

> As families moved into the wilderness, they moved into a world bearing little resemblance to the one they had left. Far from the city marketplaces and factories, far from the country peddler with his pack of manufactured goods, the pioneer family had to become self-sufficient. Much of the model of appropriate female behavior had to be disregarded. . . . And although the sex division of work generally remained, necessity could cause a blurring of sexual boundaries. Pioneer women's lives were less rigidly circumscribed than domesticity allowed and their activities suggested the flaws in its analysis of woman's nature.[6]

The concerns raised in Jeffrey's passage suggest the instability in stratified gender constructs as women moved to the frontier. Similarly, Whedon's female characters display this pattern as they flee to the edge of civilization, a place where gender constructions are fluid. Since *Firefly* has a long tradition of feminine social constructs to draw from, I examine their stereotypical place in the western canon, and explore the deconstruction of those stereotypical traits of these characters in the series. Consequently, by understanding his remapped feminine, readers can dissect the western tradition from which Whedon draws so much of his material to gain a richer conception of the narrative.

Zoe: Regendering the Sidekick

The character of Zoe Washburn is complex and enigmatic. Zoe has fled the battlefield to move to the space frontier. She is Captain Reynolds's right-hand (wo)man, his sidekick in western terms. And she is married to Firefly's pilot, Wash. In all of these facets of her character, Zoe breaks the typical western gender constructions. When the series begins, we see Zoe and Captain Reynolds in a flashback to the Battle of Serenity Valley where the rebel Browncoats are effectively defeated.[7] The defeat gives the impetus for the losers to reach for the frontier and the promise of a new life. The western often dealt with the same circumstances in post–Civil War era westerns. Wanting to flee a sense of defeat, many westerns are set up with southerners moving west in a hope to recapture some dignity on the wild fringes of the country. This device is fairly common. Perhaps the most famous example of this device is found in Owen Wister's novel *The Virginian* (1902). Wister develops the well-mannered southerner, known only as the Virginian, who heads to the West and finds trouble because he lives by the gun. *The Outlaw Josey Wales* (1976) chronicles an ex-Confederate soldier, played by Clint Eastwood, as he seeks revenge in the frontier of the desert southwest, and a more recent example is the Academy Award–winning *Dances with Wolves* (1990), starring Kevin Costner as a battle-fatigued Union officer who seeks solace on the plains after the Civil War.

Zoe is no different. She has fled with Captain Reynolds to the edge of civilized space to find work and make a place for herself. But she cannot divorce herself from her military past. She still clings to the military code of conduct even though the war has been over for six years at the time of the series. But keep in mind that these post–Civil War narratives are always gendered male. The metaphors are always gendered in typical male occupations of war. Yet here is Zoe on the "raggedy edge" (quote from *Serenity*) of space, a woman and a warrior who is driven by the same need for a new start just as much as Josey Wales or Malcolm Reynolds. In *Firefly*, the landscape is not made for men alone to conquer, but for those who are able to conquer it, including women.

Moreover, Zoe occupies the usual male role of sidekick to the protagonist. Early TV westerns are replete with sidekicks, from the Cisco Kid's Pancho and the Lone Ranger's Native American friend Tonto, to Hopalong Cassidy's faithful Red Connors. Even in the Roy Rodgers westerns, Dale Evans is not the sidekick, though many people mistakenly think so. Gabby Hayes is Roy's sidekick, and in many episodes Trigger, his horse, functions as more of the sidekick than Dale Evans. These sidekicks are always gendered male in typical westerns. But while sidekicks usually act as a foil for the male lead, in *Firefly* Zoe is skilled and more accomplished than the "hero," Mal Reynolds. According to Peter Stanfield, "the base function of the sidekick is to keep the hero in the realm of the common man, not to confirm his preeminence."[8] Zoe achieves this function by outshining him; thus, the foil is reversed, and Mal is centered in the place of the common man. The incidents when Zoe outshines Mal are often quite comical. Starting from the first episode ("Serenity"), we see the interaction of Mal and Zoe as an imbalanced relationship where she defers to Mal as the "hero" but she seems more capable. After the shoot-out with Patience on Whitefall, the banter afterward illustrates this:

ZOE: Armor's dented.

MAL: Well, you were right about this being a bad idea.

ZOE: Thanks for saying, sir.

The recurring theme of Zoe outshining Mal is shown in many episodes. During the bar fight scene in the lead-in to "The Train Job" (2002), Mal is thrown out of the holographic window, while Zoe leaves the bar beating the other patrons. She even rescues Mal from Niska's station in "War Stories" (2002). Zoe's competence and ability shouldn't be diminished because she occupies the station of western sidekick. The philosophical differences between Zoe and Mal can further be explored in a flashback in the episode "The Message" (never aired). Zoe instructs a young recruit, Tracey, on the code of battle, which, of course, Mal fails to follow:

ZOE: They had two scouts sniffin', but I took 'em down.

TRACEY: Why, I didn't hear a thing.

ZOE: First rule of battle, little one, don't ever let them know where you are.

[Mal enters, guns blazing, whooping and hollering]

MAL: Woo hoo! I'm right here. I'm right here. You want some of this. Yeah, ya do. Come on. Come on. Woo hoo.

ZOE: 'Course there're other schools of thought.

Viewers may want to relinquish Zoe to an ancillary role in *Firefly*, but this characterization would be incorrect. Her character shows that she is at least the equal to, and at best superior to, Captain Malcolm Reynolds. She is not a typical sidekick in the tradition.

In the episode "Our Mrs. Reynolds" (2002), the crew is hired to stop bandits who are ambushing wagon shipments. Mal disguises himself as a woman while Zoe hides in the back of a wagon waiting for the ambush. When Mal is questioned by Inara about why he was wearing the dress, and not Zoe, he responds that it was "tactics," and he liked the "airflow thing." The transgression of typical western male/female social roles continues with the relationship of Zoe and Wash. The western landscape is a very masculine place. Gunfighters, sheriffs, cattle rustlers, and bank robbers are traditionally male. The men are the active participants in the world. The wives and lovers of these men are almost always left behind on the homestead. Zoe and Wash reverse this role. She is constantly leaving with Mal to fight crime while Wash, in a sullen manner, waits for his love to return. Even in the realm of sexuality, Wash defers to Zoe's superiority. The episode "Bushwhacked" (2002) features a scene where Wash is interrogated by an Alliance commander and he quips, "Have you ever been with a warrior woman?" Clearly he is associating Zoe as a strong sexual partner and a warrior. This is an unusual way in most westerns to describe a female character, but not at all uncommon in describing a strapping male lead.

In the *Firefly* series, Wash and Zoe have effectively flipped roles. But this reversal does not go unnoticed. Wash, for instance, comments on Zoe's work in "Serenity": "I always worry when Zoe's on a job." In a later episode, "War Stories," Wash forces Mal to take him along on a deal instead of Zoe because he wants to be able to tell the stories that they tell. He wants to know what it is like in the realm of the space "man."

Inara: Trapped between Society and the Frontier

Inara Serra's unique position in *Firefly* allows her character to explore the complexities of being caught between worlds. This is a fairly common trope in science fiction.[9] In Inara's case, is she loyal to the Alliance that gives her social status and power, or is she a secret fugitive, fleeing some remote sin? The series is purposely ambiguous in this aspect. Inara never clearly articulates why she has fled to the frontier and taken refuge aboard Serenity. Whatever her reasons, Inara allows the viewer to see the duality of the "verse between Malcolm Reynolds's" world, filled with small-time criminals such as Badger, and her glamorous world of lords and ladies and floating chandeliers. This mixing of classes shows the viewer the decadence of the Alliance imperialism, and why men with a moral compass might want to flee to the hinterlands to avoid places that glorify cultural elitism.

Inara's character is wonderfully portrayed by the talented and beautiful Morena Baccarin. Inara occupies a strange role on the ship, trapped between the stereotypes of the old West and the courtesan role taken from the Asian tradition. This may seem an odd mix, but in reality the blending makes perfect sense, both thematically in *Firefly* and historically when looking at the American West. The Alliance in *Firefly* is a melding of Anglo-Chinese culture. It is the two superpowers going into space, so the blending of traditions seems fairly plausible in the context of the series. Viewers will also note that the languages have blended as well: most of the curse words are uttered in Mandarin, so there is a precedent in the series. In the old West, Chinese workers were widely used to build the western half of the transcontinental railroad.[10] In the West, Chinatowns popped up all over the map, from Virginia City's Comstock Load boom, to San Francisco, to Seattle. The influx of Chinese laborers cannot be understated in the creation of the American West. But neither can the racism. It was not uncommon for Chinese laborers to be run off or murdered once the rail lines were completed. Richard Harris's character in *Unforgiven*, English Bob, has made his reputation from killing "Chinamen." The conflict between these cultures is played out through Inara.

Inara is a registered companion, a high-class courtesan from the Asian traditions. The most prominent comparison would be that of a geisha, and she does have several elements to support that. First, Inara dresses in Asian patterns of clothing, usually made of silk. Her boudoir is decorated in Asian designs, and she has been trained in a house the way geishas are trained. At first the Anglo-Chinese connections are not prominent, but we must remember that the geisha tradition in Japan was imported during the Ming Dynasty, and its roots are in the dynastic courts of the mainland. *Geisha* in literal terms means "person of the arts." This is certainly true in Inara's case. Besides being trained in the fine arts of sexuality, Inara has skills in medical training ("Serenity"), sword fighting ("Shindig" [2002]), the tea ceremony ("Jaynestown" [2002]), and archery (*Serenity*). Inara's claim as person of the arts is easily backed up by these episodes where we see her cultural upbringing.

Her training supports her elevated social status in this society. Yet her association with the geisha tradition offends the sensibilities of Captain Reynolds, who has a typical Western morality of right and wrong that does not fit with Asian mores. Mal views Inara with the typical Western viewpoint that prostitutes are of a low social status and that their actions are immoral.

However, Leslie Downer argues in her essay about the geisha that since they were "unafflicted with Judeo-Christian guilt, the Japanese had no concept of sin, and therefore of sex being sinful."[11] Mal, we see in the pilot episode, is a Christian. And in later episodes, we see him as a disillusioned Christian in his philosophical discussions with Shepherd Book. Inara, on the other hand, comes from a more liberal tradition where sex is celebrated as a holy union. She even rebukes Mal in the episode "Heart of Gold" (never aired), after she catches him leaving a local prostitute's room and he is completely embarrassed by the situation. Inara tells him, "One of the virutes about not being puritanical about sex is not feeling embarrassed afterwards. You should look into it." Of course she is lying. She and Mal have a complicated relationship that is understood, but never mentioned. Inara's character flaw in the geisha tradition is that she cares about him. Downer also comments on the morality of the Japanese tradition:

> According to the Neo-Confucian code which governed society, it was un-thinkable to marry someone you loved. As Naomi Tamura wrote in *The Japanese Bride* as late as 1904: "It is very clear that we do not marry for love. If a man is known to have broken this rule, we look upon him as a mean fellow, and sadly lacking in morality. His own mother and father would be ashamed of him. Public sentiment places love for a woman very low in the scale of morals."[12]

Considering Inara's upbringing, her hesitance to openly profess her love for Mal, and her anger at his tryst with a lowly prostitute, is understandable. She views her authentic emotion as a moral failing. She is trying to navigate the geography of her own feelings with what is expected from her traditions and his. The chasm that divides them is deep.

This division of ideas between Inara and Mal is glaring. Mal fought against the Alliance; she supported unification. Although Inara has a high social class because of her occupation as a high-society courtesan, Mal has Western sensibilities, which casts prostitution in a very low social role. He sees her as a typical whore and calls her such on several occasions. He chooses not to see the cultural differences in their belief systems. The hatred or belittling of Asians is quite common in westerns. From the 1937 western *Border Phantom*, to the Chinese-killing gunfighter English Bob in *Unforgiven*, the depiction of Asians in westerns has been less than favorable.

Even though Mal sees her as occupying a lower moral position because of her occupation, nothing could be further from the truth. Inara holds the highest social position on the ship. In the pilot episode, Mal refers to her as the "ambassador" in a contemptuous way. His assessment isn't far off, though; she has the social standing of at least a minor political figure, and on several occasions in the series she exercises her power. She is able to walk into a sheriff's office in Paradiso in the episode "The Train Job" and basically walk out with Mal and Zoe, who have been questioned for robbery. In "Shindig," after the swordfight scene where Mal defeats Atherton Wing, a local noble, we see her power in the following short dialogue:

ATHERTON: Inara. Inara!

SIR WARWICK: You've lost her, lad. Be gracious.

ATHERTON: You set this up, whore, after I bought and paid for you. I should've beat you up good, so no one would want you.

MAL: See how I'm not punching him. I think I've grown.

ATHERTON: Get ready to starve. I'll see to it you never work again.

INARA: Actually, that's not how it works. You see, you've earned a black mark in the client registry. No companion is going to contract with you ever again.

Inara uses her power as a companion when she needs to—and make no mistake, her social class grants her an inordinate amount of power. This isn't the only time she uses her power to thwart an overbearing man. In "Jaynestown," she throws out Magistrate Higgins from her shuttle. She doesn't use the power in an offensive way, however. She has a restraint to her that keeps her in control, so when men cross that boundary, and she flexes her power, the audience is well aware that a line has been crossed. Inara is caught between the civilized society she represents and the frontier. The change in geography makes her navigate through uncharted territory to remap the frontier. This gives her an inordinate amount of power, both personally and socially. She is much more than the "whore" that some of the men label her.

Kaylee: The Radical Redirection of the Pioneer Woman

Kaylee is an intriguing character on board the Serenity. If you took the stereotypical pioneer woman, infused her with twentieth-century feminism, and launched her into outer space, you just might get Kaylee. Joss Whedon has drawn from several traditions to develop her character. The Western pioneer woman has a long literary and film tradition from which to draw. Perhaps the two most famous examples in literature of life on the frontier come from Laura Ingalls Wilder and Willa Cather.

Laura Ingalls Wilder's *Little House on the Prairie* series recalls her life growing up in the 1870s and 1880s and has been a perennial favorite in America since its publication. There was, of course, also a TV series loosely based on the *Little House* books that ran from 1974 to 1983. The life described by Wilder is rough, and she describes a frontier that is not the kindest of places, but the folks are honest and hardworking people. She also describes the social positions of women: the careers they can have, and the work that they do. Hard work by both genders is a virtue on the edge of civilization, where famine and hardships were always lurking if laziness overtook the pioneers.

Willa Cather describes a frontier Nebraska in the waning years of the 1800s in such works as *O Pioneers!* (1913) and *My Ántonia* (1918). Both of these novels center on love stories that are unrequited, which fits into the pioneer flavor of Kaylee and her love for Simon Tam. Cather's sweeping stories chronicle the struggles on the frontier. Her novels specifically deal with the loneliness in the landscapes and in the human heart. Cather seems to be a prominent source for Kaylee's character since space and the heart in *Firefly* are equally as lonely. Kaylee shows herself to be an unsophisticated, yet charming, pioneer girl. Her innocence helps draw the viewer's interest and sympathy in her character.

Underneath this innocent exterior is a woman who is sexually liberated. Kaylee is not ashamed of sex and freely embraces the pleasures of her body. This is a radical redirection of the stalwart pioneer woman. This openness about her sexuality is more often associated with feminism than with pioneer literature. In *Serenity*, Kaylee remarks to the crew that "been goin' on a year now, I haven't had nothin' twixt my nethers, weren't run on batteries." Her offhand remark shows how open she is with her sexuality. It's hard to even imagine that line showing up in *Little House on the Prairie*, *My Ántonia*, or even Patricia MacLachlan's *Sarah, Plain and Tall* (1985). Whedon manages to keep the innocent aspects of her pioneer upbringing, while liberating her libido from preconceived stereotypes of frontier women. Even when Kaylee is first hired on to the Serenity in "Objects in Space" (2002), she is engaged in sex with the mechanic Mal already hired. She shows an ability to fix the ship by just making a minor repair. Kaylee remarks, "I just saw it when I was on my back." But when Mal offers her the engineer's job, she lowers her head in a demure gesture and tells him, "I'll have to ask my folks." The blending of the feminist liberated attitudes toward sex and her pioneer background gives her a comical charm in the series. But by blending these two elements, she is given a freedom to act and occupy a position probably not given to many women, even in the worlds Whedon has created.

Moreover, Kaylee's character, even though she is seen as an innocent, does not fall into a subject position. She is not an object of desire defined by men. She has defined herself. Kaylee isn't subjugated by the trope of the "male gaze," so common in nineteenth-century novels. She isn't reduced to chattel by the objectifying stare of men that dehumanizes women. In Laura Mulvey's seminal essay, "Visual Pleasure and Narrative Cinema," she observes that "in a world ordered by sexual imbalance pleasure in looking has been split between the active/male and the passive/female."[13] She further states that women who have been objectified cannot advance the plot of a story. Only men can do this. Kaylee isn't objectified under a stare, and the male fails to advance the plot. Somewhat ironically, Kaylee would not mind being made a sex object, especially by her love interest, Simon Tam. On several occasions in the series, she tells Simon what he should do or say to have her, and he is so inept, he always fails to seduce his willing partner. In several episodes, she even attempts to help him seduce her. For instance, in "The Message," Kaylee tries to help Simon compliment her by offering, "Tell me more good stuff about me!"

Kaylee's unique talent as ship's engineer also makes her a fitting match for Simon. He is a well-educated doctor from the advanced inner planets, and is shown to be a remarkable doctor on several occasions.[14] Kaylee, on the other hand, lacks Simon's formal education, but she is able to operate and repair the ship as expertly as Simon can fix people. They both share an innate ability to understand the inner workings of their patients. So it is no wonder that Simon and Kaylee end up as a couple in *Serenity*. Because of Kaylee's liberated views on sex and relationships, she finds love in the end.

River: Changing the Myth of the Captivity Narrative

River Tam's character can be viewed in classic westerns as the city girl who enters the frontier only to be threatened by the "savages" who live there. The trope of threatened city girl, the girl from civilization, has existed almost as long as the United States has been a nation. James Fenimore Cooper's *The Last of the Mohicans* (1826) tells the story of Alice and Cora, two civilized girls who enter the wilderness and are confronted by the "evil savage" Magua, a Huron Indian who lusts after Cora. Opposed to Magua are Hawkeye, Chingachgook, and Chingachgook's son Uncas, who also has romantic feelings for Cora. However, by the end of the novel, civilization is "safe" once again because Magua is dead, Uncas is dead, and Cora is dead. There is no chance that any mixed racial coupling will take place.

Yet this fear gripped the imagination of writers for the next 150 years. The implicit racism of the trope is not lost on the modern viewer, but it was considered scandalous and improper to have white settler women threatened by darker-skinned heathens. When cinema took up this motif, Hollywood produced several films where women were kidnapped by Indians. In the full gamut of Hollywood westerns, women are often laid out as potential spoils for Indian raiders. One of the earliest to explore this theme was the silent movie *The Covered Wagon* (1923), which featured attacks by hostile Indians and implied ravishings by the Indian attackers. But perhaps the most famous is director John Ford's *The Searchers* (1956), starring John Wayne, which once again tackles the trope of white girls kidnapped by Indians. John Wayne's character searches for years to find them and return them to civilization. Even the more recent *Dances with Wolves* solves this problem of racial mixing by having Kevin Costner's character fall in love with and marry a white, kidnapped girl (played as a woman by Mary McDonnell), so the races are once again "protected." Even in 1990, the filmmakers couldn't overcome the mixed-race-couplings stigma, and so, conveniently, Kevin Costner finds a white woman living with the Lakota with whom he is safe to pursue a romantic relationship. Very few westerns ever had whites and Native Americans marrying or coupling in books or on film. The best known film to actually do this was *Little Big Man*, where Dustin Hoffman's character boasts to an Indian rival, "I have four wives and a horse."

When adapted to science fiction, space aliens become, Brian Aldiss argues, simply "injuns among the stars."[15] River Tam is the typically threatened, civilized girl in *Firefly*. June Namias traces this theme in her book, *White Captives*, where she explains that

> female vulnerability is a constant, a continuity embedded in all the captivity genres, even those in which women strike back. Women's generally more diminutive physical stature and role as childbearer and nurturer is used as a sign of personal and social vulnerability to evoke sympathetic response.[16]

It seems Namias could be speaking directly about River Tam. Her mental instability caused by the Alliance's experiments on her creates an even deeper sense of vulnerability in her character. The characters on the Serenity often go out of their way to protect her. In the overall story arc of the series and movie, she is inextricably tied to the Reavers, the Indians of the universe. The Reavers share many stereotypical similarities with descriptions of Indians. They mutilate themselves and others, by putting on war paint, by tattooing themselves, or by scalping their victims; mutilation is commonly associated with the "savage," and the Reavers are known by their mutilations and painting themselves with the blood of their victims. There is also the threat of rape. When Simon Tam, River's brother and protector, asks Zoe about Reavers in "Serenity," she tells him,

ZOE: You've never heard of Reavers?

SIMON: Campfire stories. Men gone savage on the edge of space. Killing . . .

ZOE: They're not stories.

SIMON: What happens if they board us?

ZOE: If they take the ship, they'll rape us to death. Eat our flesh, and sew our skins into their clothing. And if we're very, very lucky, they'll do it in that order.

The threat of savages raping the innocent pioneers on the frontier is a well-used device that played to the racist views of Americans in the early part of the twentieth century. In a time when interracial dating and marriage was illegal in many U.S. states, the threat of natives attacking "white" settlers was viewed as unthinkable. So the precedent is set for the Reavers as the space Indians. Whedon, however, plays with this stereotypical "savage" and makes them innocent victims of governmental meddling. The chemical experiments performed on the Miranda settlers created the Reavers, as we see in *Serenity*, completing the story arc and explaining the strange attachment River has to the Reavers.

The connection between River and the Reavers is set up in the pilot episode. Shortly after River is set free from her cryosleep aboard Serenity, the Reavers silently glide past, later attacking the moon, Whitefall. Another connection River has with the Reavers is in the episode "Bushwhacked" (2002). River is drawn to the cargo hold where she finds the victims of the Reaver attacks. Later, she wakes up screaming as the lone survivor of the attack wakes and begins his transformation into a Reaver. River is telepathically linked to the Reavers because, according to Malcolm Reynolds in *Serenity*, her mental instability was caused by knowing what happened to create the Reavers. River often knows what the Reavers are up to. In the final chapter of the story arc, *Serenity*, the final connections are made clear. River Tam's reality fracturing was caused by the knowledge of the Reaver conversion by Alliance experimentation. When Serenity's crew is robbing the Alliance payroll, River feels the presence of Reavers, saving the crew from certain, unpleasant death. And when the Reaver pursuer is shot dead aboard ship, she comments, "He didn't lie down. They never lie down." She is foreshadowing the tragic scene on Miranda, where the settlers became

Reavers or else would have died because of the chemicals sprayed into the atmosphere by the Alliance.

Throughout the series, there was the constant threat that this young, innocent girl needed protecting from the Reavers, but in *Serenity*, we see that she does not need protecting. In the Maidenhead bar scene, we get a glimpse of her prowess as a fighter, yet in the final battle scene with the Reavers, we finally learn that River is quite capable of defending herself. She is not a hapless victim of civilization who needs men to guard her from the "injuns among the stars." Consequently, she kills all of the Reavers that threaten the crew of Serenity, and she establishes herself as one of the crew. River has gone to the frontier and carved out a space for herself.

The Remapped Feminine

By creating the setting of *Firefly* on a new frontier in space, Joss Whedon is able to reexamine feminine stereotypes in the corpus of the western genre. He is attempting to redefine and remap the possible roles of the female characters he sees in the genre, so that they are actors and active participants in cutting a place for themselves on the frontier. Moreover, since our stories tell us something about ourselves, *Firefly* creates a narrative in which women and men live, fight, love, and die as equals. Ultimately, by remapping the feminine in the *Firefly* universe, Whedon is arguing for a new role for the western genre where sexism, racism, and bigotry are distractions made by a few instead of institutional problems affecting the many. The viewers and fans of *Firefly* are invited to blaze this trail with them, to reexamine preconceived notions, and to challenge the frontiers of their own lives.

Notes

1. For more information on Turner's ideas, see J. David Stevens, *The Word Rides Again* (Athens: Ohio University Press, 2002), 185, notes 2–5.
2. Ibid., 3.
3. Ibid., 4.
4. See Lincoln Geraghty, "Eight Days That Changed American Television: Kirk's Opening Narration," in *The Influence of Star Trek on Television, Film and Culture*, ed. Lincoln Geraghty (Jefferson, NC: McFarland Publishers), 11–21.
5. *Gunsmoke* is one of the longest running television series in America, running from 1955 to 1975. It is no wonder that the western tropes are so popular, considering the American public viewed these every week for twenty years.
6. Julie Roy Jeffrey, *Frontier Women: The Trans-Mississippi West, 1840–1880* (New York: Hill and Wang, 1979), 11.

7. The opening sequence of *Firefly* in "Serenity" (2002) sets up the Browncoats' defeat in the Battle of Serenity Valley, which establishes the reason for Mal and Zoe fleeing to the frontier, paralleling the Confederate soldiers who fled west in the post–Civil War Reconstruction era (1865–1877).

8. Peter Stanfield, *Hollywood, Westerns, and the 1930s: The Lost Trail* (Exeter: University of Exeter Press, 2001), 105.

9. Perhaps the two most recognizable characters who are caught between worlds are Mr. Spock, from *Star Trek*'s original series, and Seven of Nine, the beautiful half-human/half-Borg of *Voyager* (see Barber's chapter in this volume). For further exploration of this topic, see also Wei Ming Dariotis, "Crossing the Racial Frontier: *Star Trek* and Mixed Heritage Identities," in *The Influence of Star Trek on Television, Film and Culture*, ed. Lincoln Geraghty (Jefferson, NC: McFarland, 2008), 63–81.

10. For further research on this subject, see Stephen Ambrose's *Nothing Like It in the World: The Men Who Built the Transcontinental Railroad, 1863–1869* (New York: Ambrose-Tubbs, 2000). The chapters on the western arm of the railroad detail the plight of the Chinese workers.

11. Leslie Downer, "The City Geisha and Their Role in Modern Japan: Anomaly or Artistes?" in *The Courtesan's Arts: Cross-Cultural Perspectives*, ed. Martha Feldman and Bonnie Gordon (Oxford: Oxford University Press, 2006), 226.

12. Quoted in Downer, "The City Geisha and Their Role in Modern Japan," 227.

13. Laura Mulvey, "Visual Pleasure and Narrative Cinema," in *The Film Studies Reader*, ed. Joanne Hollows, Peter Hutchings, and Mark Jancovich (London: Arnold, 2000), 242.

14. Simon Tam is shown to be a great doctor in "Serenity," "Safe" (2002), "Ariel" (2002), "War Stories," and "Heart of Gold" (2002).

15. Brian Aldiss, *Billion Year Spree: The History of Science Fiction* (New York: Doubleday, 1973), 218. See also Gregory M. Pfitzer, "The Only Good Alien is a Dead Alien: Science Fiction and the Metaphysics of Indian-Hating on the High Frontier," in *Journal of American Culture* 18, no. 1 (1995): 51–67. I realize that the use of "injuns" and "Indians" is racist and offensive. I do not intend to be harsh in my use of language. However, I feel it is important to accurately project the stereotypes that Whedon is debunking. Please forgive me.

16. June Namias, *White Captives: Gender and Ethnicity on the American Frontier* (Chapel Hill: University of North Carolina Press, 1993), 82.

CHAPTER TWELVE

"Haven't you heard? They look like us now!": Realism and Metaphor in the New *Battlestar Galactica*

Dylan Pank and John Caro

Positive critical reaction to the "reimagining" of *Battlestar Galactica* (2003–2009) frequently praises the gritty realism that initially appears at odds with traditional television science fiction. With storylines reflecting events such as the attacks of September 11, the war on terror, and the treatment of prisoners at Abu Ghraib prison, the show has demonstrated that it is not opposed to courting controversy. *Time* voted *Battlestar Galactica* as one of the best television series of 2005: "Most of you probably think this entry has got to be a joke. The rest of you have actually watched the show."[1] *Galactica*'s meticulous visual design has eschewed previous approaches and has attempted to create a verisimilitude on screen that is heavily dependent on intertextuality. Jim Collins has suggested that the "foregrounding of intertextual references has become a marker of 'quality television.'"[2] But the allusions in *Battlestar Galactica* go beyond simply quoting other television shows and motion pictures and refer to North American values, politics, and history. In this form of "referencing-as-positioning,"[3] intertextuality goes beyond simply demonstrating knowledge of genre, format, and text. The program makers use references not only to entertain but also to express awareness and opinions on a variety of complex and difficult social issues.

Where No Science Fiction TV Show Has Gone Before

The developers of the series have enthusiastically run with the idea that the show has created a form of "naturalistic science fiction." Series creators Ronald D. Moore and David Eick have therefore indicated a clear intent to remove the series away from the antiseptic mise-en-scène of shows such as *Star Trek* (1966–1969):

> Our goal is nothing less than the reinvention of the science fiction television series. We take as a given the idea that the traditional space opera, with its stock characters, techno-double-talk, bumpy-headed aliens, thespian histrionics, and empty heroics has run its course and a new approach is required. That approach is to introduce realism into what has heretofore been an aggressively unrealistic genre.[4]

Moore was formally "a longtime laborer in the *Star Trek* mines,"[5] working on the franchise as a writer and producer in its various incarnations. His experiences have had a significant impact on his contribution to *Battlestar Galactica*. He left the production of *Star Trek: Voyager* (1995–2001) after contributing as a writer to only two episodes—"Barge of the Dead" (1999) and "Survival Instinct" (1999). Making a comparison between the two series, Moore commented:

> There are things I'm applying here that I would've like to have done in *Voyager*, i.e., lack of resources, the development of unique cultural and civil institutions, and internal strife among people trapped aboard ship(s) without any reasonable hope of finding sanctuary anytime soon.[6]

Author Brian Aldiss once described science fiction as "the new old business" of holding up a mirror to reflect the world,[7] and this has never been more evident than in the remake of *Battlestar Galactica*. Although television science fiction has (perhaps unfair and inaccurate) associations with cheap and cheesy design—meaningless flashing console lights, silver or velour jumpsuits, and generally dazzling (and quickly dated) props—Eick and Moore have deliberately avoided that aesthetic, attempting to instead portray what they have termed a "fleshed out reality."[8] The series' production designer, Richard Hudolin, describes how he set about developing this style:

> We didn't do futuristic screens or sliding doors. There's a mix of old and more modern technology on display, but there's nothing that's really state of the art. We combined retro items like the old-style telephones and maps you would see

on 1940s battleships with computer screens and other elements from the 1980s and 1990s. That gives everything a degree of familiarity to the audience.[9]

To provide an example that illustrates this approach, the season two episode "The Farm" (2005) features a typically tense showdown between the military and civilian authorities vying for control of the fleet. President Laura Roslin, in hiding with political activist Tom Zarek and Commander Adama's estranged son, Lee, ponder a strategy with which they can win the fleet over to their side. Inverting the old adage, as the sequence unfolds, the political becomes personal and they decide that Lee should record an audio message denouncing his father. At the close of the scene, Roslin fumbles with a very familiar-looking tape recorder, muttering, "How does this work?"

This sequence deals with many of the important themes inherent to the series. There is the friction between military and civilian control; the uneasy interaction between legitimate and illegitimate political movements; the traumatized and antagonistic relationship between father and son in the Adama family. However, amid the tension and the drama, what is of additional interest is the all-too-recognizable magnetic audiotape. Why, in an environment where faster-than-light travel is possible, are these people still recording on analog cassette?

The answer lies with *Galactica*'s deliberate retro-future design, which incorporates locations such as abandoned warehouses[10] and production-line factories[11] in an aesthetic that goes beyond the "down and dirty" mise-enscène and documentary camera style, but actually permeates and helps to define the overarching philosophy and attitude of the series. *Battlestar Galactica* has taken a visual approach that was previously considered indicative of low-budget and poor-quality television—the overused and overfamiliar gravel quarries of the original *Doctor Who* (1963–1989) and *Blake's 7* (1978–1981)—and given it a positive slant. In doing so the series also follows a convention that has been at the heart of twentieth-century science fiction literature.

A further explanation comes from the show's coexecutive producer and principal writer. In an early statement, Ronald D. Moore makes a remark that is clearly also intended as a criticism of the restrictions[12] he endured while working on *Star Trek*:

> I think high-tech ships with touch screens and talking computers have been done to death and also tend to take human beings out of the dramatic equation. . . . I wanted this show to be about the characters, not about the technology they use.[13]

Within *Battlestar Galactica* and its storylines, Moore's approach has been extended to encompass morally ambiguous decisions taken by ostensibly sympathetic protagonists. This permits the characters to be rather complex and to even exhibit self-contradictory behavior in a manner that may have previously been considered confusing or even as due to poor screenwriting. Moreover, to extend the intrinsic criticism of *Star Trek*, just as storylines do not always result in tidy moral lessons, neither are they resolved with *deus ex machina* revelations.

Shaky Cameras and Squeaky Doors—a Realist Aesthetic?

It is important to remain wary of these claims of realism. As Nelson Goodman remarked, "Realism is relative, determined by the system or representation standard for a given culture or person at a given time."[14] The visual motifs and devices that are read as realistic or naturalistic are often, after all, merely aesthetic effects—the *cinéma vérité* camera and lighting styles, for example, or the shaky handheld framing and snap zooms as the camera appears barely able to follow the action. It is "like a documentary crew on *Discovery Channel* is showing you the story,"[15] comments Moore. *Battlestar Galactica* has successfully challenged the idea that an aesthetic borrowed from documentary has a monopoly on what can be considered a representation of the real, especially in the genre of speculative fiction. Previously in North American television, this *vérité* style has been the preserve and signifier of a gritty realism pioneered in shows such as *NYPD Blue* (1993–2005).

Journalist Ian Jack, quoting Roland Barthes,[16] claims that "photography has been, and is still, tormented by the ghost of painting." Jack goes on to say that "the documentary has been, and is still, tormented by the ghost of the fictional feature film—the ghost of the story." The inverse is also true. Today, televisual and cinematic claims of authenticity are haunted by the ghost of the fly-on-the-wall documentary. This is a perspective certainly supported by Robert L. Strain Jr., who argues that *Battlestar Galactica*'s camera style incorporates elements of reality TV, "a medium that has changed how we watch televised fictional entertainment today."[17] To an audience now familiar with documentary forms and reality TV, breaking the fourth wall with self-conscious camera placement and movement has now become a signifier of reality, rather than an alienating and distracting device.

The program makers then have made the claim of realism to distinguish the genre and the show in particular from what they view as its more disreputable sibling—fantasy. As series director Michael Rymer comments, "Every other effects movie is getting more and more unreal and fantasy-like.

We just wanted to go the other way."[18] *Battlestar Galactica*, like *NYPD Blue*, is "important" issue-driven quality television. As *The Guardian* newspaper has enthusiastically claimed, "*Battlestar Galactica* is the only award-winning drama that dares tackle the war on terror."[19]

With its focus on external realism, it could be argued that the film *2001: A Space Odyssey* (1968)[20]—itself a thorough attempt to present realism through meticulous scientific accuracy—owed less to contemporary science fiction than it did to the Victorian novel. However, the value placed on realism did reflect a certain strain of thought within the science fiction literary community. For example, Ursula K. Le Guin has claimed that science fiction is fundamentally a realist genre[21] before the writer begins applying a particular stylistic approach. In other words, the expectation is that a science fiction text must be internally coherent in the world and cosmology it presents and cannot call upon a preexisting metaphysics as can fantasy (e.g., magic, sorcery or even a mystical "Force"). Author Robert Heinlein has also emphasized the naturalistic quality of the genre, stating that science fiction could be defined as

> a realistic speculation about possible future events, based solidly on adequate knowledge of the real world, past and present, and on a thorough understanding of the nature and significance of the scientific method.[22]

In these terms, *Star Trek*, especially in *The Next Generation* (1987–1994) and subsequent series, has become the exemplar of television science fiction realism, featuring conventions such a diegetic explanation for all the characters speaking English (the universal translator), and all plot contrivances explained by uniform, albeit mysterious, scientific discoveries (dylithium crystals, replicators, Heisenberg compensators, etc.). In *Battlestar Galactica*, however, realism is suggested by techniques more familiar to the "earthbound" crime genre: handheld cameras, urgent refocusing, whip-pans, tight framing, and the low-key, underexposed lighting suggested by practical sources. Robert Strain makes a convincing case that *Galactica*'s naturalistic, reality TV–influenced camera work has replaced television science fiction's traditional magisterial gaze with something rather more inward looking:

> For *Battlestar Galactica*, keeping a visual sense of reality, the feeling that the characters are actual people aboard an actual spaceship doing actual things means that the audience *must feel* the presence of the camera. The visual look of the series is substantively different from most made-for-TV space fiction before it.[23]

Another level of realism can be found in what Scott Bukatman, when discussing *Blade Runner*, described as a "fractal environment."[24] In defiance of the limitations of a television series' budget, *Galactica* demonstrates an extensive level of detail, with a riot of realistically rendered costumes and mechanically plausible features. Unlike *Star Trek* or the original *Battlestar Galactica* (1978–1979), the audience is not held at arm's length to admire the glistening surfaces and polished displays. Indeed, in the reimagined *Battlestar Galactica*, the audience receives a sense of detail all the way down to the particles of rust, blobs of grease, and grains of dirt found adorning the squeaky hinged doors. Of course, *Battlestar Galactica* is by no means the first moving-image science fiction text to call upon the aesthetic of rusting and broken-down technology. *Star Wars* (1977) popularized the "battered freighter" look, itself drawing on the trend (from a visual if not a narrative angle) toward a decaying dystopian aesthetic of the mid-seventies, which was a reaction to the gleaming high-tech cleanliness of the sixties, typified by *Star Trek*, *2001: A Space Odyssey* or the many Gerry Anderson television series (see Garland's chapter in this volume).

Familiar vs. Unfamiliar

In the case of *Battlestar Galactica*, taking a closer look at this fractal environment, the audience quickly notices something rather unusual—or should that be *usual*? Much of the broken-down and ragged detritus lying around the fleet looks awfully familiar to twenty-first-century Earth dwellers, especially those raised in North America and Western Europe. Such familiarities go beyond even the practicalities and budget constraints of a show produced in contemporary North America.

The design and overall mise-en-scène of the series have an undeniable link to the now. On board the *Galactica*, characters can be seen opening hinged doors, consulting documents produced on dot-matrix printers, and listening to news on analog radios. In the second-season episode "The Final Cut" (2005), D'Anna Biers records interviews with the *Galactica*'s crew using a mini-DV camcorder (albeit that the cassettes are clearly designed with the series' characteristic clipped corner feature). Adama shaves using an Ikea mirror (appropriately and amusingly enough identified as the Fräck mirror in the Scandinavian company's catalog), and the military's security force protects itself with the "Giro" range of *Bad Lieutenant* snowboarding helmets. On Caprica (once again in "The Farm"), members of the resistance battle the Cylon occupation while driving Humvee vehicles. This all ties in rather effectively and conveniently with the series' imagined world, where the protagonists paraphrase Shakespeare,[25] Colonel Saul Tigh curses by taking the Christian savior's name in vain,[26] and, in the episode "Lay Down Your Burdens: Part Two" (2006), Chief Tyrol quotes freely from a Mario Savio speech[27] to inspire the members of a burgeoning blue-collar movement.

Interestingly, it could then be argued that while this tips *Battlestar Galactica* away from the genre of science fiction, it may not be in the direction of something more realistic, but toward the "dread pit" of fantasy, for these very recognizable representations of twenty-first-century Earth, rather than putting the audience at ease with a familiar aesthetic, can actually draw attention to themselves with their sheer recognizability. This perhaps culminates with the season three cliffhanger, "Crossroads: Part Two" (2007), where several characters are revealed to be hearing the strains of Bob Dylan's song "All Along the Watchtower" (1968).[28] As the series' constant refrain has always hinted at—"all this has happened before and all this will happen again"[29]—there is a diegetic and narrative explanation for these associations with contemporary Western society. Nonetheless, some members of the audience find these identifiable tropes far too distancing and distracting. Just what on *Earth* are these items doing in a science fiction television series?

For these viewers and fans, it is simply too much to take. Within this remake of what they feel is a much-loved science fiction "classic," the production design is a huge disruption. To those expecting silver jumpsuits and green-skinned aliens, the attempts at naturalistic science fiction in *Battlestar Galactica* are actually extremely unsettling. How can it be in the *Galactica* universe, for example, that there is an inoculation against radiation sickness,[30] but no apparent cure for breast cancer?[31] The following are extracts from typical comments found on an online message board, summing up the confusion and frustration that some audience members experience:

A civilization, and technology, with Faster Than Light drives, and seamless artificial gravity would NOT use guns that not only fired bullets, but were obvious current day handguns.

How can I believe this group of Aliens (ok, humans—but not from Earth) dress just like us in 2005 (look at [the] President and her assistant) and smoke the same cigarettes? Later on, in "planet Caprica," Boomer and a fellow partner enter a basement and find a transmitter: it turns out to be a radio-cassette box just like the one I had back in the 80's.

Does the non networking philosophy of the new Galactica (which again actually makes some sense, and tries to explain the corded handsets) extend to the doors? Is it somehow illegal to have any that slide? I guess again a FTL technology can't make compact slider motors hid in walls.[32]

So, as is befitting a series with the moral complexity of *Battlestar Galactica*, when it comes to the topics of realism and naturalism in relation to fantasy and science fiction, the "sitrep" is much more complex and nuanced. For within the show, and its mise-en-scène, there is a constant oscillation or feedback loop between the familiar and the unfamiliar. Robert Strain, citing Darko Suvin, writes about the process known as "cognitive estrangement,"[33] whereby there is a balancing act between the recognizable and the unknown in the series. The familiar is made strange and vice-versa. This is a theory adapted from formalist literary criticism and in particular Viktor Shklovsky's concept of *ostranenie*. In *Battlestar Galactica* there is a continuous cycle of this alienation effect—defamiliarization to familiarization and back again—drawing attention to itself for the audience's benefit. This conforms somewhat to Shklovsky's belief that the "artist should break down the habit of automatic reaction to the outside world and force the reader to see and hear it."[34]

Form Follows Function: An Ambiguous Approach

This brings us to yet another view on the genre. Samuel R. Delany, the critic and science fiction writer, has emphasized science fiction's rhetorical nature, claiming that the genre is concerned with more than simply displacing events into a conceived or imagined future[35]; it is marked by a particular creative use of language and the use of particular verbs or adjectives in unfamiliar contexts (for example, "the door dilated"). The metaphors may suggest literal meanings ("his world exploded") or ambiguity may be created by the expanded possibility of meaning ("she turned on her left side"). The reader actively decodes what he or she reads, orienting it around his or her expectations. Delany seeks to define science fiction through its formal strategies of language, rather than through diegetic signifiers or narrative conventions. Language becomes decentered and the reader must actively decode the text to orient himself or herself within the world created by the writer, based on a knowledge and familiarity of the genre and the author.

As *Battlestar Galactica* has continued it has played increasingly with a sense of ambiguity, introducing props and references that could not be (at the time of writing) narratively justified. Diegetic explanations are suggested for some of the set designs, most notably during the opening of *Battlestar Galactica: The Miniseries* (2003), the initial broadcast that rebooted the series. It is disclosed that the *Galactica* is an outdated ship, about to be converted into a museum, and that Commander Adama has deliberately shunned advanced technology, as he feels that it was this very technology that resulted in the creation of the Cylon enemy. In his tour of the *Galactica*, public relations officer Aaron Doral (later revealed to be humanoid Cylon Number Five) explains:

> Form follows function. Nowhere is this axiom of design more readily apparent than aboard the world-famous *Battlestar Galactica*. This ship, the last of her kind still in service, was constructed over fifty years ago during the early days of the Cylon War. . . . You'll see things here that look odd or even antiquated to modern eyes: phones with cords, awkward manual valves, computers that barely deserve the name. It was all designed to operate against an enemy who could infiltrate and disrupt even the most basic computer systems. *Galactica* is a reminder of a time when we were so frightened by our enemies that we literally looked back for protection.

However, such explanations have been offered as a token and dwindling gesture as the series has progressed. Nevertheless it is a gesture that grants the show a license to employ an aesthetic that the producers have enthusiastically grasped and applied, to the extent that props can frequently even be specifically branded. For example, the aforementioned Fräck mirror and Humvee, the Panasonic DVX100 camera in "The Final Cut," and the Citroen DS and Rover P6 vehicles found in the Caprican underground car park in "Downloaded" (2006).

Overall, there is a massive collage of styles, eras, and technologies represented. The "retro-future bricolage" may evoke both the ramshackle nature of the fleet and its resources as justified by the narrative, but it also acts to decenter the audience in terms of a specific time or reference, sparking a dissonance that, as observed by the fans on the message board, actually draws attention to itself, which is in contrast to the rigorously consistent aesthetics found in other texts.

A brief action sequence in the season one episode "You Can't Go Home Again" (2004) provides an illustration of how the series draws together a range of recognizable references, and even takes the time to offer the audience a self-effacing visual pun. Colonial pilots Helo and Boomer hide out in a deserted restaurant on occupied Caprica (the actual location being a Vancouver café, *The Alibi Room*[36]). Their brief respite is interrupted by a passing Cylon centurion patrol. During the ensuing ferocious shoot-out, various noteworthy items of set decoration are seen, including a flyer posted on a notice board advertising a local social event—it would appear that Capricans enjoy cappuccinos and the occasional game of pool!

The scene emphatically draws attention to the anachronisms inherent in the series. During the 2003 miniseries a reference is made by Baltar to the Cylons (presumably the 1978 models) looking like "walking chrome toasters."[37] As Helo takes cover in the corner of the café, he furtively glances back and forth at the toast that he had earlier begun to prepare. With a jolt, the bread finally springs out of the polished chrome toaster, giving away Helo's position to his mechanical Cylon pursuers. With this simple act, the sequence refers to and gently mocks its own reference to the original show, the text brazenly drawing attention to its own allusions.

Of course, this approach leaves the series open to accusations of simply being a form of lazy anthropocentrism and North American–centrism. Conveniently for the producers, it's also a design approach that is encouraged by a corner-cutting,[38] budget-friendly production. To a degree, these accusations would be correct. After all, economic demands require that the show be designed to appeal to a North American twenty-first-century audience, and if it finds a market beyond that, so much the better. In some ways it can be argued that the series resembles the original runs of the animated situation comedies (or "anicoms"[39]), The Flintstones (1960–1966) or The Jetsons (1962–1963). Middle-class suburban North American culture and values are transferred to unfamiliar circumstances, and in doing so eternalize and reassure the audience of the power of these values. Perhaps Battlestar Galactica is not so different from Star Trek after all. Ronald Moore admits this in the Frak Party Q&A Podcast,[40] where he discusses the appearance of a distinctly American-centric Earth at the close of the "Crossroads: Part Two" episode. Why, asks a fan of the show, does the continent of North America dominate the frame in the climatic shot of the planet? Moore responds, "That's because this show is about America! If I showed you Africa do you know how many members of the audience would not even recognize this planet . . . ? That is sad (but) I needed it to read immediately. That's the quickest way to tell our folks here in North America where we are."

Moore, however, is being somewhat modest. For, as in the case of the anicoms, the act of transferring North American culture and values can also lampoon those very values. Spanning the prehistoric to the space age, The Flintstones and The Jetsons may provide some comfort to the audience with the notion that the North American way of life is enduring and immutable, but as Nichola Dobson notes, The Flintstones also had a satirical edge, offering an "amusing commentary on consumerism in America."[41] Similarly, although Battlestar Galactica may provide comfort with the thought that the pool-shooting, Humvee-driving, democratic principles of the colonies will survive the attack of an outside aggressor, those same values are also satirized and interrogated in episodes such as "Lay Down Your Burdens: Part Two," where President Roslin, with the assistance of members of the military, attempts to rig an election in her favor.

Politics and the Media

The machinations of democratic politics and the surrounding media circus is a central theme of the show. For a population that matches that of no more than a small town, Roslin's press conferences indicate a disproportionate media presence within the fleet. The episode "Colonial Day" (2004) opens with an excerpt from a Fleet News Service broadcast, an apolitical pundit "talk wireless" show entitled *The Colonial Gang*, transmitted to the fleet.[42] The format of two politically opposed commentators arguing across a genial host parodies a familiar format from U.S. media. The title is even a direct reference to the CNN political talk show *The Capital Gang*, which ran throughout the 1990s. The idea that manpower and resources in an embattled fleet would be dedicated to such a trivial endeavor would seem, deliberately, to stretch credibility. Yet its presence throughout the episode (Tom Zarek, Laura Roslin, and Gaius Baltar all give interviews) stands as a convenient metonym for the larger impact and perception of the election of a vice president across the fleet population, a familiar (and expected) point of reference in any earthbound election. Moreover, at the same time *The Colonial Gang* satirizes the trivial and often contrived nature of the debate on such talk shows and the manner in which presentation and sound bites trump serious analysis and policy review (indeed the show is a significant early step on the road to Baltar's catastrophic presidency).

The aesthetic choices in a show that places so much stock on realism moves it from a merely mimetic approach (i.e., the simple science fiction "realism") to something more. Audiences are made aware of the construction. This allows the active decoding of the text that science fiction encourages. After all, the transposition of seemingly familiar values to a distant context is a common science fiction technique. Isaac Asimov and Robert Silverberg wrote in the introduction to the their novel *Nightfall* that the reader may "imagine that the text reads 'vorks' wherever it says 'miles,' 'gliizbiiz' wherever it says 'hours,' and 'sleshtraps' where it says 'eyes.'"[43] They could almost be outlining the premise of *Battlestar Galactica* when they go on to say:

> The essence of this story doesn't lie in the quantity of bizarre terms we might have invented; it lies, rather, in the reaction of a group of people somewhat like ourselves, living on a world that is somewhat like ours in all but one highly significant detail, as they react to a challenging situation.[44]

To continue this idea to *Battlestar Galactica*, the audience may see rifles/pistols, audio cassettes, mini-DV cameras, telephones, door handles, books, and so on, but it is to read these items as representing "forms." Thus the design of the show creates a form of shorthand—a grammar—that develops an identity that a contemporary media-literate audience can recognize and engage with.

Science fiction has long grappled with the issue of representation of the day-to-day physical reality, as evidenced in the cliché that science fiction dates itself through its mise-en-scène. It would be accurate to claim that much the same is true of westerns, or any period film for that matter. However, with science fiction the case appears more pressing, as the production designers and costume departments struggle to present a future. This anxiety permeates science fiction, both written and seen. In Philip K. Dick's novel *Ubik* (1969), characters are trapped in a virtual environment where objects regress to older models of themselves: an airplane turns from a jet to a propeller-powered biplane; a car devolves into a pre–World War II Model A Ford; elevators grow into brass cages and sprout operators. Dick explicitly references Platonic ideas regarding forms that the idea of an object continues and is consistent, even as its appearance and design changes.[45] While critics may complain that the content of a text owes more to the time and culture of its writing,[46] science fiction as a formal strategy is flexible enough to absorb these anachronisms as long as the reader is given a consistent and creatively expressed world in which to place these familiar elements.

Referring back to *Nightfall*,[47] the story works as a thought experiment, taking familiar—even stereotypical—characters (scientists, politicians, religious leaders, and journalists) and placing them in an unfamiliar, defamiliarized situation: a world facing an imminent astronomical and social catastrophe. The authors then use science fiction to comment on how particular academic disciplines (astronomy, psychology, archaeology, and physics) create a particular understanding of the world. *Battlestar Galactica* takes this conceit further, peppering the series with references familiar to audiences, and establishing this not only with mise-en-scène and set and prop design, but also with references particular to the plot. This goes from the general—the much commented upon echoes of the Iraq situation in the New Caprica occupation storyline,[48] the South African Truth and Reconciliation Committee,[49] the prolife/prochoice debates in North America[50]—to references that go much deeper and sometimes require more specific or esoteric knowledge of North American political history, as in the case of Chief Tyrol's quotation of the Mario Savio speech; the Jack Ruby–like "assassination of the assassin" in the season two episode "Resistance" (2005); or suggestions of the Kent State shootings in the *Razor* (2007) television film.

Once again the presence of these references is not justified simply in terms of realism. Occasionally the allusions are stylistic; the season three episode "Unfinished Business" (2006), for example, makes unmistakable references, in terms of thematic material and visual and editing styles, to Martin Scorsese's film *Raging Bull* (1980). And those who recognize such references will be pulled up short by Savio's Sproul Hall speech shifted to a new context, although this assists the show in dealing with such issues in a largely self-conscious way.

So while the transposition makes the previously mentioned North American values appear eternal, it also allows the writers to interrogate and examine those values. Test them and apparently immutable assumptions can start to look vulnerable. Suddenly, the audience is watching a show where the heroes are justified in becoming suicide bombers, where stealing an election has a moral rationalization, or where President Roslin is forced to question her belief in a woman's right to an abortion. This makes *Battlestar Galactica* much more than a collection of historical and political allusions—or simply a "sci-fi *Simpsons*"—for people who watch CNN and subscribe to *Time*.

Unlike many previous science fiction shows, such as the various runs of *Star Trek*, or the original *Battlestar Galactica*, the reimagined series was developed in the era of high-definition television and has been broadcast in this format since its inception. In terms of the visual style, the camera work and editing reflect the approach David Bordwell terms "intensified continuity,"[51] that is to say, it is basically grounded in the classical Hollywood style, but with the faster paced editing and more aggressive, often self-conscious use of camera movement, famously (and at the time controversially)[52] introduced to television in the police drama *NYPD Blue*.

A viewing of a typical episode of *Star Trek: The Next Generation*, for example, features a much slower editing style and a preponderance of mid- to long-shot framing born of the classical master shot coverage of traditional television drama. This is often necessary to disguise the nature of the set design, for example, blank generic surfaces and computer readouts that are, in fact, static graphics. On the other hand, *Battlestar Galactica*'s high-definition format and intensified style demands an increased, "fractal" level of detail. Animated screens are magnified until the pixels can be discerned; fingers are seen pulling real triggers, pressing functioning switches, or turning working dials. While much television science fiction strives to use indicators of exotic otherness, *Battlestar Galactica* pours in references to the current and everyday, references that to the attentive viewer seem to burst out of the narrative (all the better for the fan to disentangle), even as they anchor it in the contemporary.

Notes

1. James Poniewozik, "Best of 2005: Television," *Time*, December 16, 2005, from www.time.com/time/arts/article/0,8599,1141640,00.html (accessed May 28, 2007).

2. Jim Collins, "Television and Postmodernism," in *Channels of Discourse, Reassembled*, ed. Robert C. Allen (London: Routledge, 1992), 334.

3. Ibid.

4. Ronald D. Moore, "Battlestar Galactica: Naturalistic Science Fiction or Taking the Opera out of Space Opera," *Galactica TV*, 2003, web.archive.org/web/20070208103915/, www.galactica2003.net/articles/concept.shtml (accessed May 31, 2007).

5. Scott Brown, "Why *Battlestar Galactica* Must Self-Destruct," *Wired Magazine* 16, no. 4 (2008), www.wired.com/techbiz/people/magazine/16-04/pl_brown (accessed September 4, 2008).

6. Ronald D. Moore, "Ron Moore Blog Q&A," *SciFi.Com*, 2005, blog.scifi.com/battlestar/archives/2005/01/ (accessed September 4, 2008).

7. Sandy Auden, "Aldiss and More: An Interview with Brian Aldiss," *The SF Site*, 2005, www.sfsite.com/08b/saba206.htm (accessed May 31, 2007).

8. David Langford, "Infinitely Improbable—As Others See Us," *Ansible 198* (2004), news.ansible.co.uk/a198.html (accessed May 31, 2007).

9. David Bassom, *Battlestar Galactica: The Official Companion* (London: Titan Books, 2005), 136.

10. In the season one episode "Litmus" (2004), Helo searches for Boomer in occupied Caprica, finally tracking her down in an abandoned warehouse.

11. In the season three episode "Dirty Hands" (2007), Chief Tyrol visits the fleet's tylium fuel production plant. The location used was the Vancouver-based sugar refinery Rogers Sugar. "It looks great on screen," commented director Wayne Rose: David Bassom, *Battlestar Galactica: The Official Companion Season Three* (London: Titan Books, 2007), 91.

12. Moore has subsequently identified the character Seven of Nine as one of the problems he had with the show. He felt that the skimpily attired "fan boy favorite" was merely a cynical marketing tactic: "If you want to posit a future where we wear our sexuality on our sleeves, where it's very open, and no one is put off by people being very sexual, that's great. That's very much in tune with how Gene [Roddenberry—*Star Trek* creator] saw the future. [But] the rest of *Voyager* is not like that." Interview with Ron Moore after he left *Voyager*—Part 4 in *Star Trek Homepage*, home.rhein-zeitung.de/~hascheid/artikel/rminte4.htm (accessed September 4, 2008); Gaius Baltar's relationship with the humanoid Cylon, Number Six, can be read as a response to the *Voyager* Borg character: "We're not used to seeing sex treated maturely in science fiction—nine times out of ten, any sex is either something to snigger at or to make fun of. Somehow it's okay to fetishize sex by putting women in S&M leather 'space' outfits." In *Battlestar Galactica* Moore deftly sidesteps the issue of Six's fetishized attire by having the character "invisible" to all but Baltar. See also Barber's chapter in this volume.

13. Bassom, *Battlestar Galactica: The Official Companion*, 18.

14. Nelson Goodman, *Languages of Art: An Approach to a Theory of Symbols* (Indianapolis, IN: Hackett Publishing Co., 1988), 37

15. *Battlestar Galactica: The Lowdown*, DVD (2004) [13 min., 29 sec.].

16. Ian Jack, "The Documentary Has Always Been a Confection Based on Lies," *The Guardian*, July 21, 2007, www.guardian.co.uk/media/2007/jul/21/broadcastingethics.bbc (accessed July 21, 2007).

17. Robert L. Strain Jr., "Galactica's Gaze: Naturalistic Science Fiction and the 21st Century Frontier Myth," in *Sith, Slayers, Stargates, and Cyborgs: Modern Mythology in the New Millennium*, ed. David Whitt and John Perlich (New York: Peter Lang, 2008), 56.

18. *Battlestar Galactica: The Lowdown* [1 min., 10 sec.].

19. Dan Martin, "The Final Frontier," *The Guardian*, January 13, 2007, www.guardian.co.uk/media/2007/jan/13/tvandradio.broadcasting (accessed May 28, 2007).

20. In the bonus documentary on the DVD of the miniseries, *Battlestar Galactica: The Lowdown*, David Eick identifies *2001* as touchstone for the series "because it depicted space and space travel and space living in an extraordinary realistic way" [2 min., 2 sec.].

21. Ursula K. Le Guin, "Plausibility Revisited: Wha Hoppen and What Didn't," *Ursula K. Le Guin's Website*, 2005, www.ursulakleguin.com/PlausibilityRevisited.html (accessed August 31, 2008).

22. Robert Heinlein, "Science Fiction; Its Nature, Faults and Virtues," in *The Science Fiction Novel: Imagination and Social Criticism*, ed. Basil Davenport (Chicago: Advent, 1969), 21.

23. Strain, "Galactica's Gaze," 58.

24. Scott Bukatman, *Blade Runner* (London: BFI Publishing, 2007), 58.

25. In the fourth-season episode "Faith" (2008), Baltar can be clearly heard quoting from *Hamlet* over the wireless.

26. Early in *Battlestar Galactica: The Miniseries* (2003), following an altercation with Starbuck, when visiting Adama's quarters, Tigh sighs, "Jesus!" when looking at an old photograph of Adama with his sons. "Ron Moore has stated that this was just an ad-lib by the actor, and was never in the script, and should have been removed during editing. In fact this was removed from the 'theatrical version' shown on Universal HD." Paul Gu, "Continuity Errors—Dialogue Errors," *Battlestar Wiki*, 2008, en.battlestarwiki.org/wiki/Continuity_errors_(RDM) (accessed August 29, 2008).

27. "The closing moments of 'Lay Down Your Burdens, Part II' see Chief Tyrol giving a speech which was based on a real-life public address given by the late civil rights activist Mario Savio in 1964. 'It's a speech that's very special to me,' says David Eick. 'Mario Savio's widow gave us permission to paraphrase it, and she liked the way we did it.'" David Bassom, *Battlestar Galactica: The Official Companion Season Two* (London: Titan Books, 2006), 102.

28. Series composer Bear McCreary recalls, "The idea was that an artist on one of the Colonies somehow recorded a song with the exact same melody and lyrics. . . . Perhaps this performer and Dylan pulled inspiration from a common, ethereal source." Bassom, *Battlestar Galactica: The Official Companion Season Three*, 106.

29. In the podcast of the *Battlestar Galactica Frak Party Q&A*, released April 3, 2007, Ronald D. Moore fields questions from fans of the show. He admits that the

refrain was inspired by the opening line of Walt Disney's adaptation of *Peter Pan* (1953) [23 min., 32 sec.].

30. In episodes such as "Resistance" (2005), it is established that the characters on occupied Caprica are taking medication to prevent radiation sickness caused by the Cylon nuclear detonations.

31. Early in the initial miniseries, prior to the Cylon attack, Laura Roslin is diagnosed with terminal breast cancer.

32. "*Battlestar Galactica*: IMDB User Comments," *The Internet Movie Database*, 2004, www.imdb.com/title/tt0407362/usercomments-index (accessed August 27, 2008).

33. Strain, "Galactica's Gaze," 59.

34. Edward J. Brown, *Russian Literature since the Revolution* (Cambridge, MA: Harvard University Press, 1982), 72.

35. Samuel R. Delany, *The Jewel Hinged Jaw* (New York: Berkley Publishing, 1977), 77.

36. Bassom, *Battlestar Galactica: The Official Companion*, 62.

37. Baltar has some difficulty accepting that his lover of the last two years is a humanoid Cylon. He remarks, "Well, forgive me, I'm having the tiniest little bit of trouble believing that, because the last time anybody saw the Cylons they looked more like *walking chrome toasters*."

38. Many of the documents and props seen in the series are shown with clipped corners—it is possibly another visual pun by the designers, indicating that they are literally cutting corners to meet the demands of the budget. Although the official version for the design is not quite as entertaining, it does fit with the aesthetic philosophy of the series. Production designer Richard Hudolin explains: "We were trying to come up with ways of making the *Galactica* look different and unconventional, and we decided that certain papers would have clipped corners. We thought it was a nice idea and looked cool." Bassom, *Battlestar Galactica: The Official Companion*, 140.

39. Nichola Dobson, "Nitpicking 'The Simpsons': Critique and Continuity in Constructed Realities," *Animation Journal* 11 (2003): 85.

40. *Battlestar Galactica Frak Party Q&A* podcast, released April 3, 2007 [23 min., 50 sec.].

41. Dobson, "Nitpicking 'The Simpsons,'" 85.

42. The concept of a fleetwide television broadcast is used in the episode "The Final Cut," in which television journalist D'Anna Biers (later revealed to be Cylon humanoid model Number Three) produces a video documentary. However, the only audience seen watching this program is composed exclusively of Cylons.

43. Isaac Asimov and Robert Silverberg, *Nightfall* (New York: Spectra, 1991), viii.

44. Ibid.

45. Philip K. Dick, *Ubik* (London: Voyager, 1998), 139.

46. Brian Aldiss comments on Asimov's epic of far future history *The Foundation Trilogy* that "Asimov's galaxy of 22,000 years hence is little different from the America of 1941." Brian Aldiss, *Trillion Year Spree* (London: Gollancz, 1986), 393.

47. Silverberg and Asimov's 1991 novel is an expansion of a 1940 short story by Asimov of the same name, first published in 1940 in *Astounding Magazine*.

48. Season three episodes "Occupation" (2006), "Precipice" (2006), "Exodus: Part One" (2006), and "Exodus: Part Two" (2006) feature a complex story arc that deals with suicide bombing, terrorist tactics employed against an occupying army, and the torturing of prisoners of war.

49. Following the discovery of a secret tribunal set up to punish those humans accused of collaborating with Cylons in the season three episode "Collaborators" (2006), President Roslin sets up a Truth and Reconciliation Commission, in the hope of healing the divisions in the recently reunited fleet.

50. With colonial population numbers plummeting, during the season two episode "The Captain's Hand" (2006), President Roslin is forced into the uncomfortable position of reconsidering her liberal ideology on a woman's right to choose.

51. David Bordwell, *The Way Hollywood Tells It: Story and Style in Modern Movies* (Berkeley: University of California Press, 2006), 123.

52. *USA Today* recalls how "*Blue*'s distinctive shaky camera style stirred dissent." Bill Keveney, "*NYPD Blue*: Looking Back at Its Colorful Moments," *USA Today*, September 14, 2004, www.usatoday.com/life/television/news/2004-09-14-nypd-blue-inside_x.htm (accessed September 13, 2008).

Index

Universal Studios, 10
Upstairs Downstairs, 80
utopia, ix–x, 17, 62, 71–72, 90, 117,
    139, 152, 159

vampires, xv, 136, 140, 167, 170–71,
    173, 175–77
Vancouver, 114, 118, 120, 207, 212n11
Variety, 43
Vaughn, Robert, 42, 53, 57n46
VCR, 21n25, 42, 47
Verne, Jules, 29, 37
Victor, David, 47, 51
Vietnam, 34, 57n46
Village of the Giants, 35
The Virginian (book), 186
Voyage to the Bottom of the Sea (film), 28
Voyage to the Bottom of the Sea (TV
    series), vii, 25–27, 29–32, 35, 38;
    "The Abominable Snowman," 38;
    "The City beneath the Sea," 30;
    "Eleven Days to Zero," 30; "Escape
    from Venice," 30; "The Fear-
    Makers," 30; "The Ghost of Moby
    Dick," 31; "The Mermaid," 38; "The
    Price of Doom," 31, 32; "The Secret
    of the Loch," 31; "The Sky's on
    Fire," 30; "The Traitor," 31; "Turn
    Back the Clock," 31

war, 16, 29, 68, 70, 76; U.S. Civil War,
    186, 197n7; World War I, 95; World
    War II, 79
War of the Worlds (book), 91n3
War of the Worlds (film), 161
Warden, Jack, 13
Warner Brothers, 128n2, 151
Washburn, Zoe, 186–88
Washington, D.C., 159
The Water Babies, 105
Waverly, Alexander, 41, 45
Wayne, John, 183, 194

We, 133
weapons, x, 48, 49, 71, 151, 157; bombs,
    28, 49, 69; guns, 48; nuclear, 26, 28,
    30, 76, 81, 155; rockets, 49, 68–69;
    swords, 99, 116, 119, 122–23, 125,
    129n21, 131n43, 131n45, 189, 191
Weaver, Sigourney, 158, 164n31
Wells, H. G., 33, 78
West, Major Don, 32
westerns, 33, 44, 184–88, 190, 193–94,
    210; and American culture, 3–19;
    See also genre
Westworld, 5, 184
Whedon, Joss, xv, 171, 183, 191
When Time Ran Out, 37
Whitfield, Gene, 49
The Who (pop group), 114
Widen, Gregory, 113, 116
Wilcox, Fred M., 4, 97
The Wild Bunch, 18, 22n47, 184
Wilder, Laura Ingalls, 185, 191–2
Williams, Raymond, 62
Wister, Owen, 186
Wolfram & Hart (law firm), 170–72,
    174–76, 178, 179n11
women, 75–90, 135, 140, 184, 193, 196;
    and fertility treatment, 75–76; on
    the frontier, 185–86, 192; rights of,
    75; scientists, 86–88, 134, 139
World of Giants, 35
World Without End, 9
World's Fair of 1939, 183
World's Fair of 1964, 46
Wyss, Johann David, 31

The X-Files, xvii, 139, 148n33, 148n34,
    168–9
The X-Men, 173

Zamyatin, Yvgeny, 133
Zarek, Tom, 201, 209
Zoidberg, 151, 159

About the Editor and Contributors

Lincoln Geraghty is principal lecturer in Film Studies and subject leader for Media Studies in the School of Creative Arts, Film and Media at the University of Portsmouth, with a PhD in American Studies from the University of Nottingham. He is on the editorial boards of *The Journal of Popular Culture*, *Atlantis: A Journal of the Spanish Association for Anglo-American Studies*, and *Reconstruction: Studies in Contemporary Culture*. He is the author of *Living with* Star Trek: *American Culture and the* Star Trek *Universe* (2007), editor of *The Influence of* Star Trek *on Television, Film and Culture* (2008), and co-editor, with Mark Jancovich, of *The Shifting Definitions of Genre: Essays on Labeling Films, Television Shows and Media* (2008). Forthcoming publications include *American Science Fiction Film and Television*.

Dave Allen began his academic life teaching art and design, and his PhD (1995) addressed the use of "new" technologies in visual arts teaching. Since the 1980s he has moved increasingly toward teaching and research in film, media, and popular music. He took up a post at the University of Portsmouth in 1988 and since 2004 has worked in the School of Creative Arts, Film and Media (SCAFM). In recent years most of his publications have been around popular music, and in SCAFM he is one of the leading members of an AHRC-funded research project on British film and culture in the 1970s. He was head of school from 2006 to 2008 and in 2007 was awarded a fellowship of the National Teaching Fellowship Scheme.

Trudy Barber is senior lecturer in Media Studies at the University of Portsmouth. Her background is wide ranging—from a fine art degree involving virtual reality and sexuality from Central Saint Martin's College of Art, London, to a PhD in Sociology from the University of Kent covering various sociosexual aspects of the Internet, virtual reality, and new media. Current research interests include: human-computer interaction; new media development and content; consumer-generated content; online social networking; sexuality and sexual subcultures; science fiction, cyberpunk, and the future; immersive and nonimmersive virtuality; the convergence and customization of communication technologies; and issues surrounding theory and creative digital practice.

John Caro is currently assistant head of the School of Creative Arts, Film and Media at the University of Portsmouth, where he continues to coordinate the video production strand. He graduated from the University of Newcastle at Northumbria's Media Production program in 1998. Supported by a Commonwealth Scholarship, he went on to successfully complete a master's degree in film and video at York University, Toronto. He has previously written and directed two narrative shorts: *Shake, Rattle and Roll* (1997) and *Come Again?* (1998). In 2001 he developed a personal documentary about illegitimacy, entitled *Bastard* (2001). His work has been screened at Raindance, Docupolis, and the International Tel-Aviv Film Festival. Additionally, he has toiled as a producer and editor on numerous short films. From 1983 to 1987 he was a set decorator at Pinewood Studios, working on such films as *Legend, Aliens,* and *Full Metal Jacket.* In 1997 he was on the crew of Mike Figgis's *The Death of Sexual Innocence.*

Oscar De Los Santos, PhD, is chair of the Writing Department at Western Connecticut State University. His books include *Hardboiled Egg, Infinite Wonderlands* (with David G. Mead), and the edited essay collections *When Genres Collide* (with Thomas J. Morrissey) and *Reel Rebels: Eleven Directors Who Bucked the System and Shot the Flick Their Way.* His stories and essays have appeared in *New York Review of Science Fiction, Extrapolation, Connecticut Review,* and *Saranac Review.*

Michael S. Duffy completed his MA in Cinema Studies in 2001 at New York University, Tisch School of the Arts, and earned his PhD in Film Studies in 2007 from the University of Nottingham. His thesis focused on the development of visual effects companies in Australia and New Zealand during the 1990s, and how industrial practice could influence aesthetic approach to visual effects on screen. His current interests are in aesthetic and industrial approaches to special/visual effects, music videos of the 1980s, and contemporary comic book film and television franchises.

Laurel Forster is senior lecturer in Media Studies at the University of Portsmouth. Her research interests are in women's writing, women's culture, and representations of the domestic in various literary and media forms and genres. Her publications are on a range of subjects including writing and culture of the modernist period, feminist magazines, television programs, and science fiction films and include *The Recipe Reader* (2003); "Futuristic Foodways: The Metaphorical Meaning of Food in Science Fiction Film," in Anne Bower (ed.), *Reel Food: Essays on Food and Film* (2004); "Revealing the Inner Housewife: Housework and History in Domestic Lifestyle Television," in Gareth Palmer (ed.), *Exposing Lifestyle Television* (2008). She is a member of the AHRC-supported 1970s Research Group at Portsmouth, with a particular interest in gender and culture of the period as represented in magazines and television. With Professor Sue Harper, she will coedit the collection of papers from The 1970s British Culture Conference recently held at Portsmouth. In addition, she is currently working on a longer study of women's magazines in Britain from the early twentieth century to the present day.

David Garland is senior lecturer in Media Studies in the School of Creative Arts, Film and Media at the University of Portsmouth. He has previously taught writing, film, and media in both the United States and the UK, including the University of Southern California, Ithaca College, and Coventry University. He wrote his master's thesis on the Hollywood Novel and his doctoral dissertation on David Letterman. His published work and conference presentations involve European and American film and television, reflecting particular research interests in critical theory, comedy, and the talk show.

Lorna Jowett is senior lecturer in Media and American Studies at the University of Northampton, where she teaches some of her favorite things, including science fiction, horror, and television, sometimes all at once. Her research interests are currently focused on genre and gender in horror and science fiction texts across film, television, and literature. Recent publications include articles on television shows such as *Firefly*, *Angel*, and the reimagined *Battlestar Galactica*. Her monograph, *Sex and the Slayer: A Gender Studies Primer for the* Buffy *Fan*, was published in 2005 and she is on the editorial board of *Slayage: the International Online Journal of* Buffy *Studies*.

Robert L. Lively is the department chair of English at Truckee Meadows Community College, where he teaches composition, creative nonfiction, linguistics, and science fiction/fantasy literature. He is currently pursuing his PhD in Rhetoric and Composition from the University of Nevada, Reno. His scholarly interests include ancient rhetoric and creative writing theory and pedagogy. He is currently coediting a collection exploring the history of rhetorics that lost out to the Greek and Roman traditions. He lives in Reno, Nevada, with his wife, Shelby, and his two sons, Jared and Erek.

Dylan Pank graduated from Northumbria University in 1998 with a BA (Hons) in Media Production. While there he directed a number of short films, including the first project at that university to be entirely shot and edited digitally. Subsequently he worked for five years at Istanbul Bilgi University in Turkey as a technician and instructor, while also working as, among other roles, sound recordist, editor, special effects supervisor, sound designer, and camera operator on many short films and documentary projects. His work has featured in films that have been screened and won awards at festivals around the world. Since 2003 he has been tutor in video production skills at the University of Portsmouth, and has recently completed his MA in Art, Design, and Media. He regularly organizes short film screenings in Portsmouth and is secretary for the committee of the Portsmouth Screen: Film and New Media Festival. He has been an avid science fiction fan since a young age and still dreams of electric sheep.

Van Norris has been senior lecturer in Film and Media Studies in the School of Creative Arts, Film and Media at the University of Portsmouth since 2003. His research interests lie in the American and British graphic narrative form, animation history and theory (classical and postclassical Hollywood animation and British cinema and television animation), British and American comedy forms, and mainstream and independent American and British cinema. He is currently completing a PhD entitled "Drawing on the British Tradition: The Mapping of Cultural Attitudes and Identity and Their Intersection with Comedy Modes Employed within British Television Animation." His published works include "'Yeah, Looks Like It n'All . . .': Mapping the Relationship between the 'Live Action' Universe, Abridged Figurative Design and Computer Animation within *Modern Toss*" in *Animation: An Interdisciplinary Journal*; "John Barry—007 and Counting" in *The Continuum Companion to Sound in Film and the Visual Media*; and "Internal Logic: Appropriation of Surrealism into Popular American Animation" in *The Unsilvered Screen: Surrealism and Cinema* (2006).

Cynthia W. Walker is assistant professor in the Department of Communication at St. Peter's College in Jersey City, New Jersey, where she teaches courses in journalism, public relations, media literacy, film and broadcast studies, and scriptwriting. She has written a number of *U.N.C.L.E.*-related articles including entries for The Museum of Broadcast Communication's *Encyclopedia of Television* (ed. Horace Newcomb). She also appears in *The Man from U.N.C.L.E.* DVD set, currently available from Time/Life. Her forthcoming book, *Work/Text: Investigating The Man from U.N.C.L.E.*, proposes a new dialogic model of mass communication.